TM*

 Transcendental Meditation

TM*

DISCOVERING INNER ENERGY AND OVERCOMING STRESS

Harold H. Bloomfield, M.D.
Michael Peter Cain
Dennis T. Jaffe

In Collaboration with Robert Bruce Kory

Foreword by Hans Selye, M.D.
Introduction by R. Buckminster Fuller

 **Transcendental Meditation**

DELACORTE PRESS/NEW YORK

Library of Congress Cataloging in Publication Data

Bloomfield, Harold H   1944–
TM*: discovering inner energy and overcoming stress.

"*Transcendental meditation."
Bibliography: p.
1. Transcendental meditation.   I. Cain, Michael
Peter, 1941–   joint author.   II. Jaffe, Dennis T.,
joint author.   III. Title.
BL627.B56   294.5′43   74-19289
ISBN 0-440-06048-6

CONTENTS

A NOTE ON THE BIBLIOGRAPHY
AND SCIENTIFIC CHARTS

General bibliographic references
are indicated by superior numbers.
Specific quotes are identified
within parentheses and include
the bibliographic reference
as well as the page number.

Charts referred to will be found
in the back of the book.

ACKNOWLEDGMENTS

Our greatest debt is to Maharishi Mahesh Yogi for bringing Transcendental Meditation and the Science of Creative Intelligence out into the world. We hope we have described his teaching accurately.

We are also indebted to the many dedicated individuals who have created SIMS, MIU, and their affiliate organizations.

We are extremely grateful to Al Rubottom, whose ideas and editorial assistance have been invaluable.

We would like to thank the following persons for their generous suggestions: Aleric Arenander, David Ballou, Dr. Paul Corey, Larry Domash, Dr. Bernard Glueck, Phil Goldberg, Alex Hankey, Frank Papentin, and most notably David Orme-Johnson for his assistance in structuring the presentation of scientific research.

Special thanks to Alan Cobb, Jack Forem, Jerry Jarvis, and Becky Pollack for critical readings.

We are also most grateful to David Bousfield, Charlotte Cain, Bill Reingold, Robin Spowart, and the MIU Press for art work, and to Dawn McAvoy, Jamie Michaels, Susan Pacelli, Linda Siegel, Susan Smith, and Miriam Spanier for secretarial help.

H.H.B., M.P.C., D.T.J., R.B.K.

FOREWORD

It was with great pleasure that I accepted the authors' invitation to write a Foreword to this volume. I claim no expertise in Transcendental Meditation (TM), or in the Science of Creative Intelligence (SCI), which was derived from the former. However, it was my good fortune to have spent almost an entire day with Maharishi Mahesh Yogi at one of his international symposia on SCI at Queen's University. There, joined by many meditators, we discussed the relationships between Transcendental Meditation and my work on the medical aspects of stress. Ever since then I have felt it would be an extremely fruitful development to explore in detail the obvious psychologic influence exerted by TM on somatic stress, as the latter is understood in medicine. And it is this need which is most successfully filled by the present volume.

Even a glance at the table of contents will indicate the range covered by the authors' examination of the interrelation and interaction between meditation and stress, particularly:

1) their impact upon the crisis of modern life;
2) techniques involved in contacting pure awareness;
3) the physiology of consciousness and the objectively demonstrable bodily and mental changes associated with TM;
4) the effects of TM as a means of psychotherapy; and
5) the use of this technique for developing creative intelligence and thereby approaching a solution to many of our personal and social problems.

The present work shows that TM's physiologic effects—on metabolism, breathing, skin resistance, blood lactate, brain waves and the cardiovascular system—are exactly opposite to those identified by medicine as being characteristic of the effort to meet the demands of stress. Similarly, the therapeutic effect of TM on bodily derangements is most evident in those conditions known as "diseases of stress" or "diseases of adaptation" (especially mental, cardiovascular, gastrointestinal and hypersensitivity ailments) which are caused by inappropriate adaptive responses to the stressors of everyday life. The book discusses these matters in a competent fashion.

It was only a relatively short time ago, in 1970, that Jerry Jarvis gave the first course on the principles of creative intelligence at Stanford University. It was immediately and strikingly successful, attracting the largest undergraduate enrollment of any course ever taught at that institution. Activities pertaining to this particular application of TM are now coordinated by the American Foundation for the Science of Creative Intelligence, headquartered in Los Angeles. Recently, AFSCI has tried to promote wider awareness of the relationship between TM and stress by arranging presentations of a video-taped discussion between Mr. Jarvis and myself.

By attempting to make TM available to everybody throughout the world, Maharishi hopes not only to encourage our individual self-perfection but also to facilitate the intelligent use of our environment. Specific objectives include the development of each individual's full potential, improving the accomplishments of governments, realizing the highest ideals of education and achieving solutions to the problems of family life, crime and social violence. In view of the staggering enormity of this task, current emphasis has been placed upon the training of teachers through Maharishi International University.

Transcendental Meditation has emerged at a time when we are preoccupied in rushing about from place to place, all too often with the certainty that ours is the only religion, philosophy or political trend that can solve the problems of humanity. It is particularly conducive to the success of Maharishi's program that familiarity with TM can be acquired in just a few lessons and that two daily sessions of about fifteen to twenty minutes each will suffice to reap its benefits, whatever our education or ideals may be. Furthermore, TM does not have to upset the routine of excessively goal-directed, busy people since it can be practiced anywhere, even in buses, subways and waiting rooms. The most eloquent testimony to the usefulness of this technique is the fact that TM is already practiced by about half a million Americans.

As a psychological approach to coping with the unpleasant aspects of the stress of life, TM does not conflict with my own personal views. My goal is a code of ethics based on natural biologic laws derived from the study of defense reactions during stress. Like TM, my code neither depends on nor contradicts any extant religion, philosophy or political conviction. Where TM uses pure awareness as the means to secure its intended benefits, I offer guidelines for physiologically justifiable behavior in the pursuit of happiness and security.

The point of this juxtaposition is not to expound my own doctrine but to make clear that the two approaches are not only compatible but actually complementary. TM produces a healthy, rested state of mind and stimulates creative intelligence, while the principles of "life with stress but without distress" provide a framework for using the fruits of TM to best advantage, not only to avoid the harmful side effects of stress but also to maximize the gains derived from beneficially stressful activities.

In order to clarify this very important point, we must bear in mind that the medical definition of stress is "the nonspecific [that is, stereotyped] response of the body to any demand made upon it." It does not specify whether the demands and their results are pleasant or unpleasant. The stress of anxiety or physical pain causes certain objectively measurable nervous and hormonal reactions which are essentially identical with those induced by the pleasant stress of fulfillment, victory and accomplishment.

It is from this perspective that I favor rewording the old biblical admonition: "Love thy neighbor as thyself." While obedience to this command will result in improved interpersonal relations, it provides no ultimate goal that we can respect as desirable in itself. Nor is it biologically easy to follow: big fish must eat small fish in order to survive. Yet one can reword the exhortation without forfeiting its profound wisdom, by saying:

"Earn thy neighbor's love." Here, the aim goes beyond inter-personal harmony, and success does not depend on blind obedi-ence. We are given guidelines for transforming natural egotism and the instinct to hoard into altruistic behavior. It turns the will to be strong and unassailable by accumulation of money or power into the desire to accumulate an even more effective and precious capital—love, respect, gratitude and usefulness to others. Such "altruistic egotism" removes the motives for any aggressive behavior toward its practitioner, for who would want to destroy someone who has become lovable and useful?

I think these remarks will suffice to show the compatibility of the concepts of TM with those of a code designed to achieve the pleasant stress of fulfillment (in technical language: eustress) without the harmful consequences of damaging stress (that is, distress). The point is not to abolish stress but to master it. Stress is inherent in the activity of life itself. The purpose of TM is not only to relax but to prepare for efficient creative activity. In the classic words of the Bhagavad Gita: "Not by refraining from action does man attain freedom from action . . . for not even for a moment can a man be without action. Helplessly are all driven to action by the forces born of Nature." Translated into the language of my specialty: not by avoiding stress will man attain freedom from distress.

In all, I feel that *TM* will enjoy immediate success and offer the general public a most effective explanation of how pure awareness and creative intelligence, combined with what medi-cal science has taught us about the bodily effects of stress, can help humanity face "the crisis of modern life" as outlined in the opening chapter of this volume.

Université de Montréal
Montreal, Canada 1974

Hans Selye, C.C.,
M.D., Ph.D., D.Sc. (hon.),
M.D. (hon.), F.N.A. (hon.),
F.R.S.C., F.I.C.S. (hon.)

Professor and Director

INTRODUCTION

On the occasion of Maharishi Mahesh Yogi's general meeting at the University of Massachusetts at Amherst I had the gratifying experience of appearing on the platform with him as one of his invited guests. The proceedings of that meeting were subsequently published by the Maharishi under the title "International Symposium on the Science of Creative Intelligence," published by the Maharishi International University.

Maharishi and I engaged on the stage in a protracted dialogue. The basis for my part sprang from my own 1927 discovery and private employment of self-disciplines analogous to Maharishi's meditation. My development of these techniques sprang from my pre-1927 general awareness of Yoga and of the meditative preoccupations of various well-known East Indian cases of individuals who have practiced it in depth.

My thoughts in 1927 persuaded me that the capability to practice such self-disciplined meditation was given to humans in order to implement such successfully meditating individuals' accomplishment of tasks which could bring advantage to humanity in general and which advantages could not be arrived at from other than such a cosmically comprehensive and exquisitely incisive thought advantage. For this reason, I felt that all the cases of meditation with which I was familiar as practiced by meditators in the Orient had been conducted exclusively for the meditating individual's own gratification. I thought this to be not only selfish but a short-circuited squandering of the high advantage gaining potentials of all humanity.

On that occasion of the 1972 Maharishi Amherst dialogue Maharishi responded that early in his career he, too, had come to the same conclusion. He pointed out that he had been educated in physics and as a physicist was eager to turn his knowledge to greatest advantage for humanity. Thus, he had come intuitively to the realization that the meditating disciplines might enhance his ability to make broad human contributions. He therefore sought out the greatest meditative practitioner of the times in India and studied with him. Maharishi agreed with me about the squandering of pro-social gains when the omni-humanity advantage potentials of TM are entered into exclusively for self-gratification of the meditator.

In 1927 the enhancement of my thinking processes as attained through this self-discovered mental disciplining persuaded me to undertake a comprehensive pro-humanity strategy best described in my punctuationless, one sentence statement which has since been published on several occasions, most recently in the Saturday Review of March 2, 1968, which ran as follows:

WHAT I AM TRYING TO DO

Acutely aware of our beings' limitations and acknowledging the infinite mystery of the a priori universe into which we are born but nevertheless searching for a conscious means of hopefully competent participation by humanity in its own evolutionary trending while employing only the unique advantages inhering exclusively to the individual who takes and maintains the economic initiative in the face of the formidable physical capital and credit advantages of the massive corporations and political states and deliberately avoiding political ties and tactics while endeavoring by experiments and explorations to excite individuals' awareness and realization of humanity's higher potentials I seek through comprehensive anticipatory design science and its reductions to physical practices to reform the environment instead of trying to reform men being intent thereby to accomplish proto-typed capabilities of doing more with less whereby in turn the wealth augmenting prospects of such design science regenerations will induce their spontaneous and economically successful industrial proliferation by world around services' managements all of which chain reaction provoking events will both permit and induce all humanity to realize full lasting economic and physical success plus enjoyment of all the Earth without one individual interfering with or being advantaged at the expense of another.

This comprehensive, pro-humanity strategy in turn generated a plurality of companion insights and self-disciplines. Prominent among these were the following:

A. We have but few total hours of lifetime to turn to the advantage of humanity in general. Asking others to listen to our thoughts induces a self-defensive, only half listening attitude on the part of others. As a consequence, I resolved never to speak to anyone again unless they asked me to do so, on which occasion I must give them my very best thoughts relative to the specific question posed by the other.

B. Universe is everywhere in constant, complete evolutionary transformation employing a plurality of equi-economical, inter-transformative and inter-transactive techniques as well as a myriad of different rates and magnitudes of energy and time involvement. The omni-transforming is governed by a complex of omni-interaccommodative generalized principles. Discovery of the principles enables humans to participate cooperatively in Nature's evolutionary regenerativity. All the ecological regeneration aboard our planet is matched by and geared-in with the complementarity of astro-physics and astro-chemistry. Nature accomplishes her transformations in a wordless manner, each evolutionary event inducing a host of logical, physical responses both cosmically and terrestrially. For instance, a father has left his family at some geographical location and has gone to fetch life support items for the family from another geographical point. In his absence, a flash flood of torrential magnitude occurs forming a deep mountainside gorge through which a cubic mile of theretofore dammed-in mountain lake water plunges. This roaring gorge lies between the returning father and his family. If in the tumult of such events a great rock pinnacle topples over from one high rimside to span the gorge, accidentally producing a bridge across the gorge, there is little doubt that the returning father will use the rock bridge to reach his family rather than descending into the gorge and attempting to swim across. I concluded that the human individual taking advantage of meditation-produced insights could employ the generalized principles of nature in such special case experiences and could produce artifacts such as bridges which would be spontaneously employed by humanity without the conceiving and producing individual persuading other humans wherever and whenever use of those artifacts would lead to obviously preferential degrees of human advantage. The artifacts would speak for themselves, obviating verbal persuading. I therefore resolved in 1927 to undertake solution of all problems through such artifact evolving techniques. I called this Design Science.

C. My transcendental thinking having enabled me to enter and re-enter the design inspiring realm of such of the eternal, abstract, generalized principles as humanity had thus far discovered, I was further synergetically persuaded that the eternal integrity of the principles inherently eliminated the concept of *beginnings* and *ends* in respect to principles. To qualify as principles, they can have no beginnings and ends. Like truth and virginity: *they are* or *they are not*. All females are born virgin and may die virgin. Virginity is eternal. They cannot be born non-virgin. All special case realization of eternal principles is terminal and limited. Though the mathematical principles of leverage and mechanical advantage are statable in weightless, abstract, eternal mathematical equations, "A generalized lever cannot be realized." It must always be a special, limited case lever of wood or of steel—and of such and such a length.

I saw that the word creativity assumed a "beginning", ergo, a "creation", which was induced by the inherent terminability of all physical, special case, limited experiences. The physical organisms of humans are all terminal, limited. Limited humans o'erwhelmed by all their exclusively special case experiencing have misinformedly assumed a beginning and an end to always characterize all experiences. Very few individuals have themselves discovered any of the few, thus far discovered, generalized principles. It is only another special case experience when humans learn that such generalized discoveries have been made by others. Each experience of learning that someone else has discovered a principle and has phrased its relationship characteristics in such and such a manner becomes a special case experience involving only the brain of the individual to remember that *event*. Remembering the formula or remembering in which book to find the formula does not involve mind which alone is capable of discovering the relationship existing only between and not integral to any of the special case members of the "relationship" or any of their separate integral characteristics such as dimensions, chemistries or electro-magnetics. However, it does require mind to think through and rediscover for oneself the principles existing only *between* and *not in* the separate parts as did the original discoverer. "Comprehending" or "understanding" does require mind's unique thinking in order to bring the individual to first hand awareness of the eternal cosmic verities.

Humans cerebrated and spoke falacially of the universe as a special case universe having a beginning and therefore spontaneously evolved the concept of the *creator* responsible for initiating the special case existence. Because of the plurality of misconceptions relating to "creation" and "creativity" I excluded those words from further use in my vocabulary.

Through a half-century of pursuit of my aforementioned resolutions, I have come to the working assumption that humans can always effectively employ generalized eternal principles to arrive at temporal and limited physical inter-transforming. But the results, even though new to society, are not creations. They may be properly spoken of, however, as *inventions* meaning "bringing the eternal principles into finite, limited, temporal usages" typical of all humanity's physical experiences. I would feel it wise for Maharishi to convert his phrase "creative intelligence" to "inventive intelligence."

D. As a consequence of all the foregoing thoughts in 1927, I spontaneously committed whatever I might have of capabilities to all humanity and to fulfillment of all the evolutionary events of which I had cognizance, hopefully to be in every way directly rather than indirectly compatible to and synchronous with the integrity of eternally regenerative universe events. I noted (A) that the vegetation on our planet had the function of photosynthetically converting the sun's radiated energy into orderly molecular structures as hydrocarbons which then became multiplied by all the other biologicals. And I noted (B) that the vegetation would be dehydrated in all its sun exposure had it not roots with which by osmosis to draw water from the Earth and to valve it outward into the sky to be rained earthward elsewhere on other vegetation. And I noted (C) that because the vegetation was rooted it could not reach the other vegetation to procreate, wherefore (D) all the birds, bees and insects were designed to cross traffic between the vegetational species to cross pollenize them and insure their regeneration. And I noted (E) that each of the species was given a behavioral drive to go after something inadvertently to cross pollenize. That is the honey bee goes after its nectar as a 180° straight line drive while inadvertently bringing about the regeneration of the system as a 90° inadvertency. I saw then that nature's circulatory systems are the 90° or orbital resultant of the direct 180° individual radial drives.

At the outset of the 20th Century the concept of an eternally regenerative universe had been synergetically suggested by the occurrence of a plurality of highly significant discoveries and experiments. #1 Accomplishment of the measurement of the speed of light and all other classes of then-known electro-magnetic waves, all of which proved to have the same speed. This led to Einstein's concept of an eternally transforming physical universe as co-induced by discovery of #2 the Brownian movement; #3 black body radiation; #4 light photons; #5 Boltzman's Law of the intercomplementary complex of universal entropically exporting and syntropically importing behaviors of energy; as all wrapped together by #6 the general acknowledgment by science that there was no experimental evidence of energy being either created or lost.

E. All the foregoing thoughts and my ensuing experiential adherence to them further clarified for me the concept of human mind having a local-in-universe functioning capability which is essential to the maintenance of the omni-integrity of an omni-everywhere ceaselessly transforming and only overlappingly and locally terminal physical totality. I saw humans aboard planet Earth designed by and commissioned to operate a local-in-universe laboratory for testing of the omni-complementary, interaccommodative adequacy of the family of eternal generalized principles themselves. Human brains, in contra-distinction to human minds, operate in terminal packages. Human brains are finite physio-chemical organisms limited to the functions of first differentiating into independently operative systems all the information fed into it by all the sensing mechanisms and subsequent packaging together of the differentially sorted sets and storage of the integrated sets into the neuron's memory bank with the capability of repetitive retrieval of various information sets for successive reconsiderations by the mind. The mind and mind alone can discover interrelationships operating at exponentially varying rates of change between the separate experience sets of the considered complex of individual special case experience identities which exponentially varying interrelationships are in no way implicit and foretold to be operative by any of the geometrical, chemical, or electro-magnetic characteristics of any of the special case experience sets when considered only separately. These only mutually realized interrelationships, unpredicted by any of the separate constituent members of the complex, considered only separately, are spoken of as *synergy*.

As a synergetic consequence of all the foregoing I concluded that the concept of life was the synergetic interrelatedness of all the sub-interrelationships taken overlappingly together like the progressive series of overlappings and twistings together, of the fibers and strands of a rope none of which synergetic interrelationships or sub-interrelationships are inherent in any of the special case physical experience constituents.

As a further consequence of all the foregoing, I assumed that humans had long ago made the easy-to-make error of assuming that both *inanimate* and *animate* phenomena are physical. Now the synergetic interactions of biochemistry and biophysics have made it clear that all biological organisms consist entirely of atoms and that all atoms are inanimate. Whatever life may be, it is not physical and entropically terminal as are all physicals. All the chemical constituents which mid-20th Century biochemists identified as essential to the development of biological organisms' growth on our planet have now been found present in star dust samplings taken in space. This has led these scientists to the misconception and specious pronouncement that they have identified "the chemistry of life." When, however, humans die all these chemical constituents are as yet present in the cadaver, ergo, their critical chemistry cannot be life for life is no longer present. Whatever life may be it is not physical, ergo, animation is not physical.

The phenomena life is identified exclusively with the phenomena mind and the mind's comprehensions of meanings and significant, relative interrelationships as eternally inter-existing between the pattern integrities of all the special case terminal experiences whose pattern integrities alone are regenerative.

F. In view of all the foregoing and my resolve to commit all insights and inspirations, generated by humanity's access to mind, exclusively to development of inanimate artifacts I found myself operating transcendentally: to all terrestrial national boundaries; to all competitive economical games; and to all momentarily powerful physically sustained ethnic, religious, political or aesthetical biases.

The resources of universe on inventory in our planet's physical aggregate together with its biosphere embracement as well as all its daily cosmic energy income events as derived from the intercelestial transformings and export-import energy trafficking are all designedly present by cosmic regeneration necessity to be turned to comprehensive enhancement of the local-in-universe functioning of the human mind's local-in-universe problem solving effectiveness.

In 1927 at the time of adoption of the foregoing resolutions my wife and newborn child and I were penniless and I myself discredited as a successful performer in the economic competitions of humans aboard our planet. Being penniless and without credit, but richly blessed by the love of my wife, my child and friends, I was in an eminently favorable position to serve as a "trial balloon" experiment to test the validity of such a human individual's initiation of such a grand strategy inspired only by my working assumption that if human individuals commit them-

selves to all the foregoing concepts and self-disciplines to abet
positive evolutionary regeneration that humans so committed
and operative may find themselves and those dependent upon
them to be surviving successfully but without any physically
identifiable authority to "mark their papers" or to "pay them"
for the tasks they are performing. In 1927 it was the universal
assumption of highest priority that individuals must earn their
living—like it or not—because it was assumed that there was a
fundamental inadequacy of life support. Earning a living had
to be accomplished within the economic rules and customs
adopted by society. The honey bee and the human money bee
were mutually noncognizant of nature's ecological integrity of
circulatory-cyclical inter-regeneration. Contrariwise, I had to
assume that my undertaking would be sustained in completely
unexpected ways and only if I foreswore entirely the motif of
courting rewards for anything I might do. The rewards must be
for all humanity and all universe as they apparently always have
been and always will be. There was nothing moral or noble
about the commitment, for it meant only being natural, i.e.,
normal to universe.

Our newborn daughter has long since matured and she and
her now maturing daughter and son are all in accord with the
logic and validation by the subsequent half-century of events of
the commitment that I made in 1927 whereby I have been able
to design, produce, and in every way realize a great number of
artifacts all of which eventually have found spontaneous employment by humans around our planet. This total experience
now gives me confidence that I am not misleading other humans
when I suggest that they will probably find themselves being
economically and spontaneously sustained if they, too, commit
themselves to a like set of concepts and resolves. I am equally
confident however that this will hold true only if the individuals'
experience teaches them to see problems that need attending
which are not being attended by others which problems suggest
to them artifact design solutions which have not as yet been
undertaken by any humans.

This commitment seemed ever more natural when we considered the synergetics interrelatedness of: A, precession which is the effect of bodies in motion upon other separate bodies in motion which produces 90° angular effects upon the course of the lesser such as the sun's precessing its planets into orbits about it. And B, the phenomena of complete intereffects of all the biological species' independent, chromosomically programmed, unique survival drive which are 180° forces which altogether produce the comprehensive regenerative intersupport phenomenon known as ecology, which only overlappingly and sumtotally accomplishes the continuance of omni-biological regeneration not inherent in any of the species' behaviors. Were the other species not present the honey bee would become extinct; e.g., if there were no flowers for it to exploit for food, while there could be no flowers were they not inadvertently cross-pollenized by the bee or the bee's cousins. Quite clearly the celestial regeneration of Boltzman's entropic exporting and syntropic importing together with the terrestrial biosphere's regenerative circulatory system—like the human's own heart pumping of the blood through the veins and lungs' respiratory cleansing and renewal of the blood by oxygen, etc.—altogether manifest a universe of only superficially independent circulatory systems which all interact synergetically to guarantee the integrity of eternally regenerative universe. Obviously the individual humans committing themselves directly and effectively to the omni-regenerative success would be geared in to the total regenerative system and would be inadvertently regenerated but always indirectly. Each tree puts water into the sky to be rained down on other trees—none are directly reimbursed for their functions.

I do not think, however, that individuals can irresponsibly cast off social customs evolved through all ages and expect selfishly that the universe will support them just because they have a "put-on do-gooder" attitude.

I am confident that the support which I have received would not have occurred had I maneuvered ever so surreptitiously within myself for any sustaining rewards.

As a consequence of these resolves and approximately a

half-century of experience of being unexpectedly sustained I have come to the conclusion that: *only the impossible happens.* That is to say that nothing in the rationale of the thus far acquired human experience can elucidate the indirect workings of the cosmic integrity. These are eternally transcendental to humans' inherently limited exclusively direct sensing.

With the exception of the merely semantical suggestion to Maharishi that he substitute the word *invention* for the word *creation* in respect to intellectual resource development, I subscribe unreservedly to his philosophy and his employment of meditation to evolve and augment the physical and metaphysical advantaging of others. In this same context I feel this book by Harold Bloomfield, Michael Peter Cain, Dennis Jaffe, and Robert Kory to be inspirationally conceived and lucidly developed.

R. Buckminster Fuller

PREFACE

How did it happen that a physician-psychiatrist, an artist, a social scientist and a philosopher have collaborated on a book about the unfoldment of human potentialities? We have in common the practice of a modern technique of meditation. This technique is Transcendental Meditation, which has been introduced to nearly a million people, half of them in the United States, through the efforts of Maharishi Mahesh Yogi. As a result of the practice of this technique, we saw dramatic positive change in ourselves, our friends, colleagues, patients and students. We began to explore the implications of this simple and widely used method of expanding consciousness in relation to a growing body of scientific evidence. We also investigated Maharishi's theoretical explanation of the profound effects of the technique. As we proceeded we discerned more and more clearly that this form of meditation could affect every aspect of human health and well-being. We determined to present what we had experienced and learned in a systematic report of experience, scientific evidence and theory.

Harold was a physician completing his residency in psychiatry at the Yale University School of Medicine when he learned to practice Transcendental Meditation, or TM. He saw that meditating twice a day released the accumulated tensions of daily living and brought him greater productivity and enjoyment. His meditating friends and colleagues reported similar changes in their lives. Since the reduction of anxiety is a foremost goal of psychotherapy, when scientific research corroborated his personal experience he began to recommend TM to patients, and to explore TM's uses in medical and psychiatric treatment. He has since become the first American psychiatrist to become a fully qualified teacher of TM, and successfully uses the technique in his practice as Clinical Director of Psychiatry at the Institute of Psychophysiological Medicine in El Cajon, California. Dr. Bloomfield has lectured extensively on TM throughout the United States, Canada and Europe.

When he began TM, Michael was an artist using technology to express the deeper meanings of our changing environment with an internationally known group called Pulsa. He and his wife were so impressed with the results of meditation that they traveled to India and became trained teachers of TM. Thereafter, as research associate with the Yale School of Art, Michael twice taught a college seminar on the scientific study and theory of TM. Materials selected from this course form the framework of this book. Along with his work as an artist, Michael is now a professor of art in charge of developing a curriculum in art and consciousness at Maharishi International University.

Dennis was a social scientist at Yale who had founded several innovative programs for young people, particularly drug users. After working for several years to provide counseling services for alienated youths, he began TM. Seeing changes in himself and also in young persons who had been heavy drug users, he began to recognize possibilities for widespread social change. Presently in the Department of Psychiatry at UCLA, Dennis is co-author of *Toward a Radical Therapy* and *Worlds Apart*.

Robert was studying philosophy and political theory at Yale when he began TM. The value of meditation was so immediately apparent to him that he arranged to spend a year intensively researching the relationship of psychoanalytic concepts to Vedic theories of consciousness under Maharishi's guidance. A resulting paper has been central to our formulation of the relationship of Transcendental Meditation to psychoanalytic theory in chapter seven.[159] Presently Vice-President of Expansion for the American Foundation for the Science of Creative Intelligence, he is now administrating a major grant to apply

TM in high-school education and is designing a nationwide series of seminars to introduce TM to the business community.

The authors encompass a range of disciplines and have emerged in their present commitment to TM from a variety of social movements of the last decades. We are convinced that the practice of TM by as many people as possible will be a significant step toward realizing more humane, life-supporting values on every level of life. We have written this book to present what we have experienced and understood to others who are looking for peace of mind, who feel that they have not actualized their true capacities, and who want to find a way to achieve a more harmonious, creative and fulfilled life.

TM*

 Transcendental Meditation

THE CRISIS
OF
MODERN LIFE

An inherent dynamism impels Americans toward satisfaction. People around the world have regarded America as the world's most active, productive and progressive nation. For over a century Americans have been outstandingly successful in their aggressive drive to fulfill their desires through the systematic application of technology. Why then are Americans characteristically tense inside? And why is their pervasive anxiety inseparably linked with a longing for satisfaction?

Technology is a system for fulfilling desires. America has more technology than any nation in the world. In fact Americans have largely achieved the unprecedented comfort which technology promises. The rest of the world is rapidly following suit. Though millions remain in poverty, rapid industrialization in such diverse nations as Sweden, Japan and Iran has proven that people can and will achieve material comfort through the systematic and intelligent use of technology. Despite present rising prices, widespread shortages and depletion of resources, an unprecedented percentage of the world's population is beginning to enjoy satisfaction of its basic needs and an increase in its leisure time. These many individuals, however, are falling prey to the same problems which afflict Americans, most notably anxiety, psychosomatic ailments, drug abuse, mental illness, poor quality of work, a pervasive lack of purpose and a frantic search for stimulation.

Abundance of material comfort achieved through technology

has brought a corresponding increase in anxiety and dissatisfaction. This fact constitutes a historical paradox with enormous implications. Although industrial and developing nations are committed to technological expansion, technology has so far failed to enable man to achieve personal fulfillment or social harmony. In response to this failure some social scientists have begun calling for a re-evaluation and curtailment of technological expansion,[64, 238] while others have simply withdrawn to insist on man's perennial dissatisfaction.[156, 175] The apparent insolubility of the paradoxical rise of tension throughout the world may appear to justify a pessimistic outlook on man's future. An alternative to such pessimism is to apply the technology of modern science to the study of human fulfillment.

The reason for studying human fulfillment is obvious. If science could define a means whereby people could gain access to their full personal resources and enjoy a state of complete integration, widespread application of such knowledge would not only benefit individuals but society as well. Toward this end America has spent millions of dollars on medical and psychological research. Nevertheless, aside from temporary and often damaging relief through drugs, medicine and psychology have not yet demonstrated a practical program to relieve the mounting tension which people feel.

The paradoxical rise of tension paralleling the rise of technology constitutes, however, a new point of departure for understanding why man is not fulfilled. Man's success in transforming his world has led to great changes in all aspects of life. Contemporary pressures force people to assimilate in a month what was previously a century's accumulation of information and experience.[280] People are bombarded with information and sensation to the point of damaging overstimulation. Although mass production, computerized data systems and high speed transportation have expanded man's range of influence, they have also required people's minds, bodies and senses to function beyond their available capabilities. The spiraling development of new techniques for fulfilling man's needs and desires has necessitated continuous mental and physical adaptation to overwhelming transformations in every aspect of life.

A recent book has popularized the term "future shock" to describe the disastrous effect of the accelerating pace of the modern world on human life.[280] Though "future shock" has significant psychological and behavioral implications, the term refers primarily to the inability of the human body to withstand the accelerating change presently demanded of it. Too much change too fast weakens the physical functioning of the body and causes deterioration of emotional and mental well-being. No amount of material comfort is sufficient to reverse this damage. The physiological effect of accelerating technological expansion is a primary cause of the lack of "satisfaction" in our society.

The medical term for excessive wear and tear upon the body is stress. When a person is subjected to continuous change, his body must respond to this demanding circumstance. In adapting to circumstances which challenge his faculties, an individual reacts biochemically and physiologically. This adaptation process taxes the body's essential resources and exhausts its energies. Repeated exposure to excessive stress without sufficient rest to restore depleted bodily resources triggers a process of deterioration which undermines every aspect of a person's experience. When people begin to suffer from accumulated stress, they become susceptible to disease, particularly to psychosomatic ailments.[96, 249] They also find themselves troubled by inexplicable anxiety, frustration, depression or a general feeling of dissatisfaction and aimlessness. When stress accumulates, a loss of mental clarity and emotional openness damages interpersonal relationships. Excessive stress also leads to the inability to make decisions, plan effectively and work efficiently. Because of the total interdependency of bodily, emotional and mental processes, stress affects every phase of one's life.

Medical investigation of the stress syndrome has led to increased understanding of its central role in all illness.[249] The incidence of heart disease in America illustrates how widespread and debilitating this syndrome has become. Over one-third of the adult male population suffers from hypertension and over half of all deaths result from heart and circulatory diseases.[199] Equally revealing is the tremendous sale of sleeping pills which clearly indicates that the inability to sleep is a major health problem of our times. Disturbed sleep is one of the most prominent effects of excessive stress and a precursor of mental illness. The widespread use of frequently addicting and often harmful medications for relief from insomnia must be counted as a complication of, rather than a solution to, the problem of stress. Similarly indicative of the pressing need to relieve the effects of stress is the widespread use of tranquilizers, barbiturates, amphetamines, hallucinogens, marijuana, narcotics, cigarettes and alcohol. In 1970, U.S. drug companies produced five billion doses of tranquilizers, five billion doses of barbiturates, and three billion doses of amphetamines, while U.S. doctors wrote over 200 million prescriptions for such drugs.

Although stress contributes to the growing tension in people's lives, understanding its psychophysiological nature suggests insight into the mechanics of health and fulfillment. Material comfort and achievement provide some degree of satisfaction but the state of a person's body and mind determines the overall quality of his experience. If stress can color a person's everyday activity with anxiety and dissatisfaction, the physiological opposite of stress, a rested and efficiently functioning nervous system, may be expected to support an overall experience of emotional and physical well-being. Similarly, if excessive stress limits performance and obstructs decision making, freeing the body from stress should unfold reserves of energy and intelligence for improved performance and effective thinking.

The critical need to confront the problem of stress and lack of fulfillment in our society has become painfully evident in the breakdown of people's relations to social institutions. Work, which had once provided an opportunity for achievement, has largely degenerated into a purely economic necessity. Yet recreation, which once brought ease and joy to leisure time, has become a frantic quest for ever more thrilling pleasures.[259] While the sense of community has atrophied in small towns, the anonymity and transience of urban existence has made life evanescent, rootless, and devalued.[280] Confronted with the virtually impossible task of providing an intimate and secure center for human development while the larger community is breaking down around it, the family is also under strain.[200, 280] Nearly half of all marriages end in divorce and one in four children has divorced parents. Teachers, students and parents have begun criticizing schools for their failure to equip young people with the manual, emotional and intellectual skills they need to deal with the future.[121] The apparent intractability of these generalized effects of stress has inspired growing cynicism about possible solutions. Because stress kindles antagonism and impatience among people while limiting creativity and effective thinking, it further compounds the social problems it causes.

The fast moving pace of progress demands that people quickly relieve their internal stress and begin to use their full resources to resolve the external crises of increasing social fragmentation. People must become flexible. They must learn to meet a wide variety of rapidly changing interpersonal, emotional and physical demands without incurring excessive stress. They must become acutely discriminating, and capable of making appropriate decisions amidst rapidly changing circumstances. They must become self-sufficient in finding lasting satisfaction within themselves rather than looking to rigid social roles for fulfillment. They must develop their full capability for harmonizing differences in order to sustain richness of life in the midst of accelerating change. Finally, they must tap their full measure of creativity and intelligence to insure comprehensively life-supporting design in continued technological development.

This book describes a method of achieving this growth by reducing accumulated stress, increasing the body's resistance to stress and fostering a state of psychophysiological integration. Drawing on a broad base of scientific research, we will argue that a specific technique, Transcendental Meditation (TM), is uniquely useful in reducing stress and unfolding a person's full measure of energy, intelligence and satisfaction. This technique, which is now enriching the lives of hundreds of thousands of people, has enabled scientists to identify a natural response in the body which provides stability and integration to the nervous system. When properly triggered through the correct practice of TM, this response is as automatic as a reflex. TM enables a person to gain a deep state of rest which repairs the damage of excessive stress and promotes improved health, emotional stability and performance. Recent research into its psychophysiological effects suggests that TM is a major discovery in the technology of human integration.

TM may be most significant for the wide range of impact which it provides. Researchers have reported that regular practice of the technique improves learning ability,[1, 47] perceptual motor performance[27] and reaction time.[255] Other researchers have noted improved psychological health,[71, 206] improved ability to recover from stress,[214] and improved perceptual acuity.[109, 223] Management scientists have reported that TM increases productivity and job satisfaction.[84] Doctors have reported that TM reduces high blood pressure,[24] improves asthmatic conditions[302] and is useful in treating the mentally ill.[99, 251] Among the many studies which we will discuss, these reports are suggestive of the promise which TM holds for improving people's lives by reducing stress and encouraging the integration of the nervous system.

The response which TM induces is intrinsic to the human nervous system. Growth through the practice of TM is a wholly natural process. TM involves no effort to alter bodily or mental states or to analyze or control the mind. In fact the technique is as natural and spontaneous as waking up, and its physiological effects result from deep rest achieved during its practice. The technique's corresponding psychological effects result from a spontaneous integration of the activity of the nervous system. Because of its complete naturalness and utter spontaneity, TM is totally unlike any technique of hypnosis or suggestion. For the same reason, it is entirely separate from an individual's religious attitudes.

The response triggered through TM is as old as man. A discussion of the technique can be found in the oldest records of human experience, the Vedas. This technique does not, how-

ever, have any connection with the present fashionable culti-
vation of Eastern philosophy or culture. In fact, the correct
practice of TM does not depend on any cultural orientation,
but only upon the inherent abilities of the nervous system. Furthermore, the unique state of rest achieved through TM is so
natural and valuable to personal development and well-being
that references to it appear in a wide variety of cultural traditions. However, as can be seen from currently available evidence,[289, 290] no technique of meditation is as effective as TM in
producing deep rest and consequent psychophysiological integration.

In proposing a natural rather than an artificial technique to
strengthen people physiologically and thereby unfold their innate capacities, we align ourselves with the human potential
movements in all the sciences. We will argue throughout this
book that man's failure to meet the demands of progress results
from his inability to utilize his full physical, emotional and mental potential. Correspondingly, we will suggest that a solution
to the myriad problems of our society lies in the widespread
application of a technique to psychophysiologically strengthen
the individual and unfold his untapped resources.

This thesis is closely related to the theory that man can find
tremendous resources through the development of his consciousness. Our discussion of personal development, however,
will differ substantially from the popular and polymorphous
prescription that the solution to all man's problems lies within
consciousness. We define consciousness as the basic faculty expressed in our ability to become aware of external and internal
objects and situations. Consciousness is that hard-to-describe
but utterly familiar basis of all our experience which is dull
when we are tired and which shines forth luminously when
we are alert. Consciousness is most fully experienced during wakefulness in our sharp perception, clear feelings and lucid
thoughts. In sleep and dreaming, the faculty of consciousness
is expressed in the ability to obtain the regenerative effects of
deep rest which lead to clarity in subsequent experience. Other
possible expressions of consciousness in higher states of aware-

ness will be discussed in subsequent chapters of this book. Though easily overshadowed by stress, consciousness is man's most basic and valuable resource.

Despite the obvious relationship between this basic notion of consciousness and human potential, humanists have recently used the term in so many different ways as to render it almost meaningless. One theorist has treated it as ideology,[230] another as a process,[220] another as a quality of experience[273] and another as the interface between the environment and the self.[227] To avoid confusion with these varied meanings of the term, we will discuss human potential not in terms of consciousness but in terms of a new concept, creative intelligence. We will, however, consider the relation between personal growth and states of consciousness, an idea which has specific physiological and psychological significance.

The potential of the human mind constitutes a frontier which science has barely explored. Brain researchers have identified the enormous capacities of the human nervous system,[309] while psychologists have recognized man's limited use of his mental potential even as early as the beginning of the twentieth century.[132] Within man a tremendous dynamo of energy and intelligence is constantly empowering and directing human activity. Maharishi Mahesh Yogi, the first teacher of TM in the West, has identified this potential energy and intelligence within man as "creative intelligence."[186] The term "creative" refers to the ability to cause change and the term "intelligence" refers to the ability to direct change. Therefore the term creative intelligence describes man's innate capacity to sustain progress.

In our discussion of expanding human capacity through psychophysiological integration we will use the concept of creative intelligence to describe the principle of integrated, or holistic, growth which TM catalyzes. The effectiveness of TM as a technique for unfolding creative intelligence has led to a systematic elaboration of principles through which creative intelligence operates.[186] The study of creative intelligence has gained recognition as a new science in many universities throughout the United States. In a later chapter of this book, we will discuss the impact which this new academic discipline, the Science of Creative Intelligence, is having on education.

The purpose of this book is to present the significance of TM within a coherent scientific framework. Having outlined the critical need for an approach to strengthen the individual and unfold full human capacities, we describe, in chapter 2, how TM works and how to learn it. In chapter 3, we discuss the physiology of the human nervous system and how stress affects it. In chapter 4 we review the current physiological research on TM and outline hypotheses regarding TM's physiological role in reducing stress and promoting health. Chapter 5 presents evidence of TM's psychological benefits, particularly in reducing drug abuse, while chapter 6 reports on the use of TM as an adjunct to psychotherapy. In chapter 7 we explain TM as a means of gaining continuous access to pure creative intelligence and thereby unfolding man's full potential. The final chapter reports on some of the ways TM is already being used to improve our social institutions through enhancing individual life.

2

TRANSCENDENTAL MEDITATION: THE TECHNIQUE OF CONTACTING PURE AWARENESS

Every day before breakfast and again before dinner a half a million Americans of all ages and walks of life sit in a comfortable chair and close their eyes. Effortlessly they settle into deeper and deeper states of relaxation while their minds remain alert with enjoyment. They are astronauts, senators, congressmen, a high-ranking China expert, Strategic Air Command personnel, Pentagon generals, a famous dietician, Wall Street brokers, New York Jets football players, UCLA Bruins basketball champions, Broadway playwrights, members of an eminent repertory theater, scientists, artists, businessmen, professors, doctors, teachers, housewives, students and children. They are all practitioners of Transcendental Meditation. What are they doing and why?

Neither a religion or a philosophy, nor a way of life, Transcendental Meditation is a natural technique for reducing stress and expanding conscious awareness. It was first introduced into the United States in 1959 by the Indian teacher Maharishi Mahesh Yogi. The term "transcendental" means "going beyond."[187] Maharishi chose this term to indicate that TM spontaneously takes its practitioners beyond the familiar level of their wakeful experience to a state of profound rest coupled with heightened alertness.

Maharishi's technique for achieving this state is effortless.

TM can be learned in a few hours and is then practiced for only fifteen to twenty minutes each morning and evening. The technique is a specific method of allowing the activity of the mind to settle down while one sits comfortably with eyes closed. This mental process automatically triggers a physiological response conducive to both deep rest and increased wakefulness. Because learning to meditate does not involve cultivating a new skill but instead simply allowing an innate ability of the nervous system to unfold, it requires no particular attitude, preparatory ritual, special setting or unusual postures. Though the technique is usually practiced at home, it may be done in any place where a person can sit comfortably without being disturbed. Many busy individuals meditate on planes, trains, subways, buses or in waiting rooms.

What happens during Transcendental Meditation? A person allows his mind to experience a relaxed and enjoyable state which draws his attention inward. He experiences a state in which the mind becomes very quiet, but extraordinarily alert. Though sense impressions, feelings or thoughts may be present during TM, meditators report brief or sometimes extended periods of "blank awareness," "being awake inside with nothing going on," "not being asleep, but not being aware of anything in particular" (257, p. 53). People's wakeful attention is generally engaged by the objects of their experience. Our daily experience is made up of an unending cascade of thoughts, emotions, sensations and perceptions. TM creates an opportunity for two brief daily periods of effortless disengagement from these continuous impressions. When a meditator allows his attention to shift inward, he experiences quiet levels of the mind in which he becomes increasingly aware of the unbounded nature of his awareness in the absence of objects. This state, which will be termed *pure awareness*, consists of nothing more than being wide awake inside without being aware of anything except awareness itself.

Though this experience has not been widely familiar among Westerners, it is neither difficult nor unusual. Persons learning TM and getting a sense of the experience in their first meditation often remark, "Oh yes, I've been there before," or "That happened to me several times when I was a child." Even if the experience is not explicitly remembered, it is still deeply familiar because it consists of nothing more than an intimate glimpse of the innermost aspect of the self.

If this experience is in fact natural and universal, why does a person need a special technique to experience it? As Maharishi has explained:

> Experience in TM shows that . . . pure awareness . . . is the essential basic nature of the mind. But since the mind ordinarily remains attuned to the senses . . . and their monitoring of the external . . . it misses or fails to appreciate its own essential nature, just as the eyes are unable to see themselves. (184, p. 30)

As the eyes need a mirror to perceive themselves, so the mind needs a method of becoming aware of its innermost nature. Yet even in the absence of such a technique, occasional individuals throughout history have experienced pure awareness. Their descriptions of these experiences, often in mystical, poetic or philosophical language, stand among the achievements of mankind.

The significance and value of TM is not in producing a new experience. Rather, TM provides a universally effective and systematic means of experiencing pure awareness twice a day. Through regular practice of TM, pure awareness ceases to be a vicarious idea, a distant memory or an occasional peak experience. Instead it becomes a consistent element in the ongoing process of life.

Despite the inherently fascinating nature of the experience of pure awareness, people do not necessarily practice TM for pleasure or self-knowledge, but also for significant improvements in the quality of their lives. As we will report, the regular experience of pure awareness has pronounced positive effects on physical health and psychological well-being. It also leads to the full actualization of human potentialities. Maharishi has explained these benefits in terms of the identity between pure awareness, the experience of being awake inside without thoughts during meditation, and creative intelligence, the fundamental resource of energy and intelligence underlying individual consciousness (186: I, III). By contacting pure awareness regularly a person gains direct access to that level of the mind from which all human energy and intelligence springs. In forthcoming chapters, we will consider to what extent this theory is borne out by physiological and psychological research. If TM does prove highly effective in unfolding human resources of energy and intelligence, the simplicity of this approach to human development promises a practical resolution to the crisis of stress and man's present inability to meet the challenge of progress.

THE MECHANICS OF TRANSCENDENTAL MEDITATION

TM is not an idea or a theory, but is rather a specific and unique practice. Although this section gives a sense of the technique's operation, it is essential to understand from the outset that TM cannot be learned from this book. Beginning TM requires personal instruction from a trained teacher of TM. Information on where to learn the technique is presented in the Appendix.

To explain how TM works, it is helpful to begin with an analogy. Maharishi describes the mind as similar to an ocean, with wave activity on its surface but profound stillness at its depths. Conscious activities—thoughts, emotions, perceptions— are similar to waves on the surface of an ocean; the silent depths of the mind are similar to the silent depths of the ocean. Just as silent currents underlie all the surface waves on an ocean, the silent depths of the mind support all our conscious mental activity.

To describe the relation between the silent and active parts of the mind, Maharishi includes another element in his comparison of the mind to an ocean. He asserts that thought originates in the most quiet depths of the mind just as a bubble might rise from an absolutely silent ocean floor. Compressed by the great pressure at the ocean bottom, a bubble would appear almost imperceptibly but would grow in size as it rose toward the surface. Similarly, an impulse of thought originates in the silent regions of the mind without our noticing its presence until it develops and becomes a clear and distinct experience.

While this analogy may seem too simple to describe the thinking process accurately, the basic elements of this analogy bear a striking correspondence to psychological and physiological descriptions of the thought process. Psychoanalysts refer to "preconscious elaboration" to explain what happens to thought between its first inception in the mind and its final emergence as a conscious experience (83, pp. 601-605).

Similarly, science writer Dean Woolridge concludes a description of the physiology of this process:

> We are aware of our . . . thoughts, but not of how they get there. Such unconscious activity appears to extend to complicated logical thinking—how else can we account for the sudden insight or solution of a difficult problem that sometimes comes to us when least expected? Even when it seems to us that our conscious processes are completely responsible for our mental activities we may be wrong; the real work of the brain may be that which is going on quietly behind the scenes. (309, p. 240)

Maharishi describes the process in detail:

> A thought starts from the deepest level of consciousness and rises through the whole depth of the mind until it finally appears as a conscious thought at the surface. Thus we find that every thought stirs the whole range of and depth of consciousness, but is consciously appreciated only when it reaches the conscious level; all its earlier states of development are not appreciated. That is why we say that for all practical purposes, the deeper levels of the ocean of consciousness are silent. (185, p. 64)

Figure A graphically represents the basic theory of mind upon which the technique of TM is based. Thought, represented by a bubble, rises in the mind, represented by an ocean, from the deepest part of the mind, point A. By the time a thought has emerged on the surface of the mind at level B, the thought has developed sufficiently to be appreciated as a thought. We call level B the conscious mind, because we notice thinking there. We may call level A the source of thought, because thoughts originate at this great depth within the mind.

FIGURE A

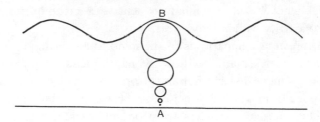

Using this comparison of the mind to an ocean, we can readily explain the mechanics of TM. The process of TM consists of simply letting one's attention settle from the active surface level of the mind to the mind's quiet depths where thinking begins. Though the very process of thinking generally stimulates the mind toward increasing activity, TM makes use of the thinking process to lessen mental activity. The key to TM's effectiveness in minimizing mental activity lies in the technique's ability to redirect spontaneously the attention of the mind from its involvement with fully developed thought to engagement in less and less elaborated levels of thought. The process of gently turning the attention inward toward quieter and quieter thought is so easy that Maharishi compares TM to diving. Just as diving into an ocean requires only taking a proper angle and then letting go, TM requires only a means of orienting the mind toward experiencing quieter levels of thought and taking it as it comes.

Once given an inward turn through TM, the attention moves toward less and less developed thought motivated by the natural tendency of the attention to shift toward increasingly satisfying experience. The tendency of the mind to move in the direction of increasingly charming experience operates in all mental activity. For example, as you read this page, there are innumerable stimuli bombarding your senses. You have probably been totally unaware of these occurrences, due to the greater enrichment found in reading. If, however, along with this book and whatever other stimuli are present, you were also exposed to your favorite piece of music, it would be difficult to continue reading attentively. Your attention would be naturally attracted by the enjoyment of listening to the music. TM applies this natural tendency of the mind to achieve a great quieting of mental activity without any effort.

Our previous comparisons of the mind to an ocean suggest a schematic representation of how the natural tendency of the attention to move toward happiness operates in TM. Just as a boat rides from wave to wave on an ocean, the attention of an individual normally wanders from one object of experience to another, always remaining on the surface of the mind. Figure B represents a normal wakeful experience of the mind moving from perceiving the moon, to the affectionate enjoyment of that sight, to an idea about photographing the moon.

FIGURE B

Figure C, on the other hand, represents the attention taking an inward turn during the process of TM. Instead of remaining on the surface of the mind, a person practicing TM begins to experience quieter and less distinct but increasingly charming stages of thought.

FIGURE C

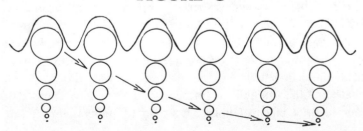

In order for this process of experiencing quiet levels of mental activity during TM to take place, the mind must first be gently disengaged from the mental activity which normally keeps it entirely involved with fully developed thoughts. However, though the mind must be freed from its superficial activities, it must be kept active in order to avoid simply falling asleep.

The technique of TM consists of giving the attention an inward turn by easily thinking a single thought. In this way, the mind remains active but is left undirected. Naturally attention begins to seek the increasing satisfaction available at quieter levels of the mind. Eventually awareness settles down completely, effortlessly transcends thinking altogether, and gains the status of pure awareness.

Theoretically it should be possible to initiate the process of TM by repeatedly experiencing any thought, emotion, sensation or perception. However, thought, as opposed to other possible experiences, constitutes the ideal vehicle for facilitating the inward shift of attention. Thought is most effective because it is the most intimate and self-contained aspect of subjective experience. But what is the nature of thought? Studies of memory and attention have shown that much of a person's thinking activity, even when dealing with recalling visual information, amounts to mentally repeating the sounds of various words. Harvard psychologist George Sperling has argued that such subvocal "rehearsal" is the basic mechanism through which consciousness directs awareness to its objects (263, pp. 87-88). Modern psychology's recognition of the importance of thought as subvocalized sound echoes a number of ancient traditions which hold that sound, especially on the subtle level of thought, is a powerful vehicle for influencing consciousness.[52]

Sound as entertained in thought provides a most effective vehicle for disengaging the mind from the everyday thinking process and turning the attention toward increasingly quiet mental activity. The thought-sounds used in TM are called "mantras." "Mantra" is a Sanskrit term which designates "a thought the effects of which are known"[187] not on the level of meaning—in fact, the mantras taught for use in TM have no denotative meaning—but on the level of vibratory effect, analogous to sound quality. Mantras are specially selected for each individual who receives instruction in TM. Once learned, the mantra is confidential and is used for only one purpose, to effect the spontaneous process of reducing mental activity during the practice of TM.

Because TM permits the meditator to experience quiet levels of the mind, where the influence of each thought is especially profound, the selection of the correct mantra for each individual is of critical importance. Maharishi and the thousands of trained teachers of TM rely on an ancient tradition through which many generations have fathomed the full depth of the mind. This tradition provides a systematic procedure for selecting the most suitable sounds for use in TM by particular individuals. Such procedure has been maintained since 5000 B.C. or earlier, the time of mankind's most ancient teachings, the Vedas.

Learning TM consists not only of learning the right mantra but also how to use it correctly. To insure correctness in every aspect of these fundamentals, personal instruction in the technique by a qualified teacher is necessary. The technique cannot be learned secondhand, from a book or from another meditator. Extensive preparation is required to qualify a teacher to guide a novice through all possible variations of personal experience. Nor is it feasible to choose a suitable mantra for oneself, by chance, by consultation of classical texts or by intuition. What seems to be an appropriate mantra on the surface level of intellectual understanding may unfortunately turn out to have inappropriate effects.

For example, the popular mantra "Om" has been described as a "universal sound" having good effects for anyone who chants it aloud or uses it internally. Many people who have used "Om" have reported, however, that its effects were reclusive or even antisocial, in contrast to the dynamic positive results of TM. This account by a 28-year-old individual is typical:

I was into other techniques, mainly an Om meditation, which created a nice mood. While I was doing it I would be in a beautiful mood, but if I left my room or had to go out and deal with just everyday things, I was definitely incapacitated. After six months I felt an incredible conflict, I got to the point where I couldn't do anything, I was so split. After I started TM every day just got brighter and brighter. I transcended right away and had many glimpses of pure consciousness. I was finally getting what I'd been looking for but was always missing. Now I'm working again and just got promoted. My energy level has increased at least 200%.

The danger of using a mantra of unknown effect is dramatized by numerous similar reports from people who have used nonsense syllables, euphonious sounds, or words with pleasing meanings. In every case, meditation with these mantras was less favorable than the correct practice of TM. In several cases the aftereffects were negative or unsettling, and included headaches, disrupted attention span and anxiety. It is unfortunate, with the increasing popularity of TM, some self-styled "experts" of relaxation or other meditative techniques have been indiscriminately advocating their own makeshift mantras, unaware that severely deleterious effects can be experienced by their unsuspecting practitioners.

Once a person learns TM correctly, he is able to practice the technique without difficulty. Effortlessly enjoying a state of profound rest and heightened alertness twice daily, a meditator becomes increasingly familiar with the full range of the mind, from the quietest to the most developed levels of the thought process.

Though researchers attribute the positive effects of TM to the profound rest gained during the meditation period, the holistic growth resulting from regular practice of the technique may be discussed in terms of increasing a person's access to quiet mental activity and underlying pure awareness. We will present this theory in detail after reviewing physiological and psychological research on TM's effects.

OTHER TECHNIQUES OF MEDITATION

Aside from TM there are two principal types of meditation: contemplation and concentration.* Techniques of contemplation involve allowing the attention to dwell upon internal or external objects of experience. Techniques of concentration involve holding or focusing attention on an object of experience.

The term contemplation describes all practices of thinking about meaning. A person may contemplate a physical object, a devotional prayer, a philosophical concept, or a generalized issue like "Who am I?" Because thinking about an issue is our basic procedure for gaining understanding, contemplation enriches a person's intellectual comprehension of whatever he contemplates.

However, this value is also contemplation's distinct limitation. Contemplation involves conscious thought and is therefore confined to the surface level of the mind. Contemplation neither quiets mental activity nor fosters deep bodily rest. Furthermore, though a person may enjoy a positive experience while thinking about a profound or delightful subject, the thought will sustain its expansive effect only as long as a person continues to think about it. Thus for example a philosopher, the professional contemplator, may find great delight in an insight gained in his study, only to be deprived of this delight when

---

*These categories tend to be more useful in distinguishing between specific practices of meditation than the tripartite classification proposed by Naranjo.[205] Naranjo's categories are "The Way of the Forms," i.e., concentration, "The Negative Way," i.e., insight and "The Expressive Way," i.e. surrender to possession states, trance, intuition, etc. The problem with these categories is that in their attempt to include all types of experience which might be considered "meditative" they indiscriminately and in some cases inappropriately lump almost every actual meditation technique, including Transcendental Meditation, into the first category of concentration. Goleman's more practical approach in his recent analysis of meditative techniques in terms of a Buddhist model has yielded a more relevant tripartite division: Concentration, Insight, and the Integration of the two.[105] His categories have some analogy to those proposed here, though they fail to make specific reference to the actual processes used, and also wind up incorrectly treating TM as a form of concentration.

dodging traffic to cross the street a few minutes later. What is constant in a person's experience is not the object of experience but the conscious experiencer. If a person wishes to make lasting change in his experience, what he needs is not a change in what he is thinking *about* but in what he is thinking *with*. To achieve this change he must use a technique which expands the range of consciousness itself.

In concentration on the other hand, an individual attempts to transform the quality of his experience by direct mental control. Techniques of concentration most often involve voluntary focusing on a particular object of experience, such as a physical object like a candle flame, a sensation-emotion like a feeling of bliss, an insoluble philosophical paradox like a Zen koan, or a more generalized state like the absence of all thought. By attempting to hold attention on a particular object, concentration interrupts the natural continuous flow of attention. Central to both human survival and development, the natural tendency of the attention to move toward greater satisfaction is a basic property of the mind. To somehow interrupt the indomitable flow of attention, a person must expend considerable energy. If he succeeds, he temporarily eliminates change, and thereby debars himself from spontaneously following the increasing charm unfolded by the expansion of quieter levels of awareness.

As scientific research reported in the next chapter suggests, in the long run concentration may produce some beneficial effects. The physiology of advanced practitioners of yoga and Zen concentration techniques has shown similarities to the physiology of practitioners of TM. But there is one important difference: the results found in Zen monks and yogis show up clearly only after fifteen to twenty-five years of practice,[146] whereas the results of TM are immediate, beginning from the first meditation. This comparison suggests that concentration provides an indirect and difficult approach to a possibility which is already accessible. It may well be that people practicing techniques involving concentration experience pure awareness because, after years of practice, they "fall backward" into experiencing what could have happened spontaneously, had they known how to just let it happen. The undirected, effortless quieting of mental activity immediately facilitated by TM may well constitute the essential process through which every experience of the pure awareness unfolds.

Psychologist Robert Ornstein has written:

> It seems that a consequence of the structure of our central nervous system is that if awareness is restricted to one unchanging source of stimulation, a "turning off" of consciousness of the external world follows. Common instructions for meditation all underscore this. . . . The somewhat bewildering superficial differences of various practices all can be understood as aids in focusing awareness on a single process, continuously recycling the same subroutine through the nervous system. When this is achieved, a common experience seems to be produced; awareness of the external environment diminishes and "turns off" for a period of time. (220, p. 169)

Ornstein misinterprets the entirely nonfocused, nonconcentrative aspect of the repetition of the mantra in TM, and also fails to elucidate what is "turned on" when consciousness of various objects of experience is "turned off." However, he presents impressive evidence that the underlying mechanism of meditative techniques is the natural tendency of the mind to settle down to its own inner nature when a single thought is experienced in an increasingly charming manner. Transcendental Meditation is unique in actualizing this ability immediately, rather than after years of practice.

If TM consists of nothing more than facilitating the natural tendency of awareness, why is it necessary to learn it at all? Most of the functions which we regard as the natural elements of human life, including sleeping regularly, eating, walking, talking and thinking are learned and are in fact specifically taught as part of our culture's built-in educational process. Since our society lacks an effective technique for taking our awareness within, our basic training of the individual has necessarily not included the means of achieving pure awareness. The utterly natural, effortless, and easily learned practice of TM readily corrects this lack.

TM is also unique among all modern techniques for altering conscious experience. TM has little in common with hypnosis or other methods which produce changes in an individual's physical or mental state through suggestion. Practitioners of TM learn to think a correct mantra innocently and do not bother about other mental intentions or external influences. In fact, making any effort or following any external direction is incorrect meditation and has the effect of holding the attention on the surface of the mind. Similarly, TM is utterly different from the various biofeedback techniques which have been developed over the last decades to permit people to train themselves to recognize and control such physiological functions as brain waves. In TM, the entire process of quieting mental activity is completely spontaneous and involves no manipulative learning processes.

NORMALIZATION THROUGH THE NATURAL RELEASE OF STRESS

The proliferation of ineffective techniques for expanding awareness has resulted in the widespread misconception that experiencing pure awareness is difficult and requires special skills. Before learning TM, people often express apprehension that they will not succeed in meditation because they cannot control their thoughts. Teachers of meditation invariably reply that anyone can master TM because it involves no control of any kind but only sitting back and letting whatever happens naturally during the practice simply happen. The effectiveness of this entirely natural and effortless procedure becomes apparent once a person has begun meditating. There is never any need to focus on the mantra because thoughts other than the mantra are no obstacle to correct meditation. If thoughts persist during TM, they are not regarded as an indication of unsuccessful meditation, but rather as a sign of success.

When a person learns TM, he receives a simple but essential explanation of the role of thoughts in Transcendental Meditation. Thoughts arise during meditation due to a principle which is as basic to the benefits of TM as the mind's tendency to seek greater happiness is to correct practice of the technique. Maharishi has referred to this principle as the "principle of the purification of the path" (186:XIII). This principle describes the automatic tendency of the nervous system to normalize itself whenever it finds an opportunity to do so.

It is the nature of the nervous system to keep itself in optimum working order through the cycle of rest and activity (300, p. 209). Activity allows the individual to express his energies and purposes. Subsequent rest restores the fatigued body and mind. After daily activity, a person lies down, relaxes and falls asleep. In this state of effortless unconsciousness, a series of complex physiological changes brings the sleeper into states of increasingly deep relaxation.[179] During this deep rest, the body's regenerative mechanisms automatically engage in repairing musculature and vital organs, balancing hormones and neurochemicals, and converting inputs from the preceding day into long-term memories. Though dreaming represents an increase in mental activity as compared with the unconsciousness of sleep, it also plays a vital role in completing the normalization of tension from the previous day. These regenerative processes require no involvement on the part of the sleeper. Restoration is achieved spontaneously by the basic tendency of the nervous system to repair itself whenever it finds an opportunity to do so. The condition which activates this natural tendency is rest.

During TM, the mind experiences quieter levels of thought and the body a corresponding state of physical relaxation. The great depth of this physical and mental rest is subjectively obvious. The rest provides an opportunity for a variety of spontaneous and regenerative changes throughout the entire nervous system. Though these changes result from rest, they necessarily involve whatever physical activity is required to accomplish the change. Thus the rest provided by TM characteristically leads to its own interruption by spontaneous activity. The activity may be gross, like a muscular twitch, or subtle like an imperceptible biochemical restructuring. In any case, the change is reported to the brain where it causes a corresponding mental activity, which may be experienced as a sensation, perception, emotion or thought. Though this mental event seems to interrupt diving, in fact it is a signal that diving has been successful, that it has permitted enough deep rest to facilitate some normalization. Thoughts during meditation are never an indication of unsuccessful meditation, but rather the experiential artifact of the beneficial result of deep rest.

Maharishi has indicated that the rest produced by TM is extremely profound (186:II). He has explained that nightly sleep is generally adequate to eradicate the negative effects of daily fatigue. However, the events of modern life frequently so greatly overload human faculties as to cause alarm and deep exhaustion. Such exhaustion is not corrected by sleep and becomes imprinted in the nervous system as stress. Maharishi has indicated that the unique deep rest provided by TM is particularly suited for the gradual but spontaneous removal of long-accumulated, deeply imprinted stresses.

During each meditation a meditator gains a particular amount of deep rest; if that amount of rest is adequate for the release of some portion of one or several stresses, then that stress will be eliminated. Since the nervous system always normalizes itself to the maximum possible extent whenever an opportunity arises, the release of stress automatically correlates with the depth of rest which each dive provides.

The benefits of TM unfold effortlessly, no matter what thoughts occur during the meditation period. Thoughts during TM may be mundane and trivial. Such thoughts may lead beginners to suspect that little is happening. However, the content of thoughts during TM provides no reliable indication of what kind of stress has been released. If thoughts are fanciful, dreamlike, or intriguing, a person should not assume that the stress dissolved was imprinted by an associated experience, but only that some stress or complex of stresses has been to some extent eliminated. An all-important procedure in TM is simply not to bother about thoughts, never to interrupt the ongoing process of meditation by analyzing thoughts which arise during the practice. Thoughts during TM are only the nonspecific report of normalization of stress.

To incorporate the benefits of this automatic normalization process fully, the optimum balance of rest and activity is essential. Along with normal sleep, the regular practice of TM at about the same time every morning and evening allows the body to take full advantage of TM's effects through consistent phasing of deep rest into the daily metabolic cycle. Effective normalization is also dependent upon daily activity to stabilize and make permanent the changes accomplished during each meditation. Maharishi has suggested that six to eight hours of normal activity are necessary to stabilize the effects of each sitting of TM.[187]

Since a person can comfortably accommodate only a limited amount of internal change while maintaining an effective relationship with changing external conditions, more than two meditations per day tend to be unproductive. The practice of TM twice daily for two brief periods brings significant change gently. Maharishi has indicated that once a meditator's nervous system has adjusted to the regular practice of TM, his body will spontaneously normalize itself at the maximum comfortable rate.

The normalizing effects of TM are cumulative over time. Maharishi has explained that the deeply imprinted stresses eliminated by TM are not just fatigue and tension, but all mental and physical abnormalities, excepting genetic defects and irreparable physical damage.[187] Because a meditator gains extraordinary deep rest in each meditation, over several years of practice he may eventually eliminate all accumulated stress and begin to enjoy the full value of normal human life.

LEARNING TO MEDITATE

The process of learning TM is simple. Introductory courses are offered regularly by the Students' International Meditation Society (SIMS) and its affiliated organizations, the International Meditation Society (IMS), the American Foundation for the

Science of Creative Intelligence (AFSCI), the Spiritual Regeneration Movement (SRM), and Maharishi International University (MIU). These organizations are established as public services in cities, rural communities and universities throughout the world. The American parent organization, SIMS, is a federally tax-exempt, nonprofit educational institution whose purpose is to make instruction in TM readily available to students. Each affiliated organization offers the same basic course of instruction, but specializes in approaching different facets of society. Respectively, as listed above, these organizations offer courses for the adult community, the business community, the retired community and the individuals interested in becoming teachers of TM.

All members of a family can learn TM. Children as young as ten can learn, though they meditate for less than fifteen minutes. Children from age four to ten generally receive a special children's technique, which helps to develop their sensory, emotional and cognative abilities. Often younger children become interested in learning to meditate after others in the family have begun TM.

The basic adult course begins with two public introductory lectures. The first introduces the nature of TM and describes the benefits of its regular practice. The second outlines the mechanics of the technique and prepares a person to learn it. After the second lecture those who wish to begin have a brief interview with an instructor and make an appointment for personal instruction.

There are three requirements for those who wish to learn TM. The first is that each person must have enough free time to complete the basic course which includes two one-to-two-hour introductory lectures, a one-hour personal instruction session, and three one-and-one-half-hour follow-up meetings on each of the three days or evenings subsequent to the day of personal instruction, and a one-hour "checking" meeting two weeks after beginning. The second requirement is a fee for the basic course and extensive follow-up program—children under ten pay two weeks' allowance, students through junior high school pay $35.00, high school students $55.00, college students $65.00, adults $125.00. The third requirement is abstinence from the use of all nonprescribed drugs for at least fifteen days prior to personal instruction. This requirement reflects the consistent finding that people who have recently used nonprescribed and illegal chemicals which alter the functioning of the central nervous system are physiologically blocked from enjoying the spontaneous effects of the technique. Since a person begins only once, the organization insists on a 15 day drug-free period if applicable to insure the best possible start.

Personal instruction takes place in private with a trained teacher. Through individual instruction, the teacher insures that the student learns the practice correctly. Each person is asked to bring some fresh flowers, fresh fruits and a new white handkerchief to this session. These are used by the teacher in a traditional ceremony which provides a preparation for teaching the technique. The ceremony is not a religious observance, but is simply a guarantee that what the student is about to learn is exactly what has been handed down from teacher to teacher for centuries. This brief ceremony also allows the teacher to express his gratitude to the tradition from which TM comes. The student is not asked to participate but only to witness.

After this brief prologue, the student learns how to meditate. He then meditates alone and afterward discusses his experience with his teacher. Since the ability to meditate is not dependent upon belief, faith, understanding or skill, but rather upon an innate human capacity, each novice is able to meditate successfully the first time. The new meditator returns home, meditates that evening, the next morning and evening, and then attends the first of the three follow-up meetings.

At the first meeting, instructors answer questions about the first "solo" meditations and make suggestions on how to meditate in various situations. The new meditators return home and, after two more meditations on their own, attend the second meeting. At this meeting, the instructors offer a detailed framework for understanding all possible experiences in meditation. The next evening, the third meeting reviews practical aids, places understanding in the light of experience, sketches a vision of future possibilities and introduces optional advanced programs.

Although TM is practiced independently after completion of the three required meetings, each new meditator is invited to attend activities at local centers designed to insure continued correct practice and offer knowledge about human development through regular meditation. These activities include "checking," a systematic procedure available from TM teachers and qualified "checkers" to eliminate any difficulties and insure the correct practice of TM. Checking is recommended as a regular supplement to the daily practice. Teachers make appointments with new meditators for checking at two-week intervals for the first several months of their practice and encourage monthly checking thereafter. Checking is available whenever needed by appointment without charge at all centers.

Another important advanced program is weekend residence courses. Residence courses are offered throughout the country to all meditators who wish to accelerate their progress. Residence courses allow for extended practice of TM as well as for deepening understanding of the process of growth through meditation. Residence courses are usually held at rural resorts, retreat houses or conference facilities over weekends. Specialized courses are given for professionals in various fields. Occasional long courses are held over holidays for both students and working adults. In the summer, week- and month-long courses are generally conducted. During these courses, repeating TM several times in a single day multiplies the usual results of regular twice-daily meditation.

After properly returning to regular twice-daily meditation the results of residence courses, like the results of meditating at home, are felt in one's subsequent activity. Coming back to their jobs, school or housework, meditators find a boost in available energy, clarity of mind and stamina which leads to greater productivity and enjoyment. For example a research physicist remarked:

> While a graduate student I found the pressure of work got
> continually heavier, week by week. I used to go to a residence

course every three months or so to refresh myself. Then I'd get five times more work done in the month after a course! It wasn't that I tried harder—I simply accomplished more. I remember the first paper I ever wrote—I'd been struggling with it for months. After attending a residence course I wrote it all out in three days! And when I was completing my graduate thesis I had to complete it within three months, so I went to two courses at five-week intervals. That had a positively pile-driving effect on my being able to complete the thesis quickly.

The response to residence courses has been so enthusiastic that plans are under way for meditator-owned residence course facilities or "Forest Academies" in every area of the country. This positive response seems to bear out the fact that residence courses facilitate a "giant step" in personal growth.

Along with residence courses, new meditators are invited to take Maharishi's introductory course on the Science of Creative Intelligence. This course consists of thirty-three video-taped lectures which coherently spell out the theory underlying the practice of TM. Specially trained teachers present the video tapes according to a fixed interactive procedure which enables easy mastery of every aspect of the material. The course includes a discussion of the operational principles of meditation, of the nature of consciousness and of the application of creative intelligence to all aspects of human experience. Available at all SIMS centers, the course is generally offered in biweekly evening meetings, each of which lasts for two hours over a three-month period. The fee for this course is currently $100.00 for meditating high-school students, $125.00 for meditating college students and $150.00 for meditating adults. This course has also been adapted to a variety of schedules and learning situations including high school and collegiate academic programs.

Meditators are also given an opportunity to become checkers of meditation through courses which are offered at all local centers. Once an individual has completed the SCI course, become a checker and received the recommendation of his teachers, he may proceed to a teacher training course. These courses include long meditation and special training in teaching TM.

THE HISTORY OF TM

To make the uniqueness of TM explicit, we will briefly recount its origin and recent organizational development. Although TM is presented in the format of its modern scientific verification, the technique has ancient roots and its effectiveness is the culmination of thousands of years of careful transmission of knowledge. Unlike the many techniques that emphasize the difficulty of attaining pure awareness, however, this tradition has always held the experience to be easily accessible to anyone. Yet according to this tradition widespread knowledge of the practice has been achieved only a few times in recorded history, most recently at the time of Krishna as related in the Bhagavad-Gita and at the times of Buddha and of Shankara (184, pp. 9–17).

Maharishi received knowledge of the technique from his teacher, Swami Brahmanada Saraswati, generally referred to as Guru Dev. Guru Dev left home at the age of nine in search of enlightenment. After five years he found a teacher, Swami Krishanand Saraswati, who lived up to his ideals. Guru Dev studied under this teacher for some years, and attained full self-realization. He then spent many years in seclusion in the Himalayas and later in the jungles of Central India.

According to monastic tradition, about 2,500 years ago, an enlightened prodigy named Shankara had revived this same ancient wisdom through which Guru Dev attained his realization. This early philosopher had established four "maths," or seats of learning, in the four geographical corners of India. In accordance with Shankara's plan, the teaching was kept widely available and maintained accurately for several centuries. In time, however, the teaching became obscured and misunderstood. In the mid-twentieth century the northern and principal seat of the knowledge, Jyotir Math, had been vacant for over 150 years due to the lack of anyone capable of filling it.

About 1920, officials approached Guru Dev to fill the seat. After twenty years of their repeated entreaties, he accepted the post of Shankaracharya of Jyotir Math in Badarinath in the Himalayas. In 1941, at age seventy-two, he came there to fulfill his responsibilities as leader of the Shankaracharya tradition. To all who came to him for guidance he taught an ancient meditation technique originating in the Vedas, the oldest Indian teachings. He made this technique available to persons leading active lives in the world and to recluses alike. He thereby established the basis for the present world-wide revival of TM.

Maharishi ascribes his personal development to the "brilliant light" and inspiration he found in Guru Dev's unbounded and perfect nature. Maharishi was Guru Dev's favored student during the "12 years that flashed by" (182, p. 10) while Guru Dev was Shankaracharya before his death in 1953.

After Guru Dev's passing, Maharishi undertook a reclusive life in Uttar Kashi in the Himalayas. After two years of virtual silence, the thought of a particular town in the south of India kept coming to his mind. The thought persisted. Finally Maharishi decided to act upon it and traveled to this town at the southernmost tip of India. One day while Maharishi was walking back to his room, the town librarian asked him if he came from the Himalayas, and if he spoke. "Yes," Maharishi replied, "I come from Uttar Kashi, but I do not lecture." Nevertheless, the man found Maharishi the next day and announced that he had arranged a series of seven public lectures, one for each night of the forthcoming week. He asked Maharishi to give the titles of his talks for newspaper publicity. Though surprised by the man's audacity, Maharishi improvised seven topics.

After the lectures, which had attracted growing crowds each night, Maharishi discovered that the librarian had arranged another series in a nearby town, and had submitted the same topics to its newspaper. Never planning not to return to Uttar Kashi, Maharishi found himself traveling from one town to another as lectures were set up throughout southern and central India. He always spoke about humanity's potential for realizing its true nature by allowing awareness to be drawn within to the inner resources of creative intelligence. After each series of talks, Maharishi taught the technique of TM to all who wanted to learn it. As the response grew, Maharishi became increasingly engrossed in teaching.

The resulting automatic progression of events brought Maharishi to Madras in 1958, to celebrate *in memoriam* Guru Dev's eighty-ninth birthday. While addressing the several thousand listeners gathered around an outdoor pavilion, Maharishi delivered a eulogy to Guru Dev and announced a plan to spread the benefits of TM all over the world. Hearing these words, the audience applauded for five minutes. After his speech the organizers asked Maharishi why he hadn't told them he was going to announce a new movement. Maharishi replied that he hadn't known beforehand what he was going to say. The next evening Maharishi spoke again on the same theme, and proclaimed the possibility of all humanity's attaining enlightenment. The response was galvanic and hundreds learned the technique. Maharishi was soon scheduled to speak in numerous cities and towns. For over a year he traveled widely, teaching TM.

One day, pondering the possibility of reaching the world's population in keeping with his professed goal, he computed his progress and realized he would need to continue for hundreds of years at his present rate. To fulfill his plan more effectively, he determined to go to the most progressive countries of the world and make TM available there. He assumed that once the populations of the world's leading nations had begun meditating, the rest of the world could follow suit. He traveled first to Burma, then to Kuala Lumpur, Singapore and Hong Kong, and arrived in Hawaii in the spring of 1959. Hundreds began meditating. He stayed there for two months before continuing on to San Francisco in April. Maharishi received a hearty reception in America and later in Europe. Many thousands of Westerners began the practice of TM.

After his first world tour, Maharishi realized that the only way to reach the entire world population would be by "multiplying himself."

He planned and conducted the first TM teacher training course in India in 1961 in rented buildings. Sixteen persons from that first course became teachers, including Mrs. Beulah

Smith of San Diego, who was the only teacher in the United States until 1966. During this period, Maharishi repeatedly toured the world, opened centers in dozens of countries and stopped each year in America.

In 1965 students at UCLA responded enthusiastically to local courses in TM and arranged for the first course on a college campus. As a result, Maharishi formed the Students' International Meditation Society (SIMS). The second International Teacher Training Course was conducted in 1966 at the newly completed Academy of Meditation in Rishikesh, in the foothills of the Himalayas, and about thirty more Americans became teachers. In 1967 Maharishi lectured at Berkeley, UCLA, Harvard and Yale. As a result, college students across the country requested courses in TM and chapters of SIMS were formed on campuses in every state under the able leadership of its national director, Jerry Jarvis. As the years passed, interest extended outside of the student community and a variety of other organizations were formed to serve the needs of specialized groups. By the end of 1970, about 35,000 Americans had learned TM. Three years later nearly ten times that number had become meditators, over half of them college students and young adults.

Meanwhile, teacher training courses have been conducted three times each year since 1970, when the numbers applying for teacher training could not be accommodated at the Academy in Rishikesh. The first teacher training course outside of India took place in Estes Park, Colorado, where 350 teachers were graduated in December 1970. The next year twelve large hotels were rented in Majorca to train over 800, and in 1972 over 2,000 were trained there. By mid-1973 a total of over 6,000 teachers had been qualified under the aegis of Maharishi International University (MIU), formed to coordinate teacher training, academic courses in the Science of Creative Intelligence (SCI) and various other educational programs.

The teacher training programs in Majorca were characteristic of recent courses, allowing meditators to train for periods ranging from twelve weeks up to eight months. Truly international, with thirty-six countries represented, most of the participants were young adults, but among them were grandmothers, middle-aged businessmen, doctors, lawyers, engineers, artists, writers, scientists, teachers and a veterinarian. Husbands and wives, mothers and daughters, fathers and sons, and brothers and sisters could be found learning to teach TM together. All these individuals have returned to their homes and become active in the common cause of making meditation available to everyone.

The future promises thousands of teachers established everywhere throughout the world. Maharishi has now formulated his early vision comprehensively as an international movement. The final chapter will consider some of the societal implications of the widespread practice of TM. At this point it suffices to envision the incredible result of one man's traveling to a town in southern India—a world movement transmitting a universal meditation technique which can bring greater health, efficiency and fulfillment to everyone.

3

THE
PHYSIOLOGY OF
CONSCIOUSNESS

Proponents of Transcendental Meditation make broad claims for the benefits resulting from regular practice of the technique. Over the past several years, reports from meditators of reduced blood pressure, abatement of tension headaches, improved productivity and so on have grown increasingly frequent, so much so that medical scientists have begun research to determine what TM has to offer. Data from the first forty studies on TM indicate that this simple mental technique may have far greater implications for the health and well-being of individuals and society as a whole than any of the original researchers had anticipated.

Just as the many reports of TM's benefits have attracted scientific attention over the past several years, the general malaise of individuals and the growing tension in our society have commanded increasing concern from medical researchers over the past several decades. With advances in technology necessary to study the relation of mental states to bodily processes, researchers have tried to explain contemporary man's larger problems in terms of specific physiological processes associated with tension in the individual. The scientific discovery of stress, the body's nonspecific response to all demands made upon it, has significantly expanded medical understanding of how chronic tension accumulates in people through repeated exposure to demanding circumstances. Though the body spontaneously adapts to excessively painful or pleasurable circumstances, such adaptations tax basic bodily resources tremendously and leave the body in need of deep rest to restore psycho-physiological equilibrium. If the body does not receive rest sufficient to restore vital bodily resources and reduce hormones which sustain hyperarousal, stress becomes excessive and destroys mental and physical well-being. The tension, poor health and chronic dissatisfaction that have plagued humanity throughout history have their roots in stress. Failing to understand the physiological costs of adapting to the demands of living, man has failed to allow himself the rest necessary to avoid accumulating stress. With our current understanding of stress, however, we may project a psychophysiological resolution to this age-old problem.

Although excessive stress has gained widespread recognition as an enemy of mental and physical health, recent brain research suggests further psychophysiological causes of humanity's continuing malaise. Over the past decade, brain researchers have identified specific functions of different parts of the brain. Some researchers hypothesize that lack of integration between certain anatomical areas of the brain may explain the growing fragmentation of modern man. Lack of integration between lower brain centers concerned with emotion and higher cortical centers responsible for thinking may contribute to general instability in bodily functioning. Unstable functioning of the part of the nervous system concerned with involuntary bodily processes may be as costly to individual and social well-being as stress.

Researchers investigating the value of TM have begun to suggest that TM may be the most effective agent available at present to reduce stress and restore psychophysiological integration. The same research tools which helped medical science define the problem of stress and brain function are being used to measure the physiological impact of TM. Scientists have found that they can map the interrelationships between states of awareness and physiology by correlating changes in subjects' heart rate, breathing, brain waves and so on, with the subjects' thought or feelings. Anxiety and despair as well as ecstasy and tranquility have their specific physiological correlates.

The notion that mental and physical events occur side by side and affect each other commands wide acceptance. Elmer Green and his associates at the Menninger Clinic have formulated this idea as the "psychophysiological principle":

> Every change in the physiological state is accompanied by an appropriate change in the mental-emotional state, and conversely, every change in the mental-emotional state, conscious or unconscious, is accompanied by an appropriate change in the physiological state. (111, p. 3)

Maharishi anticipated this notion when he stated that "any state of consciousness is the expression of a corresponding state of the nervous system" (184, p. 314). This principle offers the key to understanding how a simple mental technique can have broad implications for reducing stress and improving individual well-being. Each of the three familiar states of consciousness—waking, sleeping, dreaming—has specific physiological correlates and a unique value in our lives. Similarly, researchers are suggesting that TM produces a distinct state of consciousness with enormous value in restoring psychophysiological integration.

THE INTEGRATION OF MIND AND BODY

The human nervous system is the most complex physical structure of all known works of nature. Its billions of interconnections and electromechanical transactions allow us to think, create, love, act and become conscious of our intentions. Since humanity first became aware of the nervous system, research into its workings has sought not only greater physical health but also insight into the nature of human existence—the connection of mental activity with the physical body.

Until modern times most people assumed that they had a body and a soul. The soul was thought to govern and shape the body and, after death, depart from it. In the Renaissance, Descartes described the body as essentially mechanical and spent considerable time developing mechanical models for human functioning. His philosophical thoughts on human nature, however, forced him to look for an entry point through which the soul could transmit its formative influence to the body. He located the seat of the soul in the pineal gland, a tiny appendage of the brain now thought to be a remnant of an important sense organ, a third light-sensitive eye, in lower species such as reptiles. Using as his model the mechanical "automata" popular in Louis XVII's royal gardens for his mechanical description of physiology, Descartes concluded that the mind and body were completely separate. This duality between mind and body has persisted until modern times when brain researchers have begun bridging this gap.

The brain has remained mysterious due to its immeasurable complexity. The brain's thirteen billion interconnected cells make it virtually impossible to trace the exact circuits through which consciousness functions. It has been estimated that the number of possible circuits in the brain is greater than the number of atoms in the universe. Even more remarkably, the brain is a machine that is conscious of its own existence. Although physically the brain amounts to only a few pounds of matter, its information capacity and switching abilities considerably exceed the largest computer. The brain's remarkable capacity has been appreciated only in recent times. Until the gradual analysis of the brain through anatomical dissection, surgery, animal experiments, neurological studies and psychophysiological investigation, we knew the brain only through subjective experience, which readily supported the attribution of the brain's powers to a nonphysical soul.

Figure D is a diagram representing current anatomical knowledge of the brain. The convoluted upper portion is the cerebral cortex. This area is the site of man's highest mental and motor faculties. With surface area greatly increased by its interlocking ridges, it constitutes over three fourths of the brain's volume. Beneath the cortex lies the cerebellum which coordinates bodily movements. The brain stem, which controls our vital functions, including breathing and heart rate, is a stalklike structure which passes down between the two hemispheres of the cerebellum to join the spinal cord. The brain stem also regulates satiety, physiological hunger and thirst, but complex cortical and hormonal inputs can strongly influence these functions. The limbic system or visceral brain is a mass of differentially specialized nerve fibers which surround the brain stem and are the seat of such basic emotions as pleasure, anxiety and fear.

FIGURE D

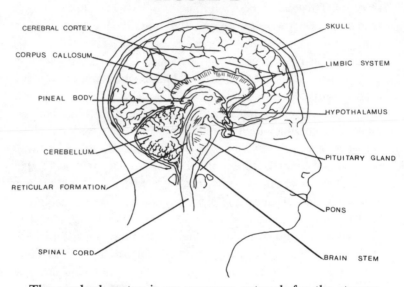

CEREBRAL CORTEX
CORPUS CALLOSUM
PINEAL BODY
CEREBELLUM
RETICULAR FORMATION
SPINAL CORD
SKULL
LIMBIC SYSTEM
HYPOTHALAMUS
PITUITARY GLAND
PONS
BRAIN STEM

The cerebral cortex is an awesome network for the storage, comparison and coding of information. By stimulating the cortex during surgery, Dr. Wilder Penfield was able to elicit both crude sensations and highly integrated memories.[225] This research constituted the first direct demonstration of cortical function in humans. Subsequent studies have provided conclusive evidence that the cortex analyzes sensory information and selects and initiates appropriate bodily responses.[224] Abstract thought, language and intentional activity have also been located in roughly separate regions of the cortex. The back of the cortex receives and organizes perceptions, while the front controls action. The cortex is divided into two hemispheres by the corpus callosum, a large bundle of fibers which relay information between the hemispheres. For some still unexplained reason, in most people the left side of the body is primarily controlled by the right hemisphere, and the right side of the body by the left hemisphere.

Neurophysiological research in the past decade has indicated specialization of function in these two hemispheres. Sperry and his colleagues experimentally severed the corpus callosum in laboratory animals.[264] They demonstrated that in an animal with a split brain each half of the brain can learn a different solution to the same experimental test. This work then led to the treatment of certain cases of severe epilepsy by severing the corpus callosum connecting the cerebral hemispheres, effectively isolating the two hemispheres from each other. The results did not produce a split personality, as is seen in some psychiatric conditions, but did produce two independent minds with distinct differences in perception, decision-making and consciousness. The study of these "split brain" patients has dramatically delineated two major modes of consciousness which seem to coexist within each person.

What are these two separate modes of consciousness? The left hemisphere generally specializes in analytic, rational thinking, especially in verbal and mathematical functions. It processes information in an orderly, linear fashion and is responsible for our time sense. The right hemisphere is predominantly concerned with synthetic and intuitive patterns of thought. It is primarily responsible for our spatial relationships, artistic endeavors, body image and recognition of faces. Its verbal ability is quite limited. In the normal person, the corpus callosum functions as the channel for an abundant flow of information between the two hemispheres.

From these findings, researchers have begun to formulate some interesting speculations. The idea of two complementary major modes of consciousness has been recognized by many philosophies, including the yin-yang principle of Taoism or the dialectic of Hegel. For the first time in history, however, a possible neurophysiological basis for our familiar psychological and cultural dualities has been identified. An expert on the two sides of the brain's functioning, psychologist Robert Ornstein speculates that the contrast between Eastern and Western modes of thought may have a neurophysiological origin.[220] He suggests that analytic Western thinkers have been subject to the dominant left hemisphere, while intuitive Eastern thinkers have been primarily subject to the more silent right hemisphere. The imbalance of modern man in both West and East may arise at least in part from relying too heavily upon either the left or right hemisphere. An integration of the rational and the intuitive is called for. A growing body of evidence, some of which we will consider later, suggests that TM may foster such integration by synchronizing the electrical activity of both halves of the brain.

Whereas the cerebral cortex is the seat of conscious thought, the brain stem enables us to maintain arousal and sustain general activity. This complex network monitors and controls nerve impulses from all parts of the brain and body. The brain stem determines what is to be attended to from moment to moment, by sending out impulses which either stimulate or inhibit other parts of the brain, the spinal cord, or sense organs. The lower portion of the brain stem contains the reticular activating system which is specifically responsible for arousal and wakefulness. Sleeping also depends on signals from the brain stem and not simply the inhibition of the arousal system.

The limbic system, or "visceral brain," located on top of the brain stem, is the apparent anatomical source of our emotions. Within the limbic system is the hypothalamus, an important region of cell groups concerned with biological rhythms, sexual behavior, hormonal control, motivation and emotions such as love, hate, fear and joy. It acts as controlling center for that part of the nervous system—the autonomic system—which directly regulates the internal environment: the heart rate, the width of blood vessels, the rate of breathing, digestion and defense against attack.

Pleasure seems to originate in the limbic system. James Olds and others implanted electrodes in specific limbic areas of rats.[210] The electrodes were connected to a lever which, when pressed, delivered a slight electrical stimulus. The animals pressed the lever at extremely high rates, some as often as every two seconds for twenty-four hours until they were overcome by exhaustion. If rewarded by stimulation of these special areas, rats will run a maze, traverse an electrical grid, and even pass up a chance to eat when starving.

Further work has demonstrated that the limbic system contains two different kinds of "pleasure centers."[211] When stimulated, one of them produces a quieting enjoyment with a corresponding decrease in arousal, lowering of heart rate, respiratory activity and blood pressure. The other produces excitement with an increase in arousal and metabolic activity. Donald O. Hebb, a physiological psychologist, has proposed that an optimum level of arousal exists for each individual.[118] If aroused beyond that level, one experiences tension; if not aroused enough, one experiences boredom. Psychologist Maynard Shelly speculates that the chronic stress of modern life leads to a gradual increase in our optimum arousal level.[258, 259] This change contributes to modern humanity's apparently insatiable thirst for higher amounts of stimulation. When constant excitement is required to maintain a higher level of arousal necessary for happiness, daily activities simply become boring. Our dependence on higher levels of stimulation for pleasure also explains why quieting forms of enjoyment which reduce arousal in a pleasing way have become increasingly ignored or devalued. This hypothetical neurophysiological model for modern humanity's chronic unhappiness suggests that a more stable happiness might be achieved by lowering our optimum level of arousal. If a natural low level of arousal could be established, people might experience more enjoyment in daily activity without boredom. As we will see in succeeding chapters, this lowering of arousal level is one way to explain the effects of TM on the nervous system. Furthermore, this physiological effect of TM may explain the increase in general psychological wellbeing reported by TM practitioners.

Our emotions and basic drives are not simply determined by activity in the limbic system. Our "higher" centers in the cerebral cortex also influence emotions and instinct. Stanley Schachter suggests that expectations determine much of the character of an emotional response. He argues:

. . . given a state of physiological arousal for which an individual has no immediate explanation, he will "label" this state and describe his feelings in terms of the cognitions available to him. To the extent that cognitive factors are potent determiners of emotional states, it could be anticipated that precisely the same state of physiological arousal could be labeled "joy" or "fury" or any of a great diversity of emotional labels, depending on the cognitive aspects of the situation. (243, p.53)

To test this notion Schacter and Singer injected adrenalin into subjects who were exposed to different social situations—one in which a companion (in the employ of the experimenters) acted euphorically, and another in which the companion displayed anger which built into rage.[244] The investigators found that the emotion which the subjects displayed was dependent on the social situation in which they were placed: i.e., determined by their companion's emotional display. This research suggests that cognitive manipulations through the cortex may transform the same state of adrenalin-induced arousal in the limbic system onto experiences as antithetical as euphoria or anger.

The interplay between the cortex and limbic system in determining emotional states and behavior continues to be researched and debated. Arthur Koestler contrasts the homeostatic and balancing tendency of the limbic system with the functioning of the cerebral cortex.[156] He proposes that humanity's self-destructive urges may be explained in terms of a pathological split between emotion and reason, the result of a faulty coordination between ancient and recent brain structures. Koestler attributes a major portion of human physical and psychological ailments to an imbalance between these two sometimes conflicting command posts. He points out that the unique ability of human beings to drive themselves to complete exhaustion, to become addicted to chemicals such as alcohol and narcotics, to commit suicide, and to wage massive war are found in no other animal species. Koestler suggests that this emotional imbalance results from lack of integration between the visceral brain and the cerebral cortex. Koestler states:

... There is nothing particularly improbable in the assumption that in the course of the explosive growth of the human neocortex evolution erred once more. The Papez-MacLean theory offers strong evidence for the dissonant functioning of the phylogenetically old [i.e., limbic system] and new cortex, and the resulting "schizophysiology" built into our species. This would provide a physiological basis for the paranoid streak running through human history, and point the direction of the search for a cure. (156, p. 296)

Is Koestler correct in attributing human suffering and destructiveness to an error in evolution? His argument implies that humanity is biologically flawed, permanently and irretrievably cast out of harmony with nature. Koestler holds that the only cure for this "mental illness" is an "artificially stimulated, adaptive mutation to bridge the rift," that only pharmacology can save humanity by "synthesizing a hormone which acts as a mental stabilizer" (156, p. 337).

Koestler's frightening vision is born of desperation. Humanity's repeated failure to achieve its social ideals may suggest a fundamental lack of psychophysiological integration and a corresponding imbalance in the individual. Nevertheless, the present widespread lack of individual psychophysiological integration so prevalent in our society does not necessarily imply that this imbalance is evolutionarily intrinsic to man. Furthermore, this thesis need not imply that people must resort to the artificial manipulation of bodily chemicals to restore sanity in our civilization. The historical lack of evidence of a natural means of regaining and maintaining psychophysiological integration does not rule out the possibility of such a procedure. Although Koestler is familiar with meditative techniques, he fails to appreciate the psychophysiological impact of the meditative state. Koestler apparently has not considered the natural evolution of consciousness through meditation as a possible solution to the problem he poses. In subsequent chapters, we will review evidence which suggests that TM is a powerful and natural tool for reinstating a dynamic equilibrium between thought and emotion, between the cortex and the limbic system.

The brain communicates with the body and the body with the brain by means of the network of nerve fibers extending from the spinal cord. The nervous system is divided into two general systems, which are themselves divided into subsystems. The voluntary (or cortical) and involuntary (or autonomic) systems comprise two major divisions of the nervous system. The cortical system is concerned with our willed regulation of muscular activity while the autonomic system, pictured in Figure E, is responsible for regulating all the involuntary activities such as breathing, heartbeat, blood pressure, digestion, perspiration, hormonal balance and reproduction. Generally we are aware of those activities directed by the cortical system and unaware of those activities regulated by the autonomic system.

Nevertheless, branches of the cortical system do interact with the autonomic system. For example, we can become aware of and control our breathing rate; however, we rarely bother to do so because the autonomic system naturally regulates this activity. Furthermore many sensory nerves located in the autonomic nervous system transmit signals to the cortex, permitting us to become aware of our internal state. For example, we know when we are hungry. Research in training individuals to control involuntary functions through bio-feedback suggests the possibility of developing our sensitivity to internal stimuli beyond this rudimentary level.[179, 254]

Because it plays such a key role in regulating our vital functions, the autonomic nervous system has come under increasing investigation. The autonomic nervous system is divided into two subsystems, the sympathetic and the parasympathetic systems, which operate in dynamic equilibrium in healthy individuals. They are symmetrical and complementary; when one subsystem dominates, the other subsides. When the organism feels threatened, the sympathetic subsystem dominates the autonomic nervous system, mobilizing the body to deal with the threat. The heart, lungs and muscles are rapidly brought into alarm readiness and work rapidly, forcefully, in what is called the fight/flight, or defense alarm reaction. As we will see in the next section, this reaction is a major component of stress. On the

FIGURE E

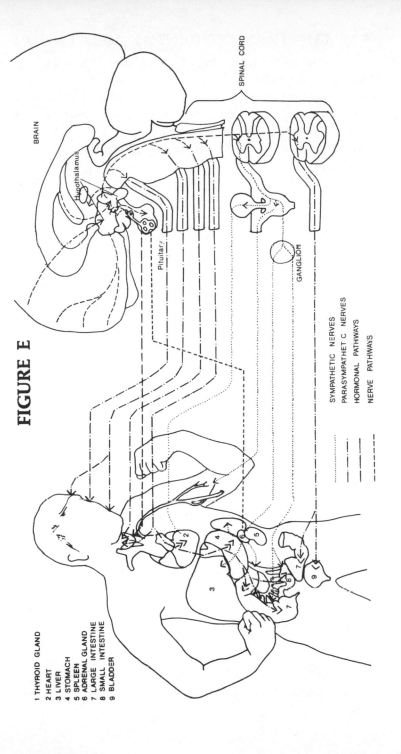

1 THYROID GLAND
2 HEART
3 LIVER
4 STOMACH
5 SPLEEN
6 ADRENAL GLAND
7 LARGE INTESTINE
8 SMALL INTESTINE
9 BLADDER

BRAIN

Hypothalamus

Pituitary

SPINAL CORD

GANGLION

SYMPATHETIC NERVES
PARASYMPATHET C NERVES
HORMONAL PATHWAYS
NERVE PATHWAYS

other hand when we are resting, digesting food or sleeping, the parasympathetic subsystem dominates, allowing the heart and lungs to relax and work at a decreased rate. Researchers have recognized that the complementary interaction of these systems is critical to health. Data on the physiology of TM suggest that it can restore balance to the functioning of the autonomic nervous system.

Despite these and other scientific advances, a vast and perhaps unbridgeable gulf still exists in our understanding of the physical processes of the nervous system and consciousness. While we can study certain links and correlations between mental processes and physical phenomena, the nature of the link between mind and matter remains a mystery unpenetrated by scientific inquiry. Present understanding of the complex mechanisms functioning on the atomic, cellular, brain and organismic levels staggers the imagination. Each moment of consciousness has an incalculable complex physiochemical substrate underlying it. One can study, as neurophysiologists do each day in their laboratories, the correlations between consciousness and neurochemical events. Brain phenomena are bound by the same physical and chemical laws which determine the behavior of all matter and energy. Each of the neurosciences has its own particular tools for generating information: neuroanatomy, the electron microscope; neurochemistry, radioactive tracers; neurophysiology, electrode implantation. But it would be extremely pretentious to think that the mystery of consciousness will ever be unraveled by such analytic tools alone.

Neurophysiologist Seymour Kety notes that when a mother hears the sound of her baby calling "Mama," a remarkable sequence of biological processes is initiated.[152] Many of the underlying mechanisms have been discovered, and perhaps someday physiologists will be able to describe them all—from the sound of a specific wave length striking an eardrum to its emergence as electrical signals along specific auditory fibers. In the future it may be possible to trace accompanying signals through other neutral pathways leading to the reticular activating system and visceral brain. Perhaps scientists will eventually have mod-

els of how these impulses produce the thought "how remarkable and lovable is this baby." But the conscious experience
underlying love will not be found in the scientific description
of this electrochemical sequence. This awareness, says Kety, "is
neither wave length, nor nerve impulse, nor spatial arrangement
of impulses; it is not necessary to any of these processes and,
though dependent on many of them, is explained or even described by none" (152, p. 1862). Thus many modern investigators of the nervous system have come to realize that there is
a quality of mind which transcends the biological. Though
modern science has displaced the dualism of body and soul, its
investigation of the brain has left it in awe of the mind.

STRESS

Though recent brain research has revealed a number of psychophysiological imbalances underlying man's present problems, stress remains the most thoroughly understood cause of
modern man's chronic tension, ill health and dissatisfaction.
Medical theory suggests that excessive stress and resultant anxiety currently play a leading role in disease and emotional illness. When stress was still but vaguely recognized forty years
ago, the medical historian Henry E. Sigerest foresaw its importance. Every epoch, he observed, has its characteristic ailments:

> It seems as though the powers that ordain the style for and
> stamp their impress upon a certain epoch affect even diseases
> . . . the nineteenth century, with its tremendously increased in-
> dustrialization, the development of great cities and the accel-
> erated life tempo, brought about industrial diseases, general
> nervousness and neuroses of many kinds. (199, pp. 105–106)

First defined as a specific syndrome in 1935 by Hans Selye,
stress commands the attention of hundreds of researchers who
publish over a thousand articles per year about it. These researchers have defined both the specific etiology and the tremendous costs of stress.

When Selye recounts his discovery of stress, he explains that his insight arose from a very simple set of observations. As a medical student, he noted that people show a characteristic fatigue and general discomfort when they are sick; in addition, this general state may arise not only during illness but also after any demanding physical or emotional event. Intrigued by these early observations, Selye began research to identify this consistent physiological response to demanding circumstances. He found that a sudden change in temperature, a bacterial infection, a loud noise or a great surprise can all trigger the same system of bodily defenses. Selye called this nonspecific reaction to any demanding circumstance stress.[249] Whenever an event triggers this reaction, that event may be termed a stressor. No one specific criterion is sufficient to determine whether or not an event will be a stressor because constitutional factors play an important role in susceptibility to stress. For example, one person may show a severe stress reaction to a situation which another person experiences with no appreciable effect. A situation may be termed stressful only with respect to a person whom it taxes sufficiently to induce the stress reaction.

The General Adaptation Syndrome (G.A.S.), Selye's medical term for stress, develops in three stages: the alarm reaction, the stage of resistance and the stage of exhaustion. The initial alarm reaction is generated by the sympathetic and parasympathetic systems working together. These subsystems adjust bodily functions to meet the stressor. The sympathetic system stimulates the adrenal glands to produce adrenaline. Simultaneously the hypothalamus activates a pattern of hormone release from the pituitary gland. Through its hormonal signals this master gland regulates the general somatic defenses of the adaptation reaction. In resisting disease or real dangers, these operations are life saving. During the second phase of G.A.S., certain of the body's neural and endocrine reactions persist until the stressful situation has abated. The expenditure of energy and vital bodily resources in the first two stages then leads to the third phase of G.A.S., the exhaustion of the individual. This fatigue persists until the body can gain deep rest and replenish itself.

If the body does not receive rest sufficient to restore its equilibrium, stress becomes a chronic condition which gradually destroys physical and emotional well-being.

Not only physical stressors but also strong emotions can increase adrenaline production. The organism experiences this state of alarm as preparedness for fight or flight. A modern person, however, is not too often confronted with a crisis which calls for either physical violence or escape from threat of harm. A man caught in a traffic jam is not making an appropriate adaptive response if he steps out of his car to fight, nor would a person receiving an unfavorable note from his boss be responding appropriately if he decided to take flight. In a civilized community stress reactions have lost much of their original adaptive purpose. Civilized people are generally compelled to suppress such impulses and make a more rational choice of action. Although the behavioral components of the fight or flight syndrome may be suppressed or modified, however, a person cannot suppress the attendant biochemical consequences. Experiments have shown that experimentally induced psychological stress may "tax" the heart and circulatory system, may decrease the clotting time of blood, inhibit certain aspects of the immune response, disturb gastric conditions, and cause urinary difficulties, sexual dysfunction and hormonal problems. Both the acute alarm reaction and the more prolonged stress reaction may contribute significantly to the development and course of mental illness.

Mental stressors are basic aspects of our psychological and social lives. For example, an unhappy marriage, business difficulties, lack of meaningful relationships with friends or the loss of a loved one may foster persistent discontent and anxiety. Again, different people experience the same or similar situations in quite different ways. To some, a financial setback is taken in stride, while to others it undermines the whole value of life, leaving them mentally unstable or frantic. The latter type of person tends to see danger lurking everywhere, and experiences severe anxiety in dealing with his problems. Such people may be suffering from anxiety neurosis, a chronic disorder that affects a significant portion of the United States population. Dr. Ferris N. Pitts suggests that between ten and thirty percent of the patients of most general practitioners and internists have ailments stemming from anxiety neurosis.[228]

Anxiety neurosis is characterized by feelings of tenseness, apprehension, shortness of breath, irritability, chest pain, heart palpitations, dizziness, trembling, faintness and easy tiring. The individual may also suffer acute anxiety attacks in which he experiences intense fear of impending doom without any apparent external cause. This reaction may lead him to fear a heart attack, cancer or insanity. The symptoms are frightening and the resultant fatigue is intense, so the anxiety neurotic frequently seeks medical attention.

Doctors are studying the biochemical basis of anxiety and anxiety neurosis. The neurotic reacts with fear out of proportion to the situation. In such people, information processed by the cortical and limbic centers appears to activate the G.A.S. inappropriately, leading to increased adrenaline production. In the neurotic, increased adrenaline is associated with excess lactate production. Lactate is a normal product of an inefficient type of cell metabolism. Dr. Pitts has been able to produce the symptoms of anxiety neurosis and even acute anxiety attacks chemically by administering enough lactate to raise the blood lactate level about as high as it is in strenuous exercise or heavy physiological stress.[228] These experiments demonstrated that lactate may in some way produce spontaneous anxiety symptoms. Anxiety symptoms also occur in normal people under stress, perhaps as a consequence of excess lactate production resulting from an increased flow of adrenaline. The anxiety neurotic is particularly vulnerable to this mechanism either because of his chronic overproduction of adrenaline, the overactivity of his central nervous system, or possibly a defect in metabolism resulting in excess lactate production. Pitts hypothesized that excess lactate causes anxiety symptoms through interference with the transmission of nerve impulses, but recent research has not substantiated this theory.[1a]

The overwhelming sense of threat in life today—the danger of nuclear war, environmental deterioration, the urban situation, the rapid rate of change—produces anxiety and somatic symptoms. The progressive accumulation of tensions makes it increasingly difficult for people to cope and make appropriate adaptive responses. Individuals frequently enter a negative spiral in which stress produces symptoms which lead to more stress. Depending on constitutional or hereditary factors, a person may develop a psychosomatic illness—such as high blood pressure, peptic ulcer or asthma—or a psychiatric disorder.

Medical researchers concerned with heart disease have recently begun exploring the role of stress in these deadly circulatory problems. Hypertension, a chronic condition in which psychic stressors apparently play an important role, is the most common of all circulatory disorders. Today close to twenty-four million people suffer from hypertension and the serious complications associated with it. Until this century heart disease was not a major medical problem; now about 700,000 Americans die each year from it. Many are men in the midst of vigorous careers. The stress and strain of modern living apparently plays a significant role in the production of coronary insufficiency and heart attack.

The biochemical changes of the alarm or fight/flight reaction include the release from the body's fat deposits of free fatty acids to be used as fuel for the coming expenditure of energy. Increase in the amount of these fats present in the blood stream apparently contributes to coronary disease. High concentration of fatty acids in the blood is associated with high blood pressure, heart attacks and strokes. Psychic stress can further aggravate these conditions by causing constriction of blood vessels and increased oxygen consumption by the heart. Of course, other factors such as heredity, body type, smoking, high-fat diets and sedentary life-styles contribute to heart disease but recent research suggests that stress plays a crucial role.

In studying the increasing incidence of heart disease, cardiologists Meyer Friedman and R. C. Rosenman turned from such factors as diet, exercise and blood type to personality and work-related factors.[86] The clue came when an upholsterer who was redoing their waiting room remarked that the chairs were only worn on the front edge. Friedman and Rosenman consistently found that almost all of their cardiac patients had in common a competitive, aggressive, ambitious, stressful life-style. They demonstrated that career men, climbing up the social ladder at a furious pace, have a higher level of fats in their blood and greater excretions of certain stress hormones. Moreover, such men are poorer risks with regard to future heart disease than people with a quieter, easier and more relaxed way of living.

Every physician and most patients suffering from ulcer symptoms know the relation between psychic stress and ulcers. Ulcers are probably the classic example of a psychosomatic disease. One out of every ten Americans will be stricken with a peptic ulcer during his lifetime. People in a "stress and strain" profession develop ulcers more frequently than others. A high incidence of peptic ulcer occurs among executives, especially those in highly competitive industries such as advertising. But the ulcer malady is not, as is commonly thought, the private preserve of executives. For instance, health surveys of the taxi drivers in New York City have shown that they develop comparatively more ulcers than any other group. The stress and constant strain of driving impatient passengers through traffic jams makes the harassed driver susceptible to ulcer formation. The ulcer is found seven times more often in whites than blacks. Some years ago it was very uncommon among black people, but its prevalence is increasing, perhaps because of their steady rise to more demanding positions. As with heart disease, peptic ulcer is least prevalent in rural communities where life is slower and more tranquil.

What is the mechanism of peptic ulcer disease? As early as 1833 the physician Beaumont observed the reddening of the stomach lining during emotional upset in a patient who had a gunshot wound which created a passageway from the stomach to outside the abdomen. More recent studies have shown that college students under the pressure of academic examinations[189] and individuals in whom anxiety, anger or resentment were elicited by a stressful interview[306] secreted excessive hydrochloric acid, the corrosive effect of which is probably one of the significant causes of peptic ulcer disease. Brady and associates studied four pair of rhesus monkeys in which both animals were shocked an equal number of times, but only one of each pair, the "executive," could control the shock and avoid it by learning to press a lever. The "executive" monkeys showed a rise in gastric acidity which was directly proportional to the length of the preceding shock-avoidance sessions. Impressively, the "executive" monkeys all died within seven weeks of continuous exposure to these experimental conditions, as a result of severe ulceration and its complications. The control monkey of each pair, who had no control in determining whether the shock would occur, showed no evidence of such peptic ulcer disease.[97] While the exact mechanism of this disease still remains unknown, psychological stress appears to be a major contributing factor.

Excessive stress disrupts the natural biorhythms on which health and productivity depend; it disturbs waking, dreaming and sleeping. While awake, the stressed person feels anxious and exhausted. He is easily aggravated. His vision is narrow and his effectiveness limited. When he dreams, the stressed person has nightmares. While asleep, he is restless. He may have difficulty falling asleep or waking up, and generally gets out of bed feeling unrefreshed. Doctors estimate that as many as ninety percent of their patients complain that they are just too fatigued to perform their work and enjoy their lives. Insomnia and fatigue are consistently associated with stress; nearly all mental patients' problems are complicated by sleep disorders. Doctors and psychiatrists invariably seek to restore this all-important function, but unfortunately the sleeping pills so often prescribed are a mixed blessing; most of these medications interfere with the ability to dream, a necessary component of successful rest.

As a result of research into stress, doctors have become increasingly concerned with helping their patients to relax. Tranquilizers are frequently prescribed but may only mask the stress response. They provide ineffective rest and may be addicting. Vacations may take people away from their responsibilities, but many people find that even during a vacation they cannot unwind. Doctors are still searching for an effective means to achieve deep relaxation. In the meantime, stressed individuals are desperately seeking solutions of their own. Despite overt warnings about its dangers, cigarette smoking continues to increase and contribute to the rising incidence of lung cancer and heart disease. Many thousands of individuals have become addicted to barbiturates, amphetamines or heroin, and alcoholism affects one out of every ten families.[76] Drug abuse induces auto accidents, diseases of all sorts and suicide.[34] In the sum total of its effects, drug abuse is the second most frequent cause of death in the United States after heart disease.

To restore the health and general well-being so absent from our crisis-ridden society, we need a program for correcting the pathophysiology of modern man. We must find a means of relieving excessive stress which radically disturbs emotional and physical health, causes poor performance and fosters tension in human relations. We must also find a means of restoring balance within the autonomic nervous system. We cannot continue to absorb the enormous cost of psychosomatic diseases, to the millions suffering from them and to society which is losing many of its most productive members. To restore people's ability to find pleasure in their simple daily tasks, we need a natural means of lowering people's optimal arousal level. This normalization of man's emotional thermostat must reduce tension and increase baseline happiness. Finally, we must find a means of eliminating the disharmony between the cerebral cortex and the limbic system to begin resolving humanity's age-old inner struggle between reason and emotion. Increasing communication and integration between the brain hemispheres may also be very important in achieving humanity's long-held spiritual goal of inner wholeness. In short, we need a program to regenerate humanity's collective psychophysiology.

Despite the growing malaise of our time, regeneration is intrinsic to living. Medicine has long recognized that rest is the basic precondition for all regenerative processes. We are all intimately familiar with the natural regenerative process in our alternation of wakefulness, sleeping and dreaming. Though we expend our energies while awake, we naturally replenish our bodily resources when asleep. Deep rest may be the most powerful agent to reduce stress. Considerable evidence suggests that TM can provide more profound and natural rest than psychoactive drugs or other relaxation techniques. Furthermore, TM appears to provide profound, effective rest to any person who learns the technique properly, regardless of his mental or physical condition. In the following chapters we will consider scientific evidence which suggests that TM induces a psychophysiological state of great regenerative value. To make the significance of this research explicit, we must first describe the physiology of the ordinary states of human consciousness.

WAKING, DREAMING AND SLEEPING

Until the last two decades, physiologists could only distinguish two normal states of consciousness: wakefulness and sleep. Researchers have since gathered evidence that dreaming is a third physiologically distinct state of consciousness. Our understanding of the three ordinary states of consciousness—waking, sleeping and dreaming—is largely dependent on data obtained from the electroencephalograph, or EEG. Experiments using this ultrasensitive voltage meter, developed in the 1920s, revealed that the cerebral cortex gives rise to faint electrical activity called brain waves. Electroencephalography is a technique of recording the electrical activity of the surface of the brain through the intact skull. Electrodes are applied to the scalp and low intensity electrical activities are amplified and recorded on an inked tracing or computer tape. The EEG is a crude but safe and easy measure.

The normal adult, physically relaxed with his eyes closed, but not asleep, produces a rhythmical wavelength with a frequency of about 8 to 13 cycles per second (c.p.s.)—about as fast as you can move a finger back and forth. This wavelength represents a pattern of electrical activity which appears when the cortex is not processing visual information. The pattern usually disappears when the eyes are open, but can occur even then if the person is in a state of extreme relaxation or boredom.

Since these brain waves were the first to be observed, they were labeled as alpha waves. In addition, the normal adult brain displays beta waves, which have frequencies higher than 13 c.p.s. and amplitudes smaller than those of alpha waves. Beta waves generally signify that the brain is intently active and are typical of concentration, tension and thinking. Young infants display an EEG dominated by generalized slow wave activity in the frequency range of 3 to 5 c.p.s., known as the delta. When the infant matures, this rhythm is replaced by theta rhythms of 4 to 7 c.p.s. and subsequently by alpha rhythms. During drowsiness and quiet sleep in adults, theta and delta waves reappear. Theta activity has also been associated with serene pleasure,[197] and also with creativity.[36]

We can now consider the relevance of these EEG patterns to delineating the states of waking, sleeping and dreaming. In a sleep laboratory in Chicago in 1953, Eugene Aserinsky and Nathaniel Kleitman conducted a series of experiments which began the scientific exploration of sleep and dreaming.[12, 153] Their subjects slept with electrodes pasted on their scalps to record EEG and other electrodes attached to their eyelids to record eye movements. Heart rate, breath rate, temperature, blood pressure, muscle tension and biochemical changes were also measured. The subjects were also under direct observation; at any time the experimenter could waken them and ask what they were experiencing. The researchers discovered that sleep consists not of one simple state, but of a complex process indicated by a series of characteristic EEG events, classified roughly into stages labeled 1 through 4. Stage 1 appears in the first few moments of sleep. It is followed by stages 2, 3, and 4, during which relaxation and unconsciousness deepen. Sleep had previously been thought to be a continuous transition from wakefulness to drowsiness to increasing depth of sleep, followed by a gradual reawakening. Aserinsky's and Kleitman's research demonstrated this assumption to be false. Their all-night EEG recordings showed that sleep is cyclical, with four or five periods of emergence from the deeper stages to stage 1 sleep.

They further observed periods when the sleeping subject displayed an EEG reading quite similar to that of wakefulness. These periods were usually accompanied by disturbed breathing and restlessness, apparently indicating very light sleep. These periods occurred four or five times each night, during the sleeper's transition from stage 4 back to stage 1. One of the few conditions which distinguished this state from wakefulness was the fact that the musculature of the sleeper retained a state of total relaxation which prevented him from beginning to move about and awaken.

For two reasons this state has been called paradoxical sleep. First, total muscular relaxation accompanied by an EEG characteristic of wakefulness appeared contradictory. Second, despite the brain's apparent wakefulness, the subject often proved more difficult to arouse than in any other stage of the entire sleep cycle. Another interesting characteristic of this state is that the sleeper's eyes dart rapidly back and forth beneath his closed eyelids.[12] Because these rapid eye movements (REM) are another conspicuous earmark of this unique physical state, paradoxical sleep is also known as REM sleep. When subjects were awakened during REM sleep they almost invariably reported dreaming, whereas subjects aroused at other (non-REM) times only rarely reported dreams. Periods of non-REM sleep and REM sleep alternate during the night. After the first long non-REM period, the REM periods appear about every ninety minutes. The duration of REM sleep changes during the course of the night. The first REM period is short with only five to six minutes of dreaming, while later periods are longer with dreams that may last from twenty to forty minutes.

This research disposed of many misconceptions about dreaming, especially the belief that some people never dream, while others dream all night. In normal adults about twenty percent of sleeping time is spent dreaming. Every person dreams for several periods every night, whether or not he recalls his dreams when he awakes. For reasons which we do not yet understand, infants spend about eighty percent of their sleeping time in REM sleep during the first few weeks of life. REM sleep has also been observed in many mammals and even in some birds.

Studies of sleep deprivation have shown that a person must have sleep if he is to function effectively.[77] The behavior of sleep-deprived persons resembles drunkenness. They speak in a slurred, rambling way, as if wakefulness intoxicates them. Their speech is listless, lacks normal inflection and is inappropriate to the situation. Loss of sleep also causes irritability and irascibility. If individuals are kept awake for extended periods, they become mildly psychotic or paranoid.

Sleep deprivation also causes increased REM sleep during the next night of undisturbed sleep, as if more dreaming were needed to replenish a person's psychic resources. It also appears that the period of intense mental activity which characterizes REM sleep and alternates with the calm of deep sleep is a necessary part of the physical and psychic restoration which occurs during sleep. Hartmann has shown that during sleep the lower the metabolic rate becomes, the longer the periods of dreaming.[115] Since dreaming is important for the release of emotional stress, Hartmann's finding suggests that low metabolism fosters this process. It may well be that the deeper phases of sleep permit the spontaneous normalization of stress and that the subjective experience of dreaming is the mental artifact of this process.

Sleep deprivation experiments have been designed to arouse subjects at the moment of transition into REM sleep.[77] In early experiments researchers found that subjects deprived of REM sleep became confused, anxious and paranoid. Some even became psychotic. These results seemed to confirm Freud's notion that dreams are a critical mechanism for discharging psychic tension. In more recent experiments, however, in which subjects were awakened carefully to minimize their loss of non-REM sleep, subjects were not so profoundly upset, though they became irritable and emotionally unstable. Despite variations from one REM-sleep deprivation experiment to another, dreaming does appear to play a significant role in maintaining emotional stability.

The physiological description of sleeping, dreaming and waking has led to an appreciation of their essential interdependence. Sleeping regenerates the body and provides sufficient rest to normalize psychic tension through dreaming. Dreaming is a by-product of the release of stress accomplished by sleep and permits further deep sleep. Sleep restores the physiological resources necessary to sustain the waking state. The accumulated fatigue of a full day's activities naturally leads back into sleep. The regenerative interaction of the states of consciousness should optimally lead to health and integration. Unfortunately, dreaming and sleeping do not seem sufficient to counterbalance the stresses incurred by most people during their wakeful activity in the modern world.

We may question whether another state of consciousness in addition to waking, sleeping and dreaming may not be necessary to counterbalance the effects of stress. Throughout the body, physiological processes interact to maintain a dynamic balance. The heart and lungs operate in a cycle of rest and activity in maintaining their vital functions. Similarly the restorative operations of the parasympathetic system must complement energy-depleting sympathetic activities. One might infer, therefore, that since the body displays a stress reaction, it would also be capable of a complementary restorative reflex. Whereas stress brings hyperarousal, alarm and fatigue, this reflex would bring deep rest and great calm. Just as the accumulation of stress leads to disease and a general breakdown of all the individual's activities, repeated exposure to this restorative reflex ought to bring health and a generalized improvement in performance.

Since early in the twentieth century, psychologists have expressed interest in meditation as a possible key to triggering a unique restorative reflex in the body (132, pp. 275–276). Traditional accounts of meditation have discussed its effect not only in terms of its physical value but also as a unique state of consciousness. With advances in medical technology necessary to define the three ordinary states of consciousness, medical researchers began to investigate the reported benefits of meditation.

THE PHYSIOLOGY OF TRANSCENDENTAL MEDITATION

PIONEERING RESEARCH

For centuries mystics and philosophers from all cultural traditions have held that people may attain "higher" states of consciousness through meditation techniques. A variety of Indian texts, which date back at least several thousand years, indicate that in addition to the three ordinary states of consciousness, sleep, dreaming and wakefulness, a fourth state exists. Gained through the practice of meditation, this fourth state has been regarded as "higher" and valuable because repeated experience of it presumably enables a person to unfold increased energy, intelligence and satisfaction.[124]

Nearly seventy-five years ago, William James, the father of American psychology, anticipated current scientific interest in meditation when he wondered

> whether the yoga discipline may not be . . . a methodical way of waking up deeper levels of will power than are habitually used, and thereby increasing the individual's vital tone and energy. I have no doubt whatever that most people live, whether physically, intellectually or morally, in a very restricted circle of their potential being. They make use of a very small portion of their possible consciousness, and of their soul's resources in general, much like a man who, out of his whole body organism, should get in to a habit of using and moving only his little finger . . . may the yoga practices not be, after all, methods of getting at our deeper functional levels? (132, pp. 275–276)

The search for a physiologically definable fourth state of consciousness began as early as the 1930s. The French cardiologist Thérèse Brosse took her electrocardiograph to India in 1935, to test whether certain yogis could actually control the activity of their autonomic nervous systems.[35] Her findings seemed to authenticate the possibility of the voluntary control of several autonomic functions. A follow-up study with more elaborate equipment by Indian neurophysiologists Wenger, Bagchi and Anand,[296] however, repudiated the claim that yoga practitioners could completely determine such functions as heart rate. In another study, however, Wenger and Bagchi found a subject who, on command, demonstrated direct voluntary control over one autonomic process in his ability to perspire from the forehead.[295] Though Bagchi and Wenger were among the first physiologists to study people during meditation, they reported to the American EEG Society in 1958 that genuine meditative experts were hard to find.[15] After carting a portable electroencephalograph 4,000 miles across India, they were able to report on only thirteen subjects. On the basis of their admittedly limited data, they concluded that meditation may represent a unique state of deep rest, particularly for the autonomic nervous system.

Later studies offered evidence that the meditative state lowers the metabolic rate. On a small number of subjects, Japanese physiologists Sugi and Akutsu found an indication of very deep rest in some experts who decreased their consumption of oxygen and elimination of carbon dioxide by about twenty percent during meditation.[269] Indian physiologists Anand, Chhina, and Singh studied an Indian meditator, Sri Ramanand Yogi, who was sealed in an air-tight box in their laboratory for a period of ten hours.[8] The researchers analyzed a sample of air from the interior of the box every half hour. Sri Ramanand decreased his oxygen intake more than any recorded reduction of oxygen consumption during sleep. Remarkably, over the ten-hour period, Ramanand consumed oxygen at only seventy percent of what was thought to be the minimum rate for sustaining life and, during a period halfway through the experiment, at only fifty percent of this projected minimum rate. The researchers considered these results significant because they challenged the basic principle of modern physiology that vital functions within the body are beyond voluntary control. Because recent research indicates that the physiological effects of meditation occur naturally and spontaneously, it may be questioned whether Sri Ramanand could actually control involuntary bodily functions. Anand's study is more significant for the unprecedented state of rest reported than for any implication of control over involuntary bodily processes.

Other early studies of meditation have reported brain-wave patterns not seen in other states of consciousness. Anand studied four Indian meditators who showed prominent alpha-wave activity in their normal resting periods, and a marked increase in the amplitude of their alpha waves during meditation.[7] The Japanese neuropsychiatrists Kasamatsu and Hirai reported the appearance of alpha waves in Zen meditators within fifty seconds after the beginning of the meditation period.[146] These alpha waves generally increased in amplitude even though the monks meditated with their eyes open. In some of the monks, the alpha pattern slowed down in an unusual manner to become rhythmical theta-wave trains with a frequency about half that of alpha activity. The researchers classified these EEG changes in four stages: the appearance of alpha waves (I), the increase in alpha amplitude (II), the decrease in alpha frequency (III), and the appearance of rhythmical theta trains (IV). Further research demonstrated the more years a subject has spent in Zen training, the more likely are pronounced EEG changes during meditation. Those subjects meditating less than five years show stage I predominantly, while those practicing Zen more than twenty years show primarily stages III and IV. The monks' level of spiritual development, as evaluated by a Zen master, correlated closely with the degree of EEG change. The researchers concluded that "the degrees of EEG changes during Zen meditation are parallel with the disciples' proficiency in Zen training. The four stages of EEG changes reflect physiologically the mental state during Zen meditation" (146, p. 493).

Several researchers have also noted an interesting EEG pattern in meditators' responses to noise.[4, 146] When a person is producing alpha waves while resting quietly, a sudden noise will interrupt the alpha rhythm. If that sound is repeated, however, the person will habituate to it and the alpha train will return and continue without interruption. Some early and inconclusive studies suggest that meditators do not show this habituation response outside of meditation, indicating a heightened awareness of their environment. Arthur Deikman, psychologist and theorist on meditation, draws on this EEG data to suggest that meditation causes "deautomatization"

> . . . permitting the adult to attain a new, fresh perception of the world by freeing him from a stereotyped organization built up over the years and by allowing adult synthetic and associative functions access to fresh materials, to create with them in a new way that represents an advance in mental functioning . . . The struggle for creative insight in all fields may be regarded as the effort to deautomatize the psychic structures that organize cognition and perception . . . In this sense, deautomatization is not a regression but rather an undoing of a pattern in order to permit a new and perhaps more advanced experience. (55, p. 217)

Though these early studies suggested that meditation produces a unique state of consciousness, the researchers freely admitted the inconclusive nature of their findings due to the small numbers of subjects and in some cases poor testing conditions. Systematic psychophysiological definition of the meditative state of consciousness had to await the rise of interest in meditation among Americans late in the 1960s.

THE PHYSIOLOGY OF THE MEDITATIVE STATE

Robert Keith Wallace was the first American scientist to undertake the scientific exploration of the state of consciousness experienced in Transcendental Meditation. His 1970 Ph.D. thesis at UCLA Medical School on *The Physiological Effects of Transcendental Meditation* is a landmark investigation.[287] He subsequently continued his investigation into the potential application of TM to health at Harvard Medical School with Herbert Benson, a cardiologist and associate professor of medicine.

To date, Wallace and Benson's experimental efforts comprise the most comprehensive and accurate mapping of the physiological characteristics of a meditative state. [24, 289, 290, 291] They selected TM for study because its practitioners were readily available normal Americans, who learned a uniform technique. Because anyone can learn TM, the researchers easily located a fairly random sample of practitioners willing to be tested in a laboratory. Furthermore, unlike previously tested Japanese and Indian meditators, the TM subjects were free from special religious, dietary or ritualistic practices which might account for the observed effects of the technique.

Thirty-six subjects, some in Boston and some in the Los Angeles area, without physical or mental disabilities, of both sexes, ages seventeen to forty-one, were selected to participate in the initial study. They had been practicing TM from one week to nine years and for an average of about two and a half years. Because TM requires no special environmental setting, the subjects could easily meditate in the laboratory without feeling disturbed, inhibited or uncomfortable, even while being monitored by many imposing physiological testing systems. These testing devices included a mask over the lower portion of the face which permitted the measurement of oxygen consumption, a catheter inserted into the brachial artery in the arm to continuously monitor changes in blood chemistry, and electrodes on the scalp to measure EEG.

The experimental procedure was simple. Subjects came to a laboratory where the researchers connected them to the variety of instruments. After a thirty-minute period during which subjects became habituated to the experimental apparatus, the researchers began taking measurements. Initially the subject sat quietly, just relaxing with eyes closed, for about twenty minutes. After this relaxation period, the subject meditated for thirty minutes. Thereafter, he sat just relaxing for another fifteen minutes. Physiological changes which occurred during the meditation period were compared with the initial measurements taken during the pre-meditation control period. The post-meditation measurements were compared with those from the initial control period and from the meditation period.

Wallace and Benson's findings added considerably to the sketchy and often contradictory information reported in previous studies of meditation. They also provided remarkable insight into the physiological value of TM. One of the most dramatic changes registered during the practice of TM was in oxygen consumption. Oxygen consumption is generally regarded as a reliable index of a person's physical activity. For example, when a person runs or climbs a long flight of stairs, this accelerated activity requires an increased consumption of oxygen. In contrast, when a person sits quietly, breathing tends to become lighter, leading to a decrease in oxygen consumption. Though breathing is deep when a person sleeps, oxygen consumption drops greatly. Typically, a person's oxygen consumption gradually drops during a night's sleep to its normal low point in the daily twenty-four-hour cycle, by an average of ten percent and occasionally by twenty percent below daytime resting values.

During the first few minutes of meditation, Wallace found in all meditators an immediate, spontaneous reduction in oxygen consumption of sixteen to eighteen percent. This level of reduced oxygen consumption was sustained throughout the entire twenty minutes of meditation. After the meditation period, oxygen consumption returned to its normal resting level, indicating a return to a metabolic level suitable for initiating activity. Comparing their results with reported changes in oxygen consumption during sleep and hypnosis (Chart 1), Wallace and Benson concluded that TM produces a state of rest deeper than sleep and distinctly different from the subjectively reported relaxation during hypnosis.

The drop in oxygen consumption which Wallace and Benson found during TM was so significant that they made further measurements to determine whether TM produced any respiratory abnormality. If the technique involved forced reduction in oxygen consumption, the drop in oxygen consumption would cause oxygen starvation and could be dangerous. To test this critical hypothesis, the investigators measured the amount of carbon dioxide in arterial blood during the meditation period. Respiration consists of inhaling oxygen, passing it through the arterial system where, at the cellular level, it participates in the metabolic process. Energy for bodily activity is produced at the cellular level where carbon compounds derived from digested foods are metabolized. During this process oxygen is consumed and converted to carbon dioxide, which is then passed through the venous system, to be exhaled. If the body is starved of oxygen, reduced oxygen consumption does not lead to a parallel reduction in carbon dioxide elimination because the cells continue to metabolize remaining oxygen in the blood at a constant rate. Oxygen starvation causes a decrease in the concentration of oxygen and an increase in the concentration of carbon dioxide in arterial blood. The relative amount of oxygen and carbon dioxide in the blood is called the respiratory quotient. During normal respiratory processes, this quotient remains constant. In abnormal respiratory situations, such as the forced reduction of oxygen consumption through inhalation of nitrous oxide (laughing gas), the reduction in available oxygen and increase in carbon dioxide starves the brain of oxygen, producing lightheadedness and eventually unconsciousness.

Benson and Wallace found, however, that during the practice of TM the amount of carbon dioxide exhaled drops in proportion to the amount of oxygen consumed. In addition, the respiratory quotient remains constant. These two findings indicate that TM does not produce any respiratory abnormality. The drop in oxygen consumption during TM apparently results from a natural reduction in metabolic activity at the cellular level and not from forced reduction of breathing. When cellular metabolic activity drops naturally, the cells throughout the body burn less oxygen and consequently produce less carbon dioxide. The absence of reports by meditators of lightheadedness or unconsciousness during the practice of TM further corroborates the data suggesting that oxygen consumption drops naturally during TM.

Further measurements indicated that oxygen consumption was reduced in terms of both the volume of air breathed and also the rate of breathing. Dr. Wallace remarked that the mask and flow meter which he used to measure respiratory changes inevitably interfered with the subject's shallow breathing and thus probably masked a possibly greater reduction in respiratory function.

In England Dr. John Allison conducted a study which corrected this experimental limitation and corroborated Wallace and Benson's findings on respiratory changes during TM.[6] Instead of a bulky mask and flow meter he used small nasal thermistors, electronic temperature sensors adapted for the nose. Allison asked his experimental subject to read a book for a few minutes while he recorded his respiration. The subject then meditated for about thirty minutes and afterward read again for some minutes. Recording was continuous throughout this period. Control measurements were also made while the subject relaxed watching television. (The changes in breathing rate which Allison recorded are illustrated in Chart 2.) Allison's study supports Wallace's finding that the changes at the beginning and end of meditation are immediate. The rate of respiration during TM is about half the resting rate, occasionally falling quite remarkably to as little as four breaths per minute. Despite the marked decrease, the subject showed no compensatory overbreathing afterward, a further indication that reduction in metabolic rate during TM takes place naturally.

Wallace's findings on reduced oxygen consumption during TM have been further confirmed by Dr. Paul Corey. In a recent study of specific airway conductance, the inverse of resistance to air flow in the passageways to the lungs, Corey found a 19.5 percent increase in conductance during the practice of TM.[48] Corey conducted his experiments at the National Jewish Hospital and Research Center in Denver, where considerable pioneering work has been done with asthmatic patients. He had meditating and nonmeditating subjects sit in a "body box" (plethysmograph). After each subject performed standard panting and forced volume maneuvers, Corey was able to measure changes in conductance with considerable accuracy. Medical literature reports no significant increase or decrease in airway conductance among normal subjects under normal resting conditions. Therefore, his finding that meditators exhibit a nearly twenty percent increase in conductance is highly significant and suggests that TM may have therapeutic applications for patients suffering from asthma and other pulmonary diseases in which conductance is decreased. Corey emphasizes that his findings are preliminary and merely suggestive of a potential therapeutic value; he plans to conduct further research into the effects of TM on respiration in order to specify the mechanism involved in producing these dramatic changes.

Cardiac output, the rate of blood flow from the heart, is another accurate means of measuring metabolism, since blood from the heart carries oxygen to the site of the metabolic process in the tissues. Wallace, by means of venous catheters inserted in the arms of meditating subjects, determined that an average decrease of about twenty-five percent occurs in the cardiac output during the practice of TM. Simultaneously heart rate slows down by about five beats per minute. These decreases correlate with the reduction of oxygen consumption and indicate a state of deep metabolic rest. Similar changes are found during sleep, but are achieved only over a period of several hours; whereas the deep relaxation of TM is gained almost immediately.

Wallace and Benson also found an increase in the Galvanic Skin Response (G.S.R.), an incompletely understood but accurate measure of relaxation. The G.S.R. is measured by placing electrodes on the skin surface and measuring the resistance to a mild electric current. In the past, physiologists thought that the G.S.R. depended upon the amount of perspiration on a person's skin. Recently physiologists have identified more complex mechanisms underlying changes in G.S.R. In any case, the G.S.R. has long been known to decrease with anxiety or stress and increase during relaxation. This easily measurable change has been used for several decades by law enforcement agencies as a basis for "lie detector" tests. If, after answering a particular question, an individual's skin resistance decreases, this decrease indicates that he is anxious, possibly because he is lying. If in the same situation a person relaxes, possibly because he is telling the truth, he will tend to show an increase in skin resistance. During deep sleep, the relaxation of the body promotes an average but slow increase in skin resistance of about 250 percent. During the short period of TM, however, subjects have shown an increase in G.S.R. of as much as 500 percent (Chart 3). This increase indicates a rapid reduction in anxiety and a state of very deep relaxation.

Wallace and Benson also found a significant decrease in the concentration of arterial lactate (Chart 4), the apparently stress-related blood chemical discussed in chapter 3. During TM, the subject's lactate level declined nearly four times faster than the rate of decrease in people normally resting in a supine position or in the subjects themselves during their pre-meditation control period.[289, 291] This decrease in blood lactate is almost three times faster than the decrease during sleep.[123] Though lactate concentration increased with the rise in metabolic activity at the end of the post-meditation period, it remained considerably below the pre-meditation level. The physiological mechanisms involved in this decrease in lactate level bear further investigation.

In medical laboratories in Germany, other circulatory system changes have been studied which offer insight into the mechanism of reduced lactate. Using an infrared radiometer, Ritterstaedt found an increase of 0.4 to 1.6°C. in the forehead skin temperature of all subjects practicing TM.[234, 235] Reichart reported forearm blood flow may increase as much as 300 percent.[232] This increased skeletal muscle blood flow may account for the lowered lactate level and may also explain the subjective feelings of muscular relaxation regularly reported by meditators. During TM the heart can apparently deliver more blood with less effort to the musculature, as indicated by the simultaneous increase in peripheral blood flow and decrease in heart rate and cardiac output.

Summarizing their study, Wallace and Benson note that TM apparently produces a unique state of deep rest coupled with mental alertness. They refer to the constellation of changes resulting from TM as an integrated, psychophysiological response which restores energy and equilibrium to the body. Contrasting the hypometabolic state achieved during TM with the hypermetabolic state which results from stress, Wallace and Benson write:

> There is good reason to believe the changing environment's incessant stimulations of the sympathetic nervous system are largely responsible for the high incidence of hypertension and similar serious diseases that are prevalent in our society. In these circumstances the hypometabolic state, representing quiescence rather than hyperactivation of the sympathetic nervous system, may indicate a guide-post to better health. (289, p. 90)

BRAIN WAVES OF THE MEDITATIVE STATE

Wallace and Benson's research demonstrated that TM produces an integrated physiological response. Subsequent studies have aimed at identifying the underlying mechanism of this response. The variety of simultaneous physiological changes during TM have suggested to several researchers that the practice must somehow trigger a restorative reflex in the brain. Wallace was the first to seek a clue to this unknown mechanism through EEG studies in TM practitioners. He found a consistent increase in the amplitude of 8 to 9 c.p.s. waves, or slow alpha waves, in the frontal and central regions of the brain. In some practitioners of TM, this increase was accompanied by occasional theta trains, 5 to 7 c.p.s. waves in the front of the brain. These brain waves clearly distinguish TM from sleep and dreaming. Wallace noted that his subjects, some of whom had been practicing TM only a few months, showed EEG patterns very similar to those reported by Kasamatsu and Hirai in their studies of expert Zen monks who had meditated for twenty to thirty years.[147]

Researchers Brown, Stewart and Blodgett studied the EEG's of eleven practitioners of TM and an equal number of nonmeditating control subjects.[37] They found the presence of frontal-cortical alpha waves during most of the meditation period in ten of the eleven subjects. In contrast, only three of the eleven non-meditators occasionally demonstrated this rhythm. Consistent with Wallace's original findings, these results suggested to the researchers that TM produces significant changes in cortical activity.

Neurologist J. P. Banquet conducted the most comprehensive investigation of the EEG patterns occurring during the practice of TM to date. He used twelve meditators who had practiced TM for an average of two years, and twelve matched controls. [17, 18, 19] EEG measures were taken while the meditators meditated and the controls relaxed for thirty minutes with their eyes closed. During their meditation or relaxation all subjects had push buttons at their fingertips to record subjective events including body sensations, involuntary movements, visual imagery, deep meditation and pure awareness. Banquet used a sophisticated method of computer spectral analysis to identify component frequencies in each EEG recording and to compare readings taken simultaneously from different areas of the brain.

Pictured in Chart 5, his measurements clearly distinguished the meditative state from other states of consciousness. Banquet noted that alpha activity, which is present in the resting state of all meditators, becomes predominant during the first stage of meditation. After this first stage, he found a shift to slower frequencies, mainly theta patterns, which were totally unlike the theta and delta patterns of drowsiness. Four advanced meditators showed yet a third stage which they identified with their buttons as either deep meditation or pure awareness. This stage consisted of synchronous beta waves of an almost constant frequency and amplitude over the entire scalp. In all meditating subjects, the end of meditation repeated the stage I pattern, with an increase in alpha waves. In the advanced meditators, alpha and sometimes theta waves persisted after meditation, even with eyes open.

Banquet's other measures indicated deep relaxation with no muscular activity during the periods of deep meditation. Yet the subjects were able to make voluntary movements. For example, they were able to use the push button to signal their subjective states, even in deep meditation. Their alertness was substantiated by the fact that they memorized and answered questions during meditation. The subjects could perform such activities and perceive stimuli without disturbing the electrical pattern produced by the practice of TM. Banquet suggested that "the EEG changes of meditation are independent of the interaction between the subject and the outer world but produced by the specific mental activity of the practice" (19, p. 150).

The major finding emerging from Banquet's research is that the brain-wave patterns of meditating subjects tend to synchronize during TM. Observing a marked uniformity of frequency and amplitude in electrical activity from all areas of the brain, Banquet called this phenomenon hypersynchrony. He found that during the first minutes of meditation, alpha waves spread synchronously from the back to the front of the brain (Chart 6). After about five minutes of meditation, recordings also indicate synchrony between the dominant and silent hemispheres (Chart 7). Meditators showed hypersynchrony of alpha and even beta frequencies during TM. The nonmeditators, on the other hand, showed some synchrony of only the slower theta and delta frequencies, and then only during drowsiness and sleep. In ordinary waking consciousness, brain waves are random and chaotic, whereas during TM, they become coherent in phase and frequency (Chart 8). Further research is necessary to establish the significance of brain-wave hypersynchrony during TM. Hypersynchrony may well be the key to understanding the integrated physiological response which occurs during TM as well as the increased energy, intelligence and satisfaction reported by meditators.

Banquet's findings have been corroborated by psychiatrist Bernard Glueck and physiologist-physician Charles Stroebel in their research on TM and alpha wave bio-feedback at the Institute of Living in Hartford, Connecticut. Glueck is Director of Research at the 400-bed private psychiatric hospital, and Stroebel is director of the hospital's psychophysiology laboratory. They began research on the potential value of relaxation techniques for psychiatric patients after several researchers suggested alpha wave production may have potential therapeutic value.[100, 267]

Barbara Brown was among the first researchers to report that alpha wave production through bio-feedback resulted in rewarding subjective experiences.[36] Bio-feedback is a procedure through which the activity of an involuntary bodily function is monitored, and reported to a trainee by means of a light or sound signal. This procedure is repeated until he learns to control the function. For example, a person's EEG may be analyzed to indicate the presence or absence of alpha waves. With information about his brain-wave activity, a person can learn to maintain alpha wave activity through internal manipulation of his thoughts, feelings or mental images. Brown reported that those experimental subjects who became skilled at alpha production through bio-feedback training often noted pleasant feelings, well-being, tranquility and generally heightened alertness while producing alpha.

Having read Wallace's studies as well as reports by bio-feedback researchers, Glueck and Stroebel designed an experiment to compare the psychotherapeutic value of bio-feedback and TM. In their first EEG study of two experienced practitioners of TM, the researchers compared brain waves during meditation with those of a control period during which the subjects rested quietly with eyes closed. During meditation they found an increase in alpha and theta wave production. The alpha amplitudes recorded during meditation were generally larger than any amplitudes produced by their bio-feedback trainees. Intrigued by this early finding, Glueck and Stroebel began a study comparing TM, bio-feedback and a technique of muscular relaxation. Over a three-year period, they plan to work with hundreds of subjects, drawn from the in-patient population of their hospital.

Initial subjects were matched by age, sex and psychological testing, and then randomly assigned to receive training in bio-feedback or TM. A complete range of psychophysiological measurements were obtained prior to the subject's learning one of these techniques, then during the initial practice of the technique and subsequently at two-week intervals. In addition, behavioral indices were obtained from repeated psychological testing as well as from reports by hospital staff. One- and two-year follow-up studies are planned. Early results reported by Dr. Stroebel indicate that:

> . . . patients learning alpha biofeedback generally required more trials with a greater range of variability in achieving criterion levels and seldom reported relaxed, tranquil feelings during the alpha-on condition . . . Comparatively, the alpha-subjects experienced much greater difficulty in transferring their training to environments outside the laboratory.[267]

Most subjects practicing TM, on the other hand, produced an increase in the dominant alpha rhythm frequency, interspersed with periods of theta and beta activity. The subjects showed this ability during their first as well as subsequent sessions. In addition, the meditators tended to show hypersynchrony during their meditation period. While bio-feedback subjects reported difficulty and even frustration in their efforts to produce alpha waves, especially outside the laboratory,[268] the meditators tended to remark on the ease with which they achieved relaxation through TM.

In light of the disappointing early results with bio-feedback at the Institute of Living[267, 268] as well as similar discouraging reports from other laboratories around the world, it may be questioned whether TM and the alpha state induced through bio-feedback are comparable. While TM produces an integrated psychophysiological response resulting in deep rest coupled with mental alertness, EEG bio-feedback has not been shown to produce similarly global physiological change. Often bio-feedback subjects report a significant increase in tension even though they sustain alpha wave production. Further, TM differs from bio-feedback in its unique ability to induce brain-wave hypersynchrony at a variety of frequencies. Since no single brain-wave form has proven significant in the total physiological response occurring through the practice of TM, hypersynchrony may be regarded as the critical change in EEG patterns corresponding to the deep rest gained during TM. The consistent appearance of hypersynchrony among TM subjects has become the basis for current hypotheses about how TM affects the brain.

HOW TM AFFECTS THE BRAIN

When a person sits to practice TM, he becomes mentally more and more alert, yet settles into a state of serene relaxation which radiates from the center of his awareness to the periphery of his body. His thinking mind quiets down into a wakeful state suffused with pure enjoyment. Cellular activity all over his body slows down, reducing his need for oxygen. Increasing relaxation permits increased flow of blood to his muscles, decreasing the heart's workload. Reduction in blood chemicals associated with tension and anxiety facilitates a sense of increased ease. Finally the cells of the brain fire in a synchronous manner fostering integrated functioning between lower and higher brain centers and between left and right hemispheres. How are all these changes brought about?

Anthony Campbell, an English physician and author on meditation, notes that those parts of the brain responsible for the contents of consciousness, i.e. thoughts, feelings and perceptions, are distinct from those parts responsible for alertness (40, p. 75). Impulses from the cortex and limbic system generate the content of conscious experience. Yet though damage to either of these areas may impair thinking or feeling, it does not generally affect alertness. On the other hand anesthesia, which affects the reticular activating system in the brain stem, readily produces unconsciousness. The reticular activating system apparently determines whether a person is sleeping, dreaming or awake. The increase of alertness, and simultaneous reduction of mental activity characteristically experienced during TM suggests that TM stimulates the reticular activating system while dampening cortical and limbic activity.

In our normal waking state, activity in the limbic system colors the cognitive and perceptual activity of the cortex. During the practice of TM, impulses apparently travel throughout both cortical hemispheres downward to the limbic system where they dampen limbic activity. Such lessening of activity in the limbic system would then reduce cortical activity because cortical activity depends largely on underlying limbic activity. Regarding this change, Dr. Glueck remarked: "It seems increasingly apparent from EEG findings that the mantra is the significant element in the whole process, apparently able to markedly alter brain function within a matter of seconds."

Dr. Glueck has hypothesized that resonant derivatives of the mantra may enter the limbic system via its subvocal repetition in the speech center. Well-integrated with the limbic system, the speech center is located in Broca's area, in the temporal lobe of the dominant hemisphere. Thinking the mantra may set up a frequency modulation in the low alpha or high theta brain-wave range. These resonant derivatives may enter the limbic system at just the right frequency necessary to dampen limbic hyperarousal. Because the limbic system controls so many of the body's involuntary processes including heart rate, respiration rate and blood pressure, reduction of limbic activity probably accounts for the deep rest gained during the practice of TM.

Reduction of limbic hyperarousal may also explain how TM reduces stress and increases stability in the autonomic nervous system. By way of the hypothalamus, the limbic system directly modulates the hormonal and the autonomic nervous system. Quiescence in the hypothalamus may foster parasympathetic tone, thereby increasing autonomic stability; quiescence in the hormonal system might well lead to reduced alarm reactions, thereby reducing stress.

Research may yet prove that TM has its greatest impact on individual well-being by virtue of the hypersynchrony of brain waves which the technique induces. By encouraging synchronous functioning between the cortical and visceral parts of the brain, TM may heal the schizophysiology of the old and new brain, resolving humanity's age-old struggle between emotion and reason. By encouraging synchrony between the two brain hemispheres, TM may foster integration of analytical and intuitive modes of thinking. Man's highest achievements require the complementary workings of thought processes from both sides of the brain. The scientist and the artist, the businessman and the visionary within each of us must be able to function together if we are to realize our full individual potential and collectively attain our highest social ideals.

AUTONOMIC STABILITY AND STRESS REDUCTION

Although early research on TM's physiological effects suggested that regular practice of the technique should improve autonomic stability and reduce stress, conclusive evidence supporting this hypothesis was not available until 1972. Innumerable individual meditators had remarked on their subjective feelings of reduced anxiety and generally improved health, but such reports are not scientific evidence. Subjective reports did, however, encourage several researchers to investigate the effects of regular TM practice on the autonomic nervous system.

David Orme-Johnson, a psychologist at the University of Texas in El Paso, was the first to demonstrate improved autonomic stability and consequent resistance to stress among subjects practicing TM.[214] Orme-Johnson exposed eight experimental subjects, who had practiced TM for an average of fifteen months, and a control group to a sudden loud noise while he monitored their Galvanic Skin Response (G.S.R.). When a person is subjected to a stressor such as an unexpected loud noise, his G.S.R. decreases sharply for a few seconds and then returns to normal. If the stress is repeated often enough, the person gets used to it and stops reacting. The systematic decrease in amplitude of the G.S.R. response to repeated exposures to the same stressor is called habituation. Generally, a relaxed person habituates more rapidly than a tense person to a repeated stress which does not require immediate attention and response. Orme-Johnson found that when he subjected meditators and a control group of nonmeditators to repeated noises about as loud as a pneumatic hammer drilling pavement, the meditators displayed rapid G.S.R. habituation. The meditators stopped reacting after an average of eleven repetitions, whereas the nonmeditators required more than twice as many trials before achieving the same degree of habituation (Chart 9).

Orme-Johnson found a further indication of greater autonomic stability among people practicing TM in contrast to the control group. The more stable the functioning of a person's nervous system, the more quickly his nervous system returns to normal after adapting to a sudden stress. These findings suggest that regular practice of TM improves a person's adaptability and resistance to stress.

A second study by Orme-Johnson further supports the hypothesis that TM decreases anxiety and improves autonomic stability.[214] In this experiment, he monitored spontaneous levels of G.S.R. Spontaneous G.S.R. are measurable fluctuations in the autonomic nervous system which occur independently of any apparent external stimulus. The number of spontaneous changes appearing in a person's G.S.R. amplitude during a period when resting quietly and not exposed to any environmental stresses is a good index of his general anxiety level. Orme-Johnson found that nonmeditators produced about thirty-four spontaneous G.S.R.'s (of more than 100-ohm amplitude) per ten-minute rest period, an average amount for a normal American adult. On the other hand, meditators produced fewer than ten G.S.R. changes during a similar ten-minute rest period (Chart 10). These findings suggest that meditators have significantly less anxiety than nonmeditators.

How rapidly and efficiently can the practice of TM stabilize autonomic functioning? Orme-Johnson found that when the control subjects who had produced over thirty-five G.S.R. changes per ten-minute rest period were instructed in TM, they showed fewer than fifteen spontaneous G.S.R.'s per ten-minute test period, within two weeks after instruction. TM can apparently reduce resting levels of sympathetic activity by changing the operational style of the nervous system in a short period of time.

Thomas Routt reported further evidence of improved autonomic stability in practitioners of TM.[239] He studied twelve meditators, aged eighteen to twenty-six, with a mean experience of thirteen months, ranging from three weeks to twenty-nine months. He compared this group to a control group of non-meditators who were instructed to relax during the time when the experimental group meditated. Routt noted striking differences between the two groups' heart and respiratory rates before, during and after the meditation or relaxation period (Charts 11 and 12). The meditators' heart rates were slower by ten to eleven beats per minute and their respiratory rates were slower by two to three breaths per minute during all periods. The low heart and respiration rates observed in the TM group relative to the control group, though based on a small sample size, are a significant indicator that TM serves to maintain autonomic balance.

Because the autonomic nervous system controls all our vital functions and mediates our involuntary responses to our environment, the implications of a technique for improving autonomic balance are enormous. Autonomic stability is so critical to good health that medical science differentiates two primary personality types on the basis of autonomic stability, labiles and stabiles. The stabile person shows greater independence, less motor impulsivity, greater resistance to noise and sensory deprivation, higher measures of mental health on psychological tests, and less susceptibility to conditioning than a labile person. Autonomic lability may be a precursor of psychosomatic and mental illness. Because he expends much energy on maladaptive activities, a labile person has only limited energy available for combating stress or engaging in productive activities.

Medicine has long been searching for a means of restoring a healthy balance to the autonomic nervous system. Psychopharmacologic agents used to restore sympathetic-parasympathetic reciprocity via the limbic system and hypothalamus have played a role in the therapy of such psychosomatic diseases as essential hypertension, bronchial asthma, migraine headache and peptic ulcer. These drugs, however, have limited benefits, produce uncomfortable side effects and do not provide long-term cures.

Data presented thus far indicate that regular practice of TM restores balance to the autonomic nervous system by naturally reducing sympathetic hyperarousal. It counteracts the weakening effect of stress upon the body by activating the energy-restoring parasympathetic system. Like the rest recommended by doctors to aid recovery from an illness, TM gives the body an opportunity to restore energy and heal itself. Through regular practice, TM protects a person from debilitating responses to stressful environments. The deep rest provided by TM appears to restore the adaptability, flexibility and integration of the nervous system, and may constitute the most effective method presently available for achieving autonomic stability.

RELIEVING PSYCHOSOMATIC DISORDERS

Many psychosomatic diseases involve a disturbance in the balance of the sympathetic and parasympathetic branches of the autonomic nervous system. When the body and mind suffer from chronic overstimulation of the fight/flight response, the physiological resources of the body are depleted by energy-using sympathetic activity without corresponding energy-restoring parasympathetic activity. In this state of chronic stress and fatigue, the weakest aspect of an individual's physiology or psychology breaks down and a disease state ensues. Neurophysiologist Wenger has developed techniques for measuring the relative contribution of the two branches of the autonomic nervous system to an individual's autonomic balance.[297] He discovered that frequent sympathetic arousal is associated with a variety of diseases including schizophrenia, tuberculosis, battle fatigue, gastrointestinal ailments, dermatological disorders and other psychosomatic illnesses.

Wallace was the first American researcher to begin investigating the value of TM for improving health.[290] He surveyed a group of students who had been meditating regularly for over three months. Three hundred ninety-four subjects completed his questionnaire regarding changes in physical and mental health. Sixty-seven percent reported significant improvement in physical health and eighty-four percent reported significant improvement in mental health. Only three reported that some undesirable condition had developed in their physical health since starting TM. Improvement in physical health included fewer colds, headaches, and allergic reactions. This study suggests that TM is a safe and easy method for increasing physical and emotional well-being.

Researchers have discovered that lability in the autonomic nervous system is a precursor to hypertension.[97] Further, this disease seems to be associated with a general increase in the tone of the sympathetic nervous system. People suffering from high blood pressure tend to be defensive and view their environment as hostile. These findings have suggested to several researchers that TM might be valuable in treating the millions suffering from high blood pressure. Dr. Datey and his associates reported that forty-seven hypertensive patients doing "shavasan," a yogic breathing exercise, showed an average decrease of about twenty percent in systolic blood pressure.[53] After several weeks of practicing the exercises, this decrease in blood pressure was maintained throughout the day.

Wallace, Benson, and Wilson found that practitioners of TM have low resting levels of blood pressure: the average systolic pressure was 106 mm. Hg and diastolic 57 mm. Hg.[290] Normal blood pressure is considered to be in the range of 120 mm. Hg systolic and 80 mm. Hg diastolic. On the basis of these findings Benson and Wallace tested TM as a possible technique for treating high blood pressure.[24] They measured blood pressure 1,119 times in twenty-two hypertensive subjects before and after the subjects began the regular practice of TM. Resting control blood pressures, prior to learning meditation, were 150±17 mm. Hg systolic and 94±9 mm. Hg diastolic. After starting the daily practice of TM, resting blood pressures, outside the meditation period, were 141±11 mm. Hg systolic and 88±7 mm. Hg diastolic (Chart 13). Although this decrease in blood pressure may appear to be slight, it is statistically significant. Furthermore this finding is independent of whether or not the subjects were taking anti-hypertensive medications. The researchers expect further decreases as the patients practice TM longer. TM may therefore have clinical value in the treatment of hypertension.

Dr. Benson and co-researchers Malveila and Graham are currently investigating whether TM has therapeutic value in headache disorders.[23] They report that "since many subjects claimed decrease or cessation of headache after starting regular practice of TM, patients suffering from severe cluster, common migraine, and tension headache are being asked to practice TM" (23, p. 23). Unfortunately, there is not enough data at this time to allow these researchers to draw any final conclusions.

Wilson and Honsberger have studied twenty-two asthmatic patients among whom half started TM and the other half read related material daily but did not meditate.[302] After learning TM, ninety-four percent showed improvement as determined by measuring airway resistance. Sixty-one percent of the patients reported improvements which were confirmed by their physicians. These results indicate that meditation may be of therapeutic value in treating bronchial asthma. This finding is not surprising in light of Corey's report of increased airway conductance in practitioners of TM.

TM has also shown great promise in alleviating sleep disorders. A biological requirement for normal functioning of the nervous system, sleep is one of the guardians of health. Depriving a person of sleep greatly disrupts his psychophysiological functioning. Sleep disturbances are among the most common ailments doctors treat; the over thirty million Americans who suffer from insomnia are evidenced by the tremendous sales of nonprescription sleeping pills. But such drugs have their own hazards, including addiction, and may actually limit the quality of sleep by depriving a person of REM sleep. Since insomniacs are almost invariably overworked and overtired, sleep disturbances are clearly related to stress. To allow insomniacs to obtain their vitally necessary night's rest, some natural means is needed to correct the imbalances created in the nervous system by fatigue, strain and tension.

The twice-daily practice of TM seems to help establish an improved physiological rhythm. It tends to normalize the cycle of rest and activity by reducing tension and facilitating natural sleep. TM can also benefit people who sleep excessively but awaken unrefreshed. People who practice TM often report feeling more rested despite the fact that they reduce their amount of sleep. Initially, some people require more sleep than they typically needed before starting TM, but after a several-day or week-long "catching up" phase, meditators consistently report deep uninterrupted sleep followed by increased alertness in daytime activity.[10] After a few months, many meditators have reported sleeping fewer hours even though their activity may have increased. It should be noted here that TM cannot substitute for sleep, but rather complements it.

D. E. Miskiman at Trent University in Ontario has investigated the effect of TM on sleep deprivation.[203] He tested the hypothesis that sleep-deprived meditators, purportedly more relieved of fatigue by TM, would show less REM sleep than controls during subsequent recovery nights. Four meditators and a control group were deprived of sleep for forty hours. All night EEG recordings were taken before and after the deprivation. The nonmeditation group showed a twenty-five percent increase in compensatory REM sleep compared to only a seventeen percent increase for the TM group. These interesting findings on a small sample of meditators, however, must be qualified. Miskiman did not determine what amount of sleep meditators may have gained during their twice-daily meditative periods. It may well be that the difference found resulted from meditators "catching up" on their sleep loss during meditation. If similar future studies show that this is not the case, then these findings suggest that people practicing TM cope better with the stress of sleep loss.

Numerous cases of psychosomatic illnesses cured or greatly mitigated through regular practice of TM have been reported. Kanellakos gives an account of a woman who after a little less than one year of practicing TM discovered that she had cured a small duodenal ulcer which had troubled her for some years.[142] Another woman reported to him that before starting TM she had suffered from epileptic attacks two or three times a day, three or four times a week. After many months of TM she had no seizures and was no longer taking any medication. The authors have personally received accounts of relief from rheumatoid arthritis, severe tension headaches, angina pectoris and allergic conditions.

In light of TM's impact on stress, a primary contributor to psychosomatic ailments, such accounts are not surprising. The physiological data on the effects of TM suggest that regular practice of the technique should reduce psychosomatic illness. The unique hypometabolic state produced by TM is probably responsible for the good health reported by meditators. However, anecdotal reports are only suggestive, and never conclusive. Psychosomatic illnesses have their own spontaneous remission rates and even cures. The placebo effect of a new therapeutic technique may also account for cures, whether or not the treatment has any special value. Medical science must conduct clinical research and systematic testing of TM's therapeutic value for various diseases. The effects of TM can easily be investigated since physiological responses occur almost immediately and are easily measured. Parallel studies can be done for a period of a few days, months, or years. Because TM is easy to learn and involves no disciplines or changes in life-style, researchers can easily solicit control and research subjects from the general population. Moreover TM has never been shown to have any adverse physical effects. Large-scale investigation of the applications of TM to medicine are now being conducted at Harvard Medical School, the University of Pennsylvania, UCLA, the Illinois Masonic Medical Center and other leading medical centers throughout the world.

It should be emphasized that TM is not a miracle cure or panacea. TM should never be considered a replacement for antihypertensive medication, an ulcer diet or antiepileptic drugs. On the basis of our present knowledge, however, regular practice of TM does appear to make a significant contribution to the treatment of illness. TM may alleviate various illnesses that have a psychological component such as hypertension, peptic ulcer, asthma and some allergic conditions. There are millions of patients with some degree of organic pathology that is probably associated with emotional disturbance. TM's ability to establish autonomic equilibrium, and relieve stress, suggests its value for the prevention and alleviation of psychosomatic illnesses. The deep rest provided by TM may also accelerate all bodily healing processes. Maharishi recommends that meditators sick in bed or severely injured meditate more often than usual. Research on the effectiveness of TM as an adjunct to postoperative recovery is under way. Investigation of its usefulness for such chronic painful ailments as low back pain and arthritis also seems warranted. Because TM mobilizes energy resources and improves stability, TM might prove helpful in rehabilitation programs for the blind, the deaf and the disabled. Maharishi points out that TM can be helpful even for

> . . . purely organic diseases for which there is no evidence of a mental cause . . . it is well known that a sick man has a mental and emotional attitude towards his illness, which, while not causing the illness itself, may still have profound effects on its course. Meditation will certainly remove these anxieties. It will develop mental strength to endure and rise above suffering." (185, p. 195)

Of all the potential health benefits of TM, the most important may be that of prevention. To avoid illness altogether is the highest goal of medicine. As Maharishi states:

> To build more hospitals to alleviate sickness and suffering for people who have already fallen ill is a laudable act of charity. But it is infinitely more important to find ways and means of preventing people from falling sick and ensuring that they will enjoy good health. Since a way does exist of preventing people from becoming sick (TM), the introduction of it to people all over the world would be a much greater act of charity. (185, p. 191)

This bold claim should not be taken lightly. Modern medicine has already demonstrated that the onset of many diseases depends not so much on the presence of a pathogenic virus or bacteria, but on the receptivity of the organism. Stressed individuals are far more susceptible to all illnesses—from colds and heartburn to tuberculosis and heart disease. As further research evidence becomes available, we may very well find that TM significantly contributes to disease prevention as well as to treatment.

A FOURTH STATE OF CONSCIOUSNESS

Researchers have shown that the practice of TM induces a state of profound rest coupled with heightened alertness. They have also shown that this state has significant regenerative value for the body. Does the state of consciousness gained during the practice of TM differ sufficiently from waking, sleeping and dreaming to be classified as a fourth major state of consciousness? The significance of this question is shown by the growing interest among the world-wide scientific community in William James's observation:

> . . . our normal waking consciousness, rational consciousness as we call it, is but one special type of consciousness whilst all about it, parted from it by the filmiest of screens, there lie potential forms of consciousness entirely different. We may go through life without suspecting their existence, but apply the requisite stimulus, and at a touch they are there in all their completeness . . . no account of the universe in its totality can be final which leaves these other forms of consciousness quite disregarded. (131, p. 388)

Wallace proposed in 1970 that the psychophysiological state gained during TM was so unique that it qualified as a fourth major state of consciousness. He noted that the state had characteristic brain waves, level of oxygen consumption and blood chemistry, suggesting that this state is distinctly different from waking, dreaming and sleeping as well as altered states such as hypnosis or autosuggestion.[287] Orme-Johnson, Banquet, and Glueck have reported further evidence that TM produces a unique psychophysiological state which may merit description as a fourth major state.

In their search for a means of reducing excessive stress, scientists have sought a natural regenerative process. Many cultural traditions contain explicit references to a state of consciousness unlike waking, sleeping or dreaming which is necessary for general well-being and the unfoldment of human potentialities.[124, 205] By studying the physiological effects of TM, researchers have begun to define this fourth major state of consciousness. The ease and efficacy of TM suggest that this technique may be universally applicable as a means of alleviating stress.

THE
PSYCHOLOGICAL
EFFECTS OF
TRANSCENDENTAL
MEDITATION

The psychological correlates of excessive stress and autonomic instability have been well defined. Anxiety, poor attention span, impulsive motor behavior, drug abuse, reduced ego strength and poor performance are among a variety of negative psychological effects correlated with stress and autonomic instability. Lacking a means of significantly improving autonomic functioning and reducing stress, psychologists studying the autonomic nervous system have concentrated almost exclusively on describing the negative consequences of a labile nervous system. Until recent evidence on the possibility of improving autonomic stability and reducing stress through TM, the medical community had almost unanimously assumed that the degree of autonomic stability or instability was an invariable physiological characteristic for each person.[216]

Dr. Elmer Green's psychophysiological principle suggests, however, that the physiological effects of TM discussed in chapter 4 should have corresponding psychological effects.[111] The brain is the master regulator which controls and mediates all feelings, thoughts and behavior. Integration of brain function should lead not only to improvements in health but also to improvements across a wide range of emotional and mental processes, and ultimately to significant improvements in performance and behavior. Published research on the physiological effects of TM as well as innumerable anecdotal reports from people practicing TM have inspired over two dozen researchers to investigate the psychological effects of TM. We will review this research in this chapter.

Though psychological changes are only genuinely verified through controlled experiment, psychological data often lack meaning for people other than psychologists, because such data transform feelings into measurable quantities. To enliven our discussion of TM's psychological effects, we have included some subjective reports of the changes people have noted with the regular practice of TM. Though we received most of the reports in this chapter directly through interviews, several of the anecdotes have appeared in published articles on TM.

PERSONAL ACCOUNTS OF CHANGE

Meditators have reported a wide range of positive psychological changes in their lives which they have attributed to the daily practice of TM. The most often reported change has been improved performance at work or in school along with the growth of inner stability and general calm. In his *Yale Alumni Magazine* article, Al Rubottom presents a typical report from a geology professor who had been practicing TM for one year:

> There's been a quantum increase in the quality of my life since I started meditating. I feel that the clarity of my thinking, the enthusiasm with which I approach my work, the amount of myself I can give to my students and everyone I interact with—all have increased many times. I often feel an increased calmness in tense situations where I work. Even my co-workers say they don't understand how I can be so calm. And it's all due to meditation. Before I started TM, I was totally depressed—I was thinking of dropping out, just disappearing into the woods.[241]

Terri Shultz began TM in order to write an article on it for *Today's Health*. After three months, she reported a great improvement in her life, which eventually persuaded her skeptical husband to start TM as well:

> I was forced to notice for the first time all the gradual changes in my life. My study was cluttered with free-lance articles I had

contracted for in the last few weeks—after years of procrasti-
nation. Sewing interested me for the first time since high school,
and new drapery material lay ready for the needle. In the last
two months I had entertained more friends at home and tried
more new recipes than I had in the entire previous year. I was
drinking half as much wine with dinner. The fever and fatigue
I usually felt around five each evening had been gone for
several weeks.[246]

She found similar changes among other business and professional
people, such as this middle-aged Chicago businessman, a de-
vout Catholic, who reported meditating regularly while com-
muting by train every day.

It's as if my mind has a lever and is four times as potent, relaxed, rested. I read more, enjoy more. My mind has become a
sponge. I see people pushing in train stations, or parents berat-
ing their children, and realize I used to be like that. Now I take
more time, and almost feel sorry for people who feel a terrible
need to hurry everywhere. My religion also means more to me
now. And the change in me changes the people I touch. I am
suddenly becoming the man I always wanted to be but never
knew how.[246]

One of Dr. Kanellakos' colleagues gave an unsolicited report
of an all-encompassing improvement which took place in his
life after he began TM:

Since I began to meditate I have become less violent; I have
grown more serene and have given and received more smiles
than I ever remember. My capacity to love has been increased
and the relationships with the other members of my family
have greatly improved. Even though the output of my work has
increased (I spend more time at my desk working than before),
I feel less strain performing it.

My intuition and knowledge of myself has increased; I love
myself more, my self-esteem has gone up and my self-confidence has increased. I sleep less per night, yet I awake refreshed
in the mornings. The quality of my dreaming has changed (a
disturbing repetitive dream disappeared and most of my dreams
are not confused or disturbing as before).

More now than ever I know what I want from life and where
I am going. I am more alert to what's happening in my environment; my senses have been refined and I am aware of more
things about me. I have greatly reduced the use of alcohol and

tobacco; they have become unpleasant in taste and produce no effects. I am deepening my knowledge of my own religion. I am much calmer and things bother me less than before.

I have grown more tolerant of others and a lot of my prejudices have been either eliminated or reduced. I am developing a capacity to see an integral picture from examining or looking at the various seemingly unrelated parts.

The reduction of stress and anxiety through the regular practice of TM apparently liberates a great deal of previously blocked energy, accounting for the increased vitality which beginning meditators often report. The relief from tension automatically signals an increase in performance, as this student reports:

> Before I began meditation, I was much less tolerant of other people, and I was very nervous and easily upset. Now, after meditating 8 months, I find that I get along better with people. Problems confronting me do not seem to bother me as much as they used to; I am able to face my problems and solve them more efficiently rather than worry about them. I have found that learning is easier; since I began meditating my semester grade point average has risen from 2.6 to 3.4.

Since meditators experience themselves as growing, they anticipate the future not in terms of loss through aging, but in terms of improvement and development. Many older people who started TM have reported that since their lives become more fulfilling with each day of regular meditation, time has become a friend rather than an enemy. A 62-year-old man who has meditated for two years voiced this feeling:

> I used to suffer from loneliness, anxiety, and increasing despair as I felt my time running out. Now I feel younger and more hopeful. Rather than being preoccupied with bodily aches and pains I am pursuing new areas, carpentry and fishing. Life is more fulfilling—each day has its own rewards. I now feel an increasing sense of wisdom. I would love to live to be a hundred now but I am no longer afraid to die. TM has given me inner peace.

Meditators have also reported changes which reflect growth in ego strength. This growth has led to feelings of increased optimism and purpose. The consequences of overcoming a deep feeling of emptiness were reported by a housewife who has meditated two years:

> I was not peaceful or happy because I seemed to have continual conflict and frustration going on within myself. I was satisfied with my marriage, glad I had married my husband, had three beautiful children and all I could want in a material sense. However, I knew something was lacking. I felt always a deep uncertainty about the point of existence. Was all we have to look forward to old age, bad health and death? When I was engaged in some sports activity I thoroughly enjoyed myself, but I could never sit still for long without feelings of anxiety. The main and almost immediate benefit of TM was the feeling that there really was more to life. I would definitely say that my whole life changed the day I started meditating into one of happiness and hope. Since then I have become increasingly more stable in my own self, thoughts and feelings.

Regular practice of TM apparently enables many people to discover a positive sense of themselves which is not dependent on the esteem of others. This growth in the ego strength of TM practitioners seems to be associated with greater sensitivity to other people's needs and an increased appreciation of their environment. Friends and family members of meditators often report feeling better through the positive influence of a TM practitioner. This contagious contentment may account for the dramatic spread of TM through many communities. After one member of a family learns TM, other family members generally start the practice soon afterward. One mother of an entire family of meditators commented:

> For the first time in my married life I am enjoying my role and responsibilities as a cook, wife, mother and housewife—and mainly because of my good self-image due to my new capabilities and accomplishments. Our family used to argue a lot; now we don't. We speak more softly, with more love and understanding, patience. We enjoy each other more. The children have benefited so much, it still seems miraculous. I am less shy than before; more sure of myself and the value of my opinions and convictions.

Despite the general tendency for people to seek positive reasons for justifying whatever they happen to be doing, there are several reasons for confidence in these personal testimonials. First, the claims are often based upon specific objective changes, such as better health, higher grades, more efficient performance or decreased drug use. Secondly, the accounts converge on several common areas of increased well-being, which might be expected from the physiological changes produced by TM. Third, we obtained positive reports so readily from meditators as to suggest that such positive experiences are common to a large percentage of people practicing TM. Finally, the fact that the vast majority of people who begin to meditate continue, indicates that the regular practice of TM is rewarding. Dr. Mohammed Shafii, of the University of Michigan School of Medicine, polled a random sample of people who learned TM over a three-year period and found that seventy percent of them still meditated.[252] In informal polls reported to the authors from Yale, Trinity and Taft, a Connecticut prep school, only eighteen to twenty percent of those who learned TM discontinued the practice. Moreover, people who stop meditating very rarely report negative reasons for stopping. In interviewing a number of persons who had stopped we found that lack of time was the common reason for discontinuing regular meditation. Almost everyone who had stopped, expressed interest in resuming the practice at a later date.

The abundant reports of the positive value of TM do not constitute scientific evidence but do serve to stimulate research. From a scientific perspective, the most significant fact about the reports themselves is the wide range of effects apparently resulting from the practice of TM. If TM does foster growth in all the areas in which individual meditators have reported improvements, the technique must be regarded as unique among all the currently available human development programs. To determine the impact of the regular practice of TM on psychological health, researchers have been studying TM's effect on perception, perceptual-motor coordination, anxiety, hostility, autonomy, self-actualization, happiness, intelligence, learning ability, drug abuse and job and academic performance.

IMPROVED PSYCHOLOGICAL HEALTH

Stress and imbalance in the autonomic nervous system limit satisfaction. Psychologist Maynard Shelly has identified a clear correlation between man's search for happiness and autonomic arousal.[259] In chapter 3 we discussed Shelly's hypothesis that happiness and psychological well-being depend upon a person's ability to maintain an optimum level of arousal. If a person becomes hyperaroused, he experiences tension; if he is insufficiently aroused, he experiences boredom. Shelly describes two types of pleasure, a quiet enjoyment and an exciting pleasure associated with increasing arousal. He points out that stress raises the optimum level of arousal and that repeated exposure to stress systematically denies a person enjoyment in his activity by continually raising his level of arousal. Deprived of satisfaction in his daily routine, a person desperately seeks increasing excitement. This often frantic search for stimulation leads to a corresponding disregard for quieting pleasures. Fueled by the stress reaction, this need for excitement may become an addiction in which fleeting "highs" only lead to further exhaustion, tension, boredom and depression.

By reducing stress and restoring autonomic balance, TM may provide the physiological stabilization necessary to break this debilitating addiction. Shelly has hypothesized that by normalizing the brain's optimum arousal level, TM allows for increased enjoyment in a wide variety of daily activities. Although studies of TM's influence on autonomic stability suggested the physiological validity of Shelly's hypothesis, he decided to investigate whether people practicing TM showed greater happiness than nonmeditators.

To test his theory, Shelly distributed questionnaires to 150 practitioners of TM and to a control group of 150 nonmeditators of similar age and background. He included questions on general happiness and on specific changes commonly reported by meditators. The scales were complicated and required complex mathematical analysis, which has not yet been completed. But as reported by Landrith, the preliminary results comparing the average scores of meditators with nonmeditators were as follows:

> Transcendental meditators 1) are happier individuals;   2) are more relaxed;   3) are less sad;   4) experience the feeling of enjoyment more often;   5) seek arousal as much as do nonmeditators; however, extreme forms are avoided (extreme excitements);   6) seek social contact as often as do non-meditators in spite of the fact that they tend to spend more time alone; 7) seem to develop deeper personal relationships;   8) have more of what Shelly terms personal resources (they depend less on their external surroundings for happiness).[258]

Shelly has suggested that people practicing TM not only have developed more resources for achieving their personal goals than nonmeditators but that they also show a greater ability to mobilize these resources than people not practicing TM. More stable than nonmeditators in the face of demanding circumstances, people practicing TM apparently reflect a much greater sense of meaning and purpose in their activity than nonmeditators. In summary, Shelly has concluded that the constellation of factors that characterize meditators indicates that TM improves psychological well-being by lowering the optimum arousal level.

Further evidence that TM fosters psychological well-being has been reported in a variety of journals. Most of these early studies have been done on small samples. But when several studies, using different populations of meditators and different measures, all show similar results, then some confidence in their significance is justified. Rather than discuss each of these pilot studies in detail, we will briefly summarize their methodology and results.

1. Seeman, Nidich and Banta,[248] at the University of Cincinnati, tested the hypothesis that TM promotes self-actualization—a concept derived by Maslow from studying the most healthy, creative and successful members of society.[196] Self-actualization generally refers to the extent to which a person is applying his potential and reflecting qualities which Maslow identified as humanity's highest values. To test their hypothesis, the research-

ers administered Shostram's Personal Orientation Inventory (POI), a widely used tool for measuring the characteristics of self-actualization. The tests were given to matched experimental and control groups of fifteen subjects; the experimental group then learned TM. After two months, both groups again completed the POI, and the results of the pre- and post-tests were compared (Chart 14). The researchers found that TM promotes positive changes in personality development as measured by several of the test ratings. Increased inner-directedness suggested to the researchers that meditation permitted the experimental subjects to rely more confidently on their "psychic gyroscopes" (248, p. 185). Meditators also improved in spontaneity, self-regard, acceptance of aggression, and capacity for intimate contact. Nidich, Seeman and Dreskin have conducted follow-up studies which replicated these results.[206]

2. D. W. Orme-Johnson studied thirteen staff members of a drug-abuse program at a Texas army base. He divided the sample into an experimental group of seven who learned TM and a control group of six who did not learn the technique. Having administered the Minnesota Multiphasic Personality Inventory, a standardized measure of psychological health, to both groups before and ten weeks after the experimental group learned TM, he found that meditators showed significant decreases in measures of manifest anxiety, hypochondria and personality disorder while the nonmeditators showed no changes during the test period.[217]

3. L. C. Doucette of McMaster University in Canada noted that university students practicing TM significantly decreased their tension and anxiety, when compared with control groups of nonmeditators and of "mock" meditators practicing a simulated meditation technique.[61]

4. Boese and Berger at Pennsylvania State University Medical School studied fifteen meditators without a control group. They found that the meditators' scores of verbalized hostility as measured by the Thematic Apperception Test were significantly lower than scores of average adults.[30]

5. S. H. Tjoa of Amsterdam conducted a pilot study on

a high-school class of twenty, first before and then one year after fourteen of them began TM. He used as his experimental group the seven most regular meditators, comparing them with non-meditators on Wilde's neuroticism test and Fokkem's intelligence test. His results showed significant decreases in neuroticism and increases in intelligence among the practitioners of TM, and no significant changes among the nonmeditators.[279]

6. Larry Hjelle compared fifteen meditators (mean length of meditation, twenty-two months) and twenty-one prospective meditators four days prior to their learning TM. Experienced meditators were significantly less anxious and more internally controlled. They also scored higher on such measures of self-actualization as spontaneity, self-regard and capacity for intimate contact.[120]

7. Theo Fehr, a social science student in West Germany, compared forty-nine teachers of TM with average German subjects, using the Freiburger Personality Inventory. His results showed reduced nervousness, depression and irritability; decreased inhibition and tendency to dominate; and increased sociability, self-assuredness, emotional stability, staying power and efficiency among the meditators.[70]

8. Ferguson and Gowan used two different measures of anxiety as well as the Northridge Developmental Scale to measure anxiety, depression, neuroticism and self-actualization. They tested three groups: thirty-one students just prior to beginning meditation, a matched control group, and a group of sixteen long-term meditators who had meditated over three and a half years. Having tested all groups before the first group learned TM, the researchers found that after six weeks of regular practice, the new meditators showed significant decreases in both their anxiety scales (Chart 15) as well as in depression and neuroticism (Chart 16), but an increase in self-actualization (Chart 17). The long-term meditators showed significantly higher positive ratings on each of these scales than beginning meditators. The researchers inferred that the effects of TM are probably cumulative.[71]

Collectively, these studies suggest that the regular practice of TM has a positive impact on psychological health. The psychological effects of TM presumably arise from the increase in autonomic stability and reduction of stress achieved during meditation. Taken together, the physiological and psychological results of TM provide a basis for the hypothesis that TM may help unfold an individual's potential for psychological health. Further research on TM and psychological well-being is under way at over thirty research institutions.

IMPROVED PERFORMANCE

Contrary to popular thinking about meditation, people who practice TM insist that it does not involve withdrawal from life. In fact, they frequently assert that the rest gained during TM prepares them for increased activity. Meditators commonly report that TM improves their overall performance in practically everything they do. Because performance tests are easy to conduct, a large number of researchers have begun to investigate how the effects of the regular practice of TM relate to the ability to perform various tasks.

Anecdotal reports have led psychologists to investigate one of the most basic aspects of performance—perception. Along with heightened self-awareness, meditators have described heightened awareness of their environment. The following report of improved perceptual ability is typical:

> I have noticed a total change in perceptual awareness. I've begun to clear out the cobwebs, cut the static and see more clearly what is going on. So as a result the changes I've noticed are total.
>
> My visual, and sometimes auditory, perceptions are much clearer, and I enjoy scenery more than I ever have before, although I always have loved natural scenery. I am attracted instantly, often, by the smallest and most intricate and lovely patterns in nature that I formerly missed.

Maharishi has suggested that TM improves perception in two ways: greater breadth, or ability to scan the environment; and greater acuity, or ability to look deeply into an object (186: X, XX). Kenneth Pelletier, at the University of California at Berkeley, tried to test these assertions. He noted that the practice of all forms of meditation, particularly TM, is supposed to lead to greater sensitivity to internal cues such as physical sensations, deep feelings, and biological rhythms, and also to greater ability to concentrate on external tasks and objects. He studied changes in the deployment of attention in twenty people who were just starting meditation, and a matched control group of people interested in starting TM.[223]

He used three different measures of attention. The first, a test of autokinetic effect, consists of a point of light surrounded by a dark field. People who concentrate without interruption on the light eventually see the light begin to move, while those who scan the entire field, including the darkness, perceive less illusionary movement. Pelletier postulated that the greater concentration ability of meditators would lead them to focus more on the light and consequently to note more movement. The practitioners of TM did show significantly greater autokinetic effect than the control group. This finding suggests their improved ability to concentrate.

Pelletier's second measure was called the rod and frame test, in which subjects were asked to orient a rod within a tilted frame, so that it became perfectly vertical. People who try to orient the rod according to the frame make errors, while those who orient the rod according to their internal sense of up and down are more successful. Pelletier found that meditators were less influenced by the tilted frame, presumably because they were more in tune with internal cues. The meditators performed significantly better on the task after three months of meditation than the nonmeditating control group.

The third test of attention deployment was the embedded figure test, in which subjects are asked to locate a simple figure, such as a rectangle, inside a complex figure made up of many overlapping shapes. People who can concentrate without being distracted by the surrounding field can find the figures more quickly. Pelletier found that though improvement was less significant than on the rod and frame test, meditators performed this task better than the control group. He has hypothesized that the greater improvement in the rod and frame test resulted from its demand that the subject use physical cues rather than the purely cognitive ability required by the embedded figure test.

The ability to perform on the rod and frame and the embedded figure tests has been strongly correlated with underlying personality structures.[304, 305] Individuals who show field dependence tend to be outer-directed while those who are field-independent are more inner-directed. People who are field-dependent tend to rely on external sources for their values and view of themselves. Those who are more inner-directed, on the other hand, show greater psychological differentiation, more self-reliance and a stronger sense of identity. Field dependence-independence tests administered to young adults are considered a reliable reflection of established personality characteristics. It is therefore highly remarkable that meditators demonstrated significantly increased field independence after only a few months of practicing TM.

Researchers have also studied how accurately meditators can perceive subtle changes in their environments and whether scores on such tests improve with length of time practicing TM. For example, a study by Graham at the University of Sussex, England, reported improved auditory discrimination after the practice of TM (Chart 18).[109] Eight meditators displayed a thirty-seven percent improvement in frequency (pitch) discrimination and a twenty-eight percent improvement in amplitude (loudness) discrimination following twenty minutes of meditation. Auditory discrimination decreased slightly after the subjects read a book for twenty minutes. In another study, Brown, Stewart and Blodgett tested two-point threshold discrimination, G.S.R. and visual brightness discrimination. These tests were administered to eleven meditating subjects, before and after fifteen minutes of meditation, and to eleven controls, before and after fifteen minutes of rest. Those subjects who displayed the physiological indices of the meditative state performed significantly better on all measures studied than the control group.[37]

Other researchers have investigated the effect of TM on perceptual-motor coordination. Blasdell asked a group of fifteen meditators and a control group of nonmeditators to perform a complex tracing task which demanded rapid response to external cues.[27] She found that the meditators showed much greater hand-eye coordination in their ability to complete the tasks faster and more accurately than controls. Shaw and Kolb at the University of Texas found that the reaction time of transcendental meditators is faster than that of nonmeditators (Chart 19).[255] Nine meditators and an equal number of controls were asked to react to a flash of light by pressing a button. The researchers have reported that meditators tended to react faster than the nonmeditators by an average of about thirty percent. After many trials, both groups took a fifteen-minute break. The meditators practiced TM, while the nonmeditators sat resting with their eyes closed. The groups were then retested. The results were again significant. The meditators' reaction time was reduced by an additional fifteen percent whereas the nonmeditators' time increased about ten percent.

Allan Abrams, a psychology graduate student, devised a pilot study to test whether TM improved performance in learning. He used recall, measured by ability to learn a list of words quickly and accurately and to remember them over a period of time, as a measure of learning.[1] He noted that psychologists have not been able to increase memory by manipulating the learning environment, because this ability is dependent on the internal state of the learner. He suggested that if TM were able to increase learning ability by creating a more optimum internal environment, it could provide a unique educational tool.

Abrams recruited twelve experimental meditators and six beginners through the Berkeley SIMS Center, and a control group of twelve nonmeditators. To test their recall ability, he scheduled three sessions at one-week intervals for all subjects. The subjects were asked to memorize a nonsense word and a meaningful word to which it was paired. Twenty-five minutes later, they were asked to write down the paired meaningful word in response to each nonsense word. One week later they were requested to follow the same procedure with a new list and then to recall the original paired meaningful words of the first week in response to their paired nonsense syllables. An identical arrangement was followed the third week, with a new list at the beginning, and a test of recall of the second week's list at the end of the session.

Chart 20 summarizes the results, comparing the three experimental groups on a combined scale measuring both short-term (25 minutes) and long-term (one week) recall. On the first test, meditators remembered a significantly greater number of the pairs than the control group. In later weeks, meditating subjects recalled more pairs. Abrams also tentatively noted that when one of the pairs was given at a louder volume, an effect which tends to break concentration and interfere with performance, meditators were less negatively affected in their learning than nonmeditators. In addition, he discovered a general trend toward greater learning ability among long-time practitioners of TM. This trend suggests that the benefits of TM to learning ability are cumulative. While this pilot study gives some indication that TM increases learning ability, the low number of subjects and the low significance of the findings suggest a need for further research.

Though these early studies on improved performance among TM practitioners are more suggestive than conclusive, Banquet and Glueck's EEG studies offer grounds for a hypothesis that TM might improve performance by altering brain function. During the meditation period, brain-wave patterns synchronize between both hemispheres and between the front and back parts of the brain. This hypersynchrony suggests increased integration between different parts of the brain. Because different parts of the brain control different bodily processes, increased integration in the brain might result in improved performance. For example, the front of the brain controls voluntary movements while the back of the brain is responsible for perception. Increased integration between these two areas of the brain might explain improved perceptual-motor coordination and improved reaction time among practitioners of TM. Increased coherency in the brain's electrical activity may correspond physiologically

to the heightened awareness which meditators report as the basis
of their improved performance.

TM AND DRUG USE

Noting TM's impact on performance, a number of psychologists have become interested in directly applying TM to improve
maladaptive behavior. Because considerable evidence suggests
that TM improves self-regard, decreases anxiety and improves
self-reliance, several researchers have hypothesized that TM
might reduce drug abuse. This speculation is grounded in recent
understandings of why people abuse drugs. When a person feels
anxious, bored or aimless he naturally seeks escape. Though
vacations, movies, sports or television may provide temporary
alteration of mood, none of these activities significantly lessens
the underlying physiological causes of psychological tension. To
meet the psychological consequences of stress, our society has
developed one of the most characteristic neuroses of our age,
the reliance on drugs of all kinds.

While the illegal use of drugs has captured headlines, most
researchers on the legal and illegal use of drugs have acknowledged that drug abuse extends throughout all levels of society.
Americans consume billions of tranquilizers, amphetamines and
barbiturates in addition to hundreds of billions of cigarettes and
millions of gallons of alcohol. Psychiatrist and public health
leader Joel Fort recently completed a book in which he showed
that alcoholism is our country's most prevalent and pernicious
drug problem.[76] No other drug has led to more health problems,
broken homes, suicides, violent crimes or automobile accidents
than alcohol. Second to alcoholism, cigarette smoking has gained
recognition as the country's greatest drug addiction problem.
Despite the publicly acknowledged danger of cigarette smoking, sales of cigarettes have continued to rise. Over the past
decade, the consumption of amphetamines for energy, mood
elevators to relieve depression, barbiturates for sleeping and
tranquilizers to relieve tension has become common and even
socially acceptable. The tremendous and growing demand for

all these drugs may be the clearest indicator of how deeply stress is affecting our society.

When large numbers of young people began consuming marijuana and hallucinogenic drugs in the late 1960s, the phrase "drug abuse" became cause for alarm. Though psychiatry has gained significant insight into the psychological mechanics of drug abuse, it has not been able to deter young people from using illegal drugs. Law enforcement, education, psychotherapy and a variety of programs involving all three approaches, have proven universally ineffective in aiding young people to stop drug abuse. On the basis of the failure of these programs, Dr. Andrew Weil has concluded that people abuse drugs to meet a genuine need. Until people have found an alternate way of meeting the need which people attempt to satisfy with drugs, Weil has suggested that drug abuse will continue.[294]

To what needs is the use of drugs addressed? The tired and depressed person may take an amphetamine; the insomniac may turn to barbiturates; a bored young person may experiment with psychedelics. In each of these cases, the use of drugs expresses an underlying need to counterbalance an uncomfortable condition. Despite all the specific effects for which people take drugs, the purpose of drug abuse is the restoration of physiological equilibrium and a feeling of well-being. Because TM restores equilibrium by reducing stress and maximizes the enjoyment of life, it may well offer a plausible solution for all forms of drug abuse.

Dr. Benson was the first to report that TM might have an impact on drug abuse. After discovering that nineteen of the twenty subjects in his physiological studies of TM had abused drugs prior to TM instruction, in 1969 he suggested that TM be investigated as a tool to reduce drug abuse.[22] Later that same year, a sociology graduate student from UCLA, Thomas Winquist, reported on the drug abuse patterns of 525 students who had practiced TM for at least three months.[303] Of the 484 students who replied to his survey, thirty-two percent reported that they had used marijuana. Of the 143 students who reported regular marijuana use, eighty-four percent stated they had stopped using it; 14.5 percent, that they had decreased use of it; and 1.5 percent, that they had increased use of it after beginning TM. Of all the 111 subjects who regularly used psychedelic drugs prior to TM instruction, eighty-six percent stopped and fourteen percent decreased after learning TM. Half of the regular drug users stated that their use of drugs changed with TM because life became more fulfilling. Another fourth of the drug users said that they stopped because drug use became less pleasurable. A tenth stated that their use of drugs changed because they no longer desired them. The remaining portion was composed of individuals who did not change their drug use pattern.

The following accounts from young people illustrate how TM reduces drug abuse among young people. One twenty-year-old girl told us:

> Before TM I was attempting to find something that I could use to help me evolve and become free of the confusion which confronted me. I began taking acid. I discovered great frustration, however, in attempting to make any spiritual progress in this way. TM was the only logical step for me to take. Since learning the technique, all progress has greatly accelerated and a great factor of stability has been introduced. Things that seemed desirable yet unattainable in personal development previously have become easy and my life takes increasing shape and direction, often unexpectedly.

Another twenty-four-year-old student wrote:

> Before I began meditating, I lived in Berkeley in an ancient 5-room flat with an average of seven other drug-oriented college drop/flunk outs. We did weird things. No one worked or had money or was particularly enthusiastic about life, as shown by our generally lethargic state. I became interested in meditation at this time [Feb. '68] but was unable to reconcile myself to the $35 donation. However, my life steadily grew more depressing. My drug use increased, and I went on the old "death trip" ploy. Meanwhile, some of my friends had started meditating, and I had the opportunity to see the changes they went through in their first few months. It was this that finally convinced me that meditation was the proper direction to move in. I wound up that summer in N.Y.C., where I was initiated. . . . At the end of the summer I returned to California, enrolled in school, and

got a job, things I hadn't done in years. Since then I've continued school, raising my average to a 3.7 and I intend to graduate and go into teaching. I'm convinced that TM is the greatest thing I've ever encountered.

Winquist's early findings and numerous anecdotal reports led Benson and Wallace to study drug abuse patterns in a group of 1,862 people practicing TM.[25, 288] They asked individuals attending a teacher training course to recall their drug use, drug selling and attitudes toward drug use before and after learning TM. The subjects had practiced TM for a mean period of twenty months.

The results show the subjects progressively decreased their use of illegal drugs as their practice of TM continued; after twenty-one months of meditation, most had completely stopped (Chart 21). For example, in the half year before starting TM, about eighty percent of the subjects reported using marijuana and about twenty-eight percent of these using it heavily. After a half year of meditation, only thirty-seven percent used marijuana and only one subject was a heavy user. Twenty-one months after beginning TM only twelve percent continued to use marijuana. The decrease of LSD use was even more dramatic. Before starting meditation forty-eight percent had used LSD, fourteen percent heavily. After twenty-one months, only eight percent took LSD. Comparable changes occurred in the use of barbiturates, amphetamines and narcotics. Of those who continued using drugs following their instruction in TM, over half had been irregular in their practice of the technique. The researcher also noted a marked decrease in drug-selling activity, and an increasing tendency to discourage others regarding drug use. All subjects felt that TM had been influential in these changes.

Benson and Wallace noticed similar trends in the use of alcohol and cigarettes (Chart 22). In the six months preceding initiation, sixty percent of the subjects took hard liquor and about four percent of them were heavy drinkers. After twenty-one months of meditation, only twenty-five percent took hard liquor and almost none drank heavily. Forty-eight percent smoked cigarettes before meditation, half of them heavily, but after twenty-one months of meditation, sixteen percent smoked and only six percent smoked heavily. Nearly every subject credited TM for the decrease. A thirty-six-year-old housewife who has meditated a year offered a typical account of such a change:

> Before I started meditating I smoked [cigarettes] fairly heavily. Now I don't smoke at all. I quit easily, without any effort, and without even realizing I was doing so at first, gradually over a year's time. I also drank alcohol at parties. Now I never do, for through meditation I could feel it was damaging. I knew this before, although more vaguely, but could not stop when it was socially expected, but after meditating a year I found I could enjoy myself in any social situation without any such crutches. I have a natural strength of my own convictions.[222]

Graham, Peterman and Scarff conducted another drug study in British Columbia the summer of 1971.[110] They interviewed new meditators prior to instruction and long-term meditators at a teacher training course in Humboldt, California. They confirmed the finding that meditators decreased or stopped the use of illegal drugs, cigarettes and liquor. In addition, the 451 subjects reported a generally increased clarity of mind, improvements in relationships to others, and increased efficiency in action, which they also attributed to their practice of TM.

Shafii, Lavely and Jaffe of the University of Michigan School of Medicine have pointed out several drawbacks in Benson and Wallace's research design.[253] First, the sample was not representative of meditators in general because it consisted only of the dedicated and highly motivated meditators who had gone on for advanced training. Secondly, since the researchers did not provide a control group of drug users who did not go on to learn TM, the study gave no indication of whether the reported decrease in drug use might not have occurred in a similar group without meditation. They felt, in addition, Wallace and Benson's expectation of positive results had influenced the wording of the questions, which may have suggested to the subjects that they were expected to prefer TM to their previous drug use. Distributing the questionnaire when the subjects were in daily contact with one another may have allowed for group suggestion to further distort individual responses. While the Benson and Wallace study showed that drug use greatly decreases among a certain select group of meditators, it did not provide evidence of whether these decreases were widespread, or of whether the drug use and personal characteristics of those who practiced TM differed from other drug-using populations.

The Shafii group conducted a study of marijuana use and TM which corrected these methodological deficiencies. Using records from the local SIMS center in the University of Michigan community, they were able to contact 187 of 525 meditators. Of those contacted, thirty percent reported that they were not currently meditating and were thus disqualified from the study. In an initial questionnaire, each subject was asked to name two available people who were similar in personal characteristics to himself but who did not meditate. These named individuals were to serve as controls. The final sample consisted of 126 subjects who had practiced TM between one to thirty-nine months and a control group of ninety.

The meditators and controls were asked whether they had used marijuana during the last four years. In the meditator group sixty-nine percent were users, with a mean frequency of marijuana use of 7.3 times per month before starting meditation. Fifty-one percent of the controls, the same percentage as found by the Gallup Poll survey of college students in the same year, 1971, indicated that they were users of marijuana, at a mean frequency of 3.6 times per month. Following instruction in TM the mean of the meditators as a group fell to 2.8, whereas the control group's mean stayed the same.

Meditators were classified into five groups, according to how long they had been meditating. Shafii found that the longer a person meditated, the more likely it was that he would decrease or discontinue the use of marijuana. In group 1 (practicing TM one to three months) there was a forty-six percent decrease and a twenty-three percent stoppage during the first months after learning TM, compared to a fifteen percent stoppage in the control group. In groups 2 (practicing TM four to six months), 3 (practicing TM seven to twelve months), and 4 (practicing TM thirteen to twenty-four months) there was also a significant decrease and stoppage of marijuana use following TM instruction. In group 5 (practicing TM from twenty-five to thirty-six months) sixty-nine percent totally stopped their use of marijuana, in contrast to a fifteen percent stoppage among the controls. This latter group was most similar to the subjects of the Benson and Wallace study; the percentages of decreased marijuana were comparable.

In addition, the Shafii study reported a reduction in cigarette smoking in subjects who had been meditating thirteen months or more.[252] Seventy-one percent of the group who had practiced TM more than two years significantly decreased smoking cigarettes and fifty-seven percent totally stopped smoking. The control group figures for cigarette usage did not change.

In Sweden, Eva Brautigam conducted a pilot study suggesting that TM may be effective for hard-core narcotic abusers.[33] Through a hospital hepatitis unit, she obtained a list of twenty known heroin users. She sent them flyers suggesting that TM had been found helpful as treatment for drug abuse, urging them to sign up for the course. Those who replied were randomly divided into experimental and control groups. One group began TM immediately, and the other had a weekly counseling group. Because the second group strongly wanted to learn TM, however, they were finally instructed as well. Both groups sharply decreased their drug abuse and improved on a number of psychophysiological measures. Brautigam has suggested that in addition to the effect of TM itself, the new group contacts and new social identity as meditators contributed to the reported changes.

Though these studies on TM and drug abuse have their obvious limitations, this simple technique is apparently having a significant impact in reducing dependency on legal and illegal drugs. Governmental officials in Illinois, Michigan, New Hampshire, New York, British Columbia, Sweden, Germany, France and New Zealand have begun exploring the applied uses of TM to combat drug abuse. For example, the Illinois House of Representatives passed a resolution in May 1972, noting that TM "shows promise of being the most effective drug prevention program being presented in the world today," and recommending that the state's "mental health department incorporate the course in TM in the drug abuse program."[127]

INTEGRATED GROWTH THROUGH TM

Research findings discussed in this chapter have indicated that regular practice of TM apparently has a positive effect on a person's psychological growth. In fact, TM appears to be unique among self-development programs in the profundity and wide range of its benefits. Consistent with the scientific evidence on stress reduction and psychophysiological integration, Maharishi has offered the following analogy to show how the simple mental practice of TM can improve the entire range of individual psychology:

> If there is a fort which commands a whole territory, it is wise to go straight to the fort and capture it. Then everything in the surrounding territory, all its gold and diamond mines and other riches, will come naturally into one's possession. But if one sets out to capture each mine separately, all one's time and strength may well be exhausted in securing even one. (185, p. 107)

Having defined TM as a technique whereby a person contacts pure awareness and thereby gains access to a great reserve of creative intelligence, Maharishi has asserted that this one experience enriches every aspect of life. People often exhaust themselves trying to improve even one aspect of their psychology. Through will and a variety of mood-making techniques, they try to be good, happy, loving, powerful or creative. The inner tension created by force of will may be counted as a primary contribution to a person's failure to meet his expectations. In contrast, TM enables a person to gain access to that aspect of the mind which commands the whole psyche. By tapping his inner rescources of creative intelligence, a person begins to grow in the areas of his life which he was seeking to improve and often in unexpected areas as well. Contemporary psychologists have noted that people's most fulfilling achievements occur not through force of will but through the natural and spontaneous expression of their potential energy, intelligence, creativity and love.[196] Before discussing TM's role in unfolding human potential and placing TM in the context of current theories of the psyche, we will consider a further practical application of this technique, its use as a tool in psychotherapy.

6

MEDITATION
AND
PSYCHOTHERAPY

TM AS PSYCHOTHERAPY

Natural healing processes cure most physical and mental illnesses. Injured tissues regenerate themselves, white blood cells
repel infection and many emotionally disturbed people experience spontaneous remissions or find ways to cope with their distress. Growth too is a natural process. There seems to be a basic
urge in living things to move toward the fullest expression of
their abilities and potentialities. However, while children express
the joy derived from the discovery of new knowledge and skills,
many adults seem satisfied to spend most of their energy in
routine, repetitious or defensive activities. The stress of life and
the responsibility of living often dull people to the point of fear-
ing change and resisting growth.

During TM, meditators contact pure awareness, an energy
reservoir deep within the psyche. The reported effects of this experience include decreased anxiety and less dependence on external stimuli such as drugs and excitement for self-mobilization. Related results include increased happiness, stability, performance,
optimism, energy and good health. The practice of TM apparently brings increased well-being on physical, psychological and
spiritual levels. For example, Shafii reports that ninety-two percent of 126 meditators surveyed felt more relaxed after meditation, and seventy-five percent reported improvement in their
ability to concentrate and a decrease in tension, anxiety and ner-

vousness.[251] Can TM also be helpful to those individuals who are so seriously disturbed that they require psychiatric care? The evidence is mounting that TM can contribute significantly to the treatment of the mentally ill.

Anxiety is the common denominator of all mental illness. Neurosis is characterized by excessive anxiety which arises when there is no manifest danger, or continues long after danger has passed, and interferes with the individual's pursuit of a normal life. Chronic anxiety may precede major depressive episodes. The anxiety that portends schizophrenic reactions is extreme and incessant, leading to marked disturbances of sleep, cognition and social functioning. Hypochondriasis is often a response to anxiety as well. Alcoholism and drug abuse are destructive habits which attempt to relieve anxiety. Since anxiety is so basic to all mental illness, and since TM has been shown to relieve anxiety, there has been increasing interest by the psychiatric community as to whether TM is useful in treating severe psychic distress.

TM serves as an anti-anxiety agent by changing the response of the individual to environmental circumstances and by allowing a more adaptive response to twentieth-century living conditions. During TM, breathing becomes shallower and slower, heart rate and cardiac output decrease, muscles relax, blood lactate diminishes, skin resistance increases markedly, the brain achieves greater synchrony, and the meditator experiences a refreshing state of restful alertness. The comprehensive and integrated hypometabolic state produced by TM appears to be the opposite of a maladaptive anxiety attack.

In current practice, psychotherapy is the principal treatment for mental illness, either alone or combined with psychoactive drugs. But therapy usually requires long years of professional attention and produces results that are at best inconsistent. Psychotherapy is effective for only certain individuals, and only a select few in our society can afford the luxury of long-term psychiatric treatment. We suggest that the practice of TM offers an alternative, not necessarily to replace the interpersonal encounter which is the core of psychotherapy, but as a significant means of reducing tension, broadening awareness and making life more meaningful and pleasurable, and thereby fulfilling the goals of all forms of therapy. Furthermore, since psychotherapy also aims at removing limitations upon the mind's full range of capabilities, this process can benefit from any technique which strengthens the individual.

Psychotherapy focuses on aiding the individual to come to grips with the psychological sources of conflict. However, gaining knowledge of the source of the stress is not as important as finding ways to eliminate stress and go beyond it. Indeed, knowledge of the sources of psychic stress may be demoralizing. As many people have found after years of fruitless search, excessive analysis of previous negative experiences can lead to a loss of self-esteem rather than its enhancement. The key to successful therapy lies instead in creating psychological and physiological conditions which optimize the natural tendency of the nervous system to stabilize itself. TM appears to offer a systematic method to achieve this goal in a relatively short period of time.

Many people find that individual and group therapy are incomplete processes, leading to understanding or catharsis, but not permanent transformation and satisfaction. The following account contrasts TM with various therapies. In addition to immediate relief, this woman found that the benefits of TM increased regularly over the year she meditated:

> For all my life I was plagued by a wide variety of psychosomatic illnesses and later by depression. When I was four, I used to pick at my cuticles until they bled. A rash developed on my arms which lasted five years. When I was older I read constantly as an escape from the anxiety and loneliness I felt. I could not communicate with anyone. My parents were an affliction to suffer from and "friendship" was a charade. If I spoke at all, I was guarded. When I was fourteen, I attempted suicide. I began drinking occasionally to relieve my tension and soon developed an ulcer. I saw a psychiatrist a few times, and when I was seventeen, began a year of group therapy. It helped me understand the sources of my problems, but I still felt lonely

and afraid and angry. In college I was in many sensitivity training groups and relied heavily on friends and hallucinogenic drugs to help me analyze the sources of my anxiety.

The anxiety continued and I began having migraine headaches and taking tranquilizers and codeine to calm down. I was chronically depressed and considered suicide a real option. When I heard of meditation I was extremely skeptical, but after some investigation I decided it was worth a try. I was amazed. In my first meditation I felt a great optimism and release. I smiled so much I thought I would burst. I was euphoric: I no longer procrastinated, papers got written, books read, and exams studied for without the mental paralysis that had previously plagued me. I felt productive and happy. I wasn't afraid to talk to anybody. All my physical symptoms have left and I have not felt depressed or suicidal since I began meditating.

TM can effect profound psychological transformation. The spontaneous experience of opening up to oneself, to others and to one's environment may unfold an immediate surge of energy. New meditators may feel that they have suddenly come into contact with life. An account after almost a year of meditation suggests the power of TM to lift people out of serious psychological crises:

In April 1966 I had to leave college to enter a mental hospital. I was hypertense, overemotional, self-destructive, and was putting on weight extremely fast. I left the hospital not really able to function or to relate to reality at all. For a year or two I lived alone and took a lot of drugs—put on 35 pounds in less than three months. After that I was never able to lose the weight as it was the result of tension as well as of an emptiness inside. I did not know myself. I did not respect myself, and felt that anything that happened to me didn't matter.

I began TM. Within three months I lost over thirty pounds and felt physically and mentally as if I were able to move again. I was able to be with people, to begin to have some self-respect, and to have circumstances work out for me. Last February I returned to school, came out first in all but one class, and had to do very little work even so. I felt great about everything—there are still little hassles and some uncertainty, but I feel confident about my ability to do whatever is necessary and enjoy a lot of it. Actually I can't remember what it was like to be so unhappy and incompetent, and I don't think much about it now. I expect that everything will keep improving as it has.

Anecdotal accounts of dramatic personal change as a result of TM among psychiatric patients who were unresponsive to drug or individual psychotherapy are becoming common. Increasing numbers of psychiatrists, psychologists and other counselors have become practitioners of TM and have sought to apply it to their practice as an adjunct to therapy.

Many therapists who meditate also recommend TM to their patients. One of the authors, Dr. Bloomfield, has used TM as part of his psychiatric practice. Following are three case studies which represent some therapeutic changes he observed following the addition of TM to psychotherapy.

Joan is a twenty-five-year-old female graduate student. Prior to meditation she was chronically tense and spent a great deal of time crying because she couldn't stand "the constant pressure, pressure, pressure." She had tried tranquilizers and relaxation exercises, which offered minimal relief. As the pressure of school increased, Joan could not even get out of bed some days, yet when awake she couldn't go back to sleep. She has now been meditating for nearly a year. Since her instruction she reports gradually feeling better than she has ever felt before, and feels that she has received more relaxation and energy than from two previous years of therapy, pills and exercises. She reports that now she "knows what deep relaxation is all about."

Joan no longer has chronic insomnia, gets up every morning and looks forward to the day's activities. She still reports some tension during a particularly busy day or before a paper is due, but she feels better able to cope with such things. She states:

TM has opened up new horizons in my life. Prior to beginning TM I felt like I was on a treadmill. The strain was becoming unbearable, and I was on the verge of a nervous breakdown. Since meditating I gradually learned to be more at ease, with myself and with the situations in my life. It's not so much that my life situation has changed, but my view of these situations. I attribute a lot of these changes to the deep calm that I've obtained from meditation.

George was twenty-eight and single, and suffered from obsessive-compulsive symptoms, along with chronic anxiety. He became tense when around other people, especially in public places. He had to perform various rituals, such as having to straighten his clothes several times before he could face the world. Nonsensical thoughts constantly intruded into his mind, confusing him or arresting his attention. He has been meditating for five months, and reports a marked decrease in his anxiety. He feels "more alert and more alive." Whereas before he felt as if his mind "couldn't be turned off," he now has periods for the first time in his life where he is not thinking frantically and strenuously. George reports learning "what it means to just be," and accepts life in a more relaxed and less controlling fashion. He has been progressively less troubled by obsessional thoughts. He now is able to "let the thoughts go." In public places and with others he is less tense, and he feels a greater identification with others than ever before. He has learned that he is "not the only one trying to make a go of it in life." He states:

> I am very happy to be a meditator. It allows me to gain control over my mind rather than my mind gaining control over me as it has in the past. I also like the fact that it is such an effortless technique. Before I felt that everything in life that I got could only be obtained by trying so very hard, and that's why I frequently felt hassled and strained. It's wonderful to find a technique where, by not trying, good things happen.

The third account is of a middle-aged woman who suffered from depression and anxiety for most of her life, which had been getting worse for the four years preceding treatment. Lisa was hospitalized at a private mental hospital for a year, following a suicide attempt which was the culmination of a growing sense of desperation. TM was recommended to help alleviate the pervasive anxiety from which she suffered. Lisa describes her first meditation:

> It was wonderful. I never experienced anything quite like it. I now understand what it means to be fully relaxed and what

it means to be able to look at the world through clear eyes instead of seeing it as so tension-filled all the time. I felt better the rest of that day than I have felt in years. If meditation can help me to eventually be like that most of the time, I couldn't ask for more. No medication that I've taken, and I've taken lots, helped me to feel that way.

I find that my meditating twice daily helps me to sleep better, helps me to get out of bed in the morning and start the day. Before I started meditating, I frequently used to lay around in bed all day. I am now better able to handle suicidal impulses when I have them, and have much more hope than I did before. Don't let me make it sound, however, like it made my life all better, because it hasn't. I still find it hard to get along with other people and can't find a job, but just having meditated for six weeks I feel that it's helped me to sleep better, be less depressed, and less anxious. I'm going to stick with it because it is something I can do for myself to cope better.

Several aspects of patients' accounts of TM are noteworthy. The first is that, unlike medication and psychotherapy, TM is exclusively under the control of the patient. If he feels better, it will not be due to a pill or his relationship with a therapist, but to a natural process triggered by his own efforts. Hospitals and various forms of psychiatric treatment have been criticized for not reinforcing a patient's autonomy, but instead reinforcing negative aspects of the self through exclusive concentration on the pathological.

The struggle against total dependency characteristic of many emotionally disturbed people can find a meaningful resolution in the liberating effects of the self-administered practice of TM. This fact is highlighted in this account by an office worker who has meditated for over a year:

Before I began meditation I used drugs, methedrine and narcotics. The effects of the drugs were that I was incredibly tense. Physically, my shoulders were up so high that one could barely see my neck. To "relieve" tension I used to cry, and scream, and stamp a lot; at particularly tense moments I used to hit things with my fists and my head. I just felt that I was the most miserable "worm" in the world, and had the idea that I should keep high on drugs for as long as possible, and if I took these drugs for five years and died, it would be better than fifty years of life as I thought it was.

Finally, through my bad action, I was caught by the police, and it was decided that I should go to a psychiatric hospital where I stayed for two months. There I became very secure and didn't really want to come out. Here I could be "taken care of," no one could hurt me (mentally). I cried over any negative comment. A different kind of tension arose while I was there from just living with really sick people. I even found that I began talking like a baby. I met an aide who had just begun TM and became very interested in him (not the meditation). I wasn't about to become responsible. I had my parents sign me out so I could see Maharishi at Harvard and decided to start. Before I could start in February, I got serum hepatitis and had to wait. The reason I'm telling you all this is to give you an idea of what a physical *mess* I was. It was so bad that when a train went by or a door slammed, my whole body would shake all over. I went to New York to be initiated.

There were about fifty people there who saw me go upstairs to start with the personal instruction; when I came down (honest) everyone stopped talking and stared at me. My shoulders had dropped, all the tension in my face was gone so that my whole facial structure had changed, and most important to me, I was completely at ease. My tension didn't come back, my voice became more mature, and I began to think properly and clearly. Since then my whole family has begun TM because they saw my rapid progress.

Yale psychiatric resident David Sternberg reported to us a dramatic case involving a forty-three-year-old man who had been seeing psychiatrists since he was eighteen. Dr. Sternberg was the fourth therapist assigned to this patient in the last two years. None of the others had felt any hope for alleviation of his pervasive anxiety. Only Valium provided some relief but he had become addicted to it.

In the initial meetings, Dr. Sternberg found that nothing he tried was helpful. All the patient wanted was more medication and for the doctor to take over his life. He did not want to modify his life-style, but merely to obtain momentary relief from his constant panic-anxiety state. He had not driven his car for a year for fear of being hit, had not left his home town for fear of having a heart attack, could not hold a job, and recently had become impotent.

After two months, in frustration Dr. Sternberg asked the patient which psychiatrist had been most helpful during his twenty-five years of treatment. A behavior therapist's use of desensitization techniques, a relaxation therapy which we describe later in this chapter, had apparently provided some relief. In response, Dr. Sternberg, a meditator himself, recommended that the patient learn TM. Half of each session was then spent sitting in meditation. At first the patient complained that anxious thoughts interfered with meditation, but he gradually relaxed and let thoughts pass through his mind without upsetting emotional reactions. The ability of TM to allow a patient to experience what ordinarily would be a highly anxiety-laden image or fantasy in a state of relative calm has been noted by several therapists who have worked with TM.[43, 99, 218, 251] In marked contrast to his previous despair while dependent on tranquilizers, this patient's self-esteem increased as he was able to moderate his anxiety on his own. He took a part-time job, and for the first time since childhood, was able to travel to other cities. A most visible change occurred in his body posture from rigid and tremulous to almost relaxed and confident. He cut down his medication drastically, and his impotence disappeared. This transformation was a source of great surprise to the several therapists who had treated this patient. This result perfectly illustrates the powerful combination of psychiatric support with TM as a therapeutic technique.

Dr. Shafii recounts a long case study of TM involving a college student named Hank, who was referred to treatment after being found by police in a disoriented state due to LSD.[251] He was a bored, anxious, irresponsible, heavy drug user, who felt aimless in his life and unable to establish meaningful relationships or involvement in activity. After six months of aimless, boring, frustrating therapy, he announced that he had taken up TM.

After a few weeks, he experienced brief moments with no thoughts or pure awareness. This experience, in his words, is "very real, and not similar to any other experiences" in his life. Dr. Shafii reports that concomitantly the patient developed an unprecedented feeling of "complete trust and openness."

Hank began to take his life and therapy more seriously. He came on time, seemed less defensive and resistive in the sessions, and more committed to therapy. He slept better, stopped using psychedelic drugs and cut down on marijuana. He felt less tense and more self-confident. Dr. Shafii notes that since Hank showed no progress at all during the first six months of their work together, he attributes these positive changes to TM. Hank's feeling of inner strength and trust in himself and others blossomed dramatically, bettering his relationships and spontaneous feelings toward his therapist, girl friend and others in his life. For the first time he liked doing things, and had the energy and the motivation to complete tasks. After several years, he has happily gone on to graduate school. He no longer requires psychotherapy but continues meditating.

Dr. Shafii notes several general areas of improvement which have been characteristic of the other accounts of therapeutic change with TM. Hank learned to observe himself and became more in touch with his inner feelings and sensations. He developed empathy for others and a solid core of inner trust. His confidence increased and his performance improved. As he became more spontaneous and relaxed, his compulsive drug abuse decreased. He began to do what he wanted to do rather than struggle against the rigid demands of fixed ideas about what he should do. Shafii notes that patients like Hank are ordinarily very hard to treat, and usually have a very frustrating course of therapy because they are so highly defensive and counterdependent. TM seems to have pierced this shell gently, leading gradually to a decreased reliance on neurotic defenses without causing panic. Hank apparently contacted an energizing, positive core within himself, which provided resources for autonomous growth.

Dr. Margaretta K. Bowers believes that every psychiatric

patient can be helped by TM.[32] She has had more than fifty of her patients start. She herself has been meditating for three years, ever since she saw a sudden rapid improvement in two long-term patients after they began TM. Dr. Bowers is a member of an American Psychiatric Association committee to study the interface of meditation and psychotherapy. Her experience confirms the previous case studies and offers some useful guidelines for using TM in treatment.

She notes that a number of patients refuse to learn TM because of fears of introspection, unwillingness to help themselves, disbelief in meditation or fear of being taken over by hostile forces. Most of her patients have been pleased with TM, however, and continue the practice regularly. Some patients suffer from the intrusion of severely disturbing thoughts. When this occurs, frequent checking by a TM instructor helps the patient learn not to resist this intrusion, but rather to continue meditation easily until these thoughts lose their frightening emotional intensity. A few of her patients needed encouragement to adopt a routine of regular meditation.

The vast majority of Dr. Bowers's patients who have continued meditating twice daily have improved at an uncommonly fast rate. They need fewer therapy hours, and the sessions become more meaningful and useful. With several patients this improvement has been dramatic; some have been relieved of symptoms that were not affected by previous therapy. As judged by previous experience, progress occurs at about twice the usual rate, and sometimes even faster. Occasionally, she relates, when a patient complains about not moving at a satisfactory pace, she finds that he has stopped meditating; when he begins again, progress continues. Meditation can frequently become the principal therapy. Fewer and less frequent therapy sessions are needed. The primary focus of such sessions is understanding disturbing thoughts, and just talking things over with a concerned person. Dr. Bowers says she agrees with Maharishi that with patients who regularly meditate, the role of the psychotherapist becomes one of holding the patient's hand while TM does the healing.

Not all patients want to learn TM and not every patient who

learns it gains immediate benefit. Psychoanalysts Carrington and Ephron point out that some patient-meditators may have difficulty practicing TM correctly because their habitual defense patterns appear during meditation as efforts to resist thoughts.[43] Understanding and approval from the therapist can help a patient relax during the practice of TM.

Several therapists have reported that patients sometimes refuse to continue practicing TM because they feel themselves changing too quickly. For example, Dr. Bloomfield had a patient who wanted to stop meditating because the pleasure she derived from TM made her feel guilty. In this case, supportive reinforcement from the therapist and frequent checking by a teacher of TM enabled the patient to continue meditating comfortably.

These accounts and case descriptions suggest many clinical uses for TM. Psychiatric clinicians are finding TM valuable as an adjunct to the treatment of anxiety neurosis, obsessive-compulsive symptoms, chronic low-grade depression, identity crisis, psychosomatic illness and drug addiction. TM has many advantages over minor tranquilizers, which are all too frequently prescribed in the treatment of daily stresses and strains. Drugs may help the patient to feel less anxious but may make him feel listless and groggy, and may become addicting. TM has no adverse side effects and can promote what pills cannot, natural psychological growth. Like psychotherapy, TM encourages the resolution of emotional conflicts and allows for unacceptable aspects of the self to become integrated into the personality. It therefore seems logical to incorporate TM into the psychotherapeutic armamentarium and to research its many potential applications. Psychiatrist Robert Assagioli, the founder of an eclectic humanistic approach to therapy called psychosynthesis, extols the benefits of meditation techniques in therapy:

> Meditation helps the patient to an expanded consciousness and impersonal experience and knowledge. Meditation has an advantage in that it allows the transition to religious problems to consummate itself in a completely natural way. The course of therapy is shorter with meditation because one is not dependent upon the mood of dreams and comes more quickly, both diag-

nostically and therapeutically, to the psychic conflict. Finally, with meditation, the patient does not ordinarily transfer his problem onto the therapist and therefore the resolution of transference is usually unnecessary. Meditation has a good chance of eventually becoming one of the leading therapeutic techniques. (13, p. 314)

For therapists interested in encouraging their patients to meditate, TM is probably the best available technique. It is easiest to learn, most thoroughly researched and is available through standardized instruction anywhere in the world.

A MENTAL HOSPITAL

Half of the nation's hospital beds are occupied by mental patients. It is estimated that one out of every ten people will require psychiatric assistance at some point in their lives. The major tranquilizers discovered in the 1950s have made an important contribution to the treatment of the severely emotionally disturbed, especially those suffering from schizophrenia. Since most mental illnesses are of unclear etiology, are multidetermined and have varying degrees of severity, most psychiatrists have learned that it is inadvisable to rely on any single form of treatment. Most modern treatment programs incorporate a combination of therapeutic modalities. The best of our mental hospitals usually provide each patient with individual and group psychotherapy, a therapeutic milieu, prescribed drugs to combat specific symptoms, family meetings and recreational and occupational therapy. Of course, many state hospitals cannot provide such comprehensive care. Periodic exposés of conditions remind us that these institutions represent one of our society's most pervasive failures. The practice of TM could be of great benefit to anyone who must spend time in these stress-filled institutions.

We have mentioned that researchers at the Institute of Living psychiatric hospital are conducting a major study on the psychophysiology of TM. In September 1972, the Institute began a comparative investigation of the usefulness of alpha wave biofeedback training and TM as relaxation techniques. We noted that this research indicates TM to be more effective than bio-feedback. This section outlines the Institute's preliminary results concerning the psychological benefits of TM on hospitalized psychiatric patients.

The project is under the direction of Bernard Glueck, M.D., Director of Research, and Charles Stroebel, M.D., Ph.D., chief of the Institute's Psychophysiology Laboratory. To implement this research, the Institute of Living has a computerized system to analyze brain waves, and laboratories for studying psychophysiological functions. The hospital has also pioneered the computer storage of daily hospital records, according to standardized measures of behavior and treatment progress.

In the study, patients matched for age, sex, and personality profile are paired, and a member of each matched set is placed in one of two experimental groups. One group is assigned to alpha bio-feedback training, the other to TM. All patients receive the usual hospital treatment, which consists of intensive psychoanalytically oriented psychotherapy, group therapy, psychoactive drugs, and a regular schedule of ward activities, including a high-school program for younger patients.

Two TM teachers are on the full-time hospital staff and spend as much time as necessary with each new patient to help him or her learn to meditate correctly. The instructors have been directed by Drs. Glueck and Stroebel to give a modified introductory lecture in order to minimize the effect of expectation on outcome. Since it is often noisy on the wards, quiet and comfortable space is available for meditation on the research unit, where the TM teachers are also available. This arrangement allows patients to receive daily checking. The immediate availability of checking is important to assure the continued correct practice of TM, and is thought to contribute to the low dropout rate among meditating patients. When checked daily for a few weeks, many patients find that they are soon able to meditate quite successfully on their own without supervision. At this point, patients are allowed to continue on their own, but are required to attend weekly meetings.

The availability of the teachers also permits patients to talk informally about their progress. The treating psychiatrist and nurses on the patients' unit are in close touch with the research staff. This contact has interested many members of the hospital staff in learning TM. Dr. Glueck estimates that perhaps fifteen percent of the hospital staff now meditates.

As of May 1974, one hundred and forty-three in-patients had started TM, with a smaller number starting bio-feedback training.[103] Since the study is to be based on a sample of several hundred, and will collect long-term follow-up data, we can only report unpublished, preliminary findings. Over ninety percent of the patients taught have been able to learn the practice easily. Eleven patients stopped within the first two weeks. For at least two of these patients careful interviewing revealed that the change they experienced during their first meditation so affected their symptoms that they became frightened that they would lose all their familiar defenses if they continued.

The one hundred thirty-two patients who have continued to meditate represent a rather broad cross-section of the hospital population, ranging in age from fifteen to fifty-five and across a wide range of diagnostic categories. The researchers do not, as yet, have adequate representation in any one category to make any comments about differential response based on diagnostic label. A rather surprising early finding is a relatively uniform positive response from most of the patients.

In addition to electroencephalographic recordings and other physiological measurements, many kinds of behavioral data are gathered on each subject. At regular intervals patients take the Minnesota Multiphasic Personality Inventory (MMPI), a standardized self-report measure of psychological problems. The patients also keep a detailed psychophysiological diary in which such functions as sleeping, mood, eating and activity are recorded. The nursing staff fills out daily computerized reports of behavior on the ward, and members of the treatment unit, including treating psychiatrists, fill out standardized questionnaires on their subjective impressions of the patient. Objective indicators such as grades, length of stay and dosage of medication are also recorded.

So far, the mean MMPI scores for the meditating patients have shown a steady downward trend, indicating their own sense of a decrease in their symptomatology. Dr. Glueck presented an illustrative case study at a symposium on TM for businessmen in Hartford.[99] A middle-aged patient, whose constant anxiety was displayed for several years by tremor of the hands, began TM. On the MMPI, before learning TM, the patient scored high on depression, anxiety and on concern with unreal thoughts. After four months of meditation, all of her MMPI scales were within the normal range, and there was an increase in ego-strength. After the first meditation the tremor was gone for about an hour, but then returned. After a couple of months the tremor disappeared permanently. The patient required decreasing amounts of tranquilizers to control anxiety and after several weeks had no need for sleeping medication. The computerized nursing notes showed many ups and downs, but the general trend was a decrease in unacceptable behavior and depression, and after two months overt signs of anxiety were markedly reduced.

A major positive effect of TM seems to be the increase in self-reliance. Dr. Glueck notes that meditating patients often complain about their psychoactive medication. They know the medications are helpful in controlling their anxiety and symptomatology, but they don't like the side effects, which include a dampening of responsiveness to the environment and a vague general discomfort. These side effects make it hard to convince patients to keep taking drugs. Also, many patients say that they would rather get well on their own than rely on pills. Unlike medication, TM is completely under the patients' own control and seems to have no negative physiological or psychological side effects. Indeed, while decreasing negative feelings, such as anxiety and depression, it increases the patients' general responsiveness, sense of well-being and ability to relate to others. Meditating patients feel that they themselves are the cause of their improvements. As a result they gain self-confidence. Dr. Glueck believes that TM may be an adequate substitute for psychotropic drugs for some patients.

A decrease in the need for medication in the meditating patient group supports this belief. Middle-aged patients with complaints of chronic insomnia report improvement in their sleep patterns within the first two or three weeks of meditation. This improvement in their sleep tends to continue until night sedation is no longer necessary, even in previously severe insomnia. After about three weeks of meditation the need for all types of psychotropic medication begins to decrease.

The researchers also find that TM may increase brain-wave synchrony. With continued practice of TM, patients exhibit similar EEG patterns in all parts of the brain. Dr. Glueck cautions, however, that his findings to date do not demonstrate conclusively the synchronization of brain-wave activity during TM because he has not ascertained that brain cells are firing in phase. Using sophisticated computer techniques to analyze his data, Dr. Glueck is now conducting research to determine whether large numbers of brain cells do fire in phase during TM. If the researchers find that TM does increase brain-wave synchrony, their evidence will provide a basis for understanding how TM increases personality integration. English EEG researcher Mark Westcott has very recently reported initial data suggesting that cells from different parts of the brain do fire in phase during TM.[298a]

Further evidence of TM's value is emerging from the computerized daily nursing notes which indicate significant trends in patients' long-term progress. The data generally suggest that with the practice of TM, anxiety, depression and unacceptable behavior decrease while acceptable behavior increases. These data are corroborated by self-reports from patients as shown by improvement in their MMPI profiles.

An experimental group of adolescent patients attending the hospital high school was given academic credit for learning TM. The class met daily for a group meditation and a video-taped lecture series on the theoretical implications of the meditative experience. Thus far Dr. Glueck has noted a significant increase in the overall academic performance of the first seven students enrolled in this course. Though the IQ's of the students in the experimental group are similar to the IQ's of the rest of the students, the experimental group's mean grades have improved considerably as compared to the grades of the other students. Much more data need to be gathered, but improvement in academic performance seems to be an important objective measure of progress through TM.

The first fifty-five meditating patients who were discharged from the hospital have been compared with all of the patients discharged in the previous year. The condition on discharge is rated by the treating psychiatrist, not by members of the research project. This rating is therefore an independent and, hopefully, unbiased estimate of the patient's condition at the time of leaving the hospital. Meditating patients show a higher level of recovery than the other discharged patients. All the TM patients were rated as either "recovered," "much improved" or "improved," and none were rated "unimproved" or "worse." Another indication of TM's utility is the number of referrals the researchers are receiving from the hospital staff. Dr. Glueck reports a consistent waiting list of between seventeen to twenty-five patients who have been referred by their treating psychiatrist or have asked their therapists and received approval. The delay is due to the project's elaborate data collection procedures.

Dr. Glueck feels that the practice of TM may accelerate progress in psychotherapy. When a patient has a distressing set of thoughts in meditation, or anything unusual happens, the topic of the thoughts often comes up as part of the next regular psychotherapy session. Dr. Glueck reports:

> In working in psychotherapy with the meditating patients, the ideational content that comes up in meditation can be intensely hostile and aggressive, but there is little or no effect—that is, the ideation is there, but the intensity of the emotions that usually accompany it is reduced. This is different from what we usually see in psychotherapy. The meditating patients are able to discuss, in therapy, the ideation that came up in meditation much more easily. Both the patients and the therapists are pleased at the facilitation of psychotherapy this has provided. Some patients have covered material in two to three months that would ordinarily have taken six months to a year. Meditation appears to have a positive speed-up effect on psycho-

therapy. This may turn out to be one of the most significant aspects of the use of meditation in psychiatrically ill individuals.[100]

From the experiences at the Institute of Living, it would appear that reservations about using TM as a therapeutic adjunct for a seriously disturbed patient population are unfounded. Patients easily learn and practice TM. Indeed, Dr. Glueck reports that TM has also been used successfully with two brain-damaged patients. Carefully supervised use of TM may be helpful in calming agitated patients, reducing the need for sedation with tranquilizers. It apparently also normalizes the sleeping pattern, improves communication, accelerates the process of psychotherapy, and decreases the debilitating anxiety which is at the core of so many psychiatric syndromes. The Institute of Living study seems to demonstrate that the standardized TM instruction procedure is a valuable addition to the total therapeutic process, and can be adapted to existing programs with little modification. In addition, TM can easily be taught to large numbers of patients, making it ideally suitable for the large, poorly funded, understaffed state mental hospitals.

TM COMPARED WITH OTHER THERAPIES

Unadaptive stress and strain is the enemy of mental health. TM can help a psychiatric patient to diminish inappropriate emergency responses, and to stop perceiving benign situations as threatening. The patient grows in his ability to assess his inner and outer environment accurately, and to respond with a healthier repertoire of behaviors. The effectiveness of TM in normalizing the nervous system can be compared with other therapeutic techniques.

Because practitioners of TM are instructed not to mind thoughts during meditation and patients undergoing psychoanalysis are told to verbalize whatever thoughts come into their minds, some analysts perceive an underlying similarity between the two procedures. The mental activity caused by the release of stress in TM resembles free association, the uncensored flow of mental and emotional imagery in psychoanalysis. Despite these apparent similarities, however, TM and psychoanalysis are profoundly different in their approach to resolving conflicts in the psyche. In analysis, as the mind begins to roam freely during free association, the patient is asked to verbalize the thoughts and images which arise. This process aims at expanding the sphere of consciousness by allowing unconscious desires to be freely expressed, fully understood and eventually mastered. Psychoanalysis seeks spontaneous access to preverbal, primary mental processes but requires verbalization of thoughts in order to gain mastery over them. During the practice of TM, on the other hand, the mind naturally settles to preverbal levels, and underlying psychic conflict is resolved spontaneously without verbalization or the slightest effort to master the thoughts which arise. The reduction of metabolic rate achieved during the practice of TM is sufficient to allow a wholly physiological resolution of preverbal psychic conflict.

Charles Tart, a psychologist specializing in consciousness research, offers a psychoanalytically oriented interpretation of his personal experience of TM's automatic normalization process:

> Normally we carry out all sorts of activities with insufficient attention and/or insufficient awareness of our own reactions to them. This results in building up a tremendous backlog of partially processed experiences, unfinished business. The psychic-lubricant function of TM is to allow these things to come back into consciousness during meditation and, by virtue of now being conscious, to have the processing of them completed. Thus they no longer block other psychic processes. (273, p. 137)

Unlike the person undergoing analysis who learns that every random thought must be pregnant with meaning, the practitioner of TM learns that thoughts are simply the artifact of underlying physiological change from the release of stress. While effective analysis depends upon the patient's intention to deal with psychological conflicts which surface during analysis, the effective practice of TM depends upon the innocent lack of intention throughout the meditation period. New meditators learn not to be concerned with the content or even the presence of thoughts during TM; they learn not to waste time either resisting or analyzing thoughts which occur.

This distinction may be further explicated with reference to dreams. Freud regarded dreams as "the royal road to the unconscious" and encouraged his patients to remember dreams and master their implications through subsequent analysis. In TM, however, dreams are regarded as a mental artifact of the normalizing process of the deep rest of sleep. The only use made of dreams in TM is as a teaching example to explain how utterly automatic normalization is when adequate rest is provided. In deep sleep, the body spontaneously accomplishes restorative changes which are apparently reported to the brain in the form of dreams. As previously noted, Hartmann has found that the greater the drop in metabolic rate during sleep, the longer the subsequent periods of dreaming.[115] This finding suggests that the low metabolism of deep sleep facilitates normalization and that the mental artifact of normalization is experienced as dreaming. Similarly, the hypometabolic state of TM results in the spontaneous elimination of stress, the mental artifact of which is experienced as thoughts. There is never any need to analyze dreams to gain the benefit of sleep. The analysis of dreams may give intellectual understanding of deep-rooted conflicts, but such investigation cannot significantly aid in the physiological process of normalizing their imprinting upon the nervous system. Similarly, analyzing experiences during TM cannot add to meditation's beneficial effects.

Whereas TM is an intrapersonal process, psychoanalysis requires the interpersonal role of the analyst to help interpret the meaning of thoughts arising during the free association period. The analyst serves as a blank screen upon which the patient projects the feelings which arise out of the disturbed relationships of his childhood. The patient then has an opportunity to understand the way in which unresolved feelings toward his mother or father continue to cause psychic suffering in present-day relationships. The interpretations of the analyst are considered an indispensable aid in correcting these distortions. Psychoanalysis assumes that the individual could not possibly achieve self-integration on his own because of the likelihood of his unconsciously censoring the "true" meaning of his inner scenarios. Analysts often delve into such themes as Oedipal wishes to kill one's father and sleep with one's mother, stinginess or compulsiveness as derivatives of toilet training practices, and asthmatic wheezes as the unconscious cry for mother's breast.

Maharishi feels that delving into past miseries is an ineffective means of relieving psychic suffering:

> It should not be a function of psychology to remind a man that his past was miserable, or that his surroundings and circumstances were unfavorable, or that his associations were depressing and discouraging, or that there was lack of love and harmony with those near to him. To remind anyone of such things will only result in lowering his consciousness . . . It should be considered criminal to tell anyone that his individual life is based on the inefficient and degenerate influence of his past environment. The psychological influence of such depressing information is demoralizing, and the inner core of the heart becomes twisted by it. (185, p. 264)

Toward the end of his life, Freud too recognized the limitations of psychoanalysis; he found that the very act of verbalizing unpleasant thoughts brought resistance to their interpretation.[79] As a therapeutic tool, psychoanalysis has not lived up to the expectations of its proponents. As psychoanalyst Dr. Glueck laments:

> One of the underlying propositions of all psychotherapeutic activity has been, for some 75 years, that if we can help the individual to get rid of the memory of early painful experiences we can help him to perform in a more appropriate fashion in his present life. Unfortunately, and I say this with a good deal of chagrin, the initial promise that was perceived in the discoveries of Freud and people working with him of help for so many people has not been borne out to the extent that we would have liked. Certainly we've had some very successful responses to this kind of intervention. But in general, and this is looking back on 30 years of experience now in the field, my feeling has been that I can't do enough, continuously enough, with psychotherapy for most individuals to really undo the

damage that has been done. It appears to me that, and this is one of the major reasons for my interest in the technique of Transcendental Meditation, through this avenue the individual now may be taught to do for himself, in a remarkably brief space of time, the same kinds of things we've been trying to help him to do in our traditional psychotherapeutic approaches in the past.[100]

Talking with a therapist exclusively about problems may be futile or even counterproductive. Better that a patient move beyond concern with previous problems to enjoy growth in the present through the uplifting experience of pure awareness. Rather than "digging into the mud of a miserable past," one's vision should be enlarged to "the genius and the brightness of man's inner creative intelligence" (185, p. 265).

TM brings relief from stored-up anxiety and conflict very systematically, without the need to verbalize these sensations, or to receive interpretations from a therapist. In this way TM offers a shortcut to therapy. Whereas psychotherapy may help the individual gain intellectual insight into the sources of his stress, all too frequently the old fears persist on a visceral level, and the patient remains discouraged. Psychoanalysis too often keeps the patient preoccupied with the dark side of human nature—the cauldron of aggressive and primitive impulses—whereas meditation spontaneously enlarges the vision to a fuller appreciation of the positive, creative and spiritual possibilities of his life.

Psychoanalysis has expanded our understanding of unconscious motivation, but as a therapeutic technique it has the many failings we have outlined, and as a study of the mind it is incomplete. Through the practice of TM, one learns that the territory of the unconscious is far more extensive than Freud realized. The therapeutic effects of psychoanalysis have not received scientific validation.[26, 67, 174] Indeed, more scientific evidence of positive benefits from TM has been reported in the four years since Wallace's article in *Science* than in seventy-five years of psychoanalysis.[286]

Our criticism of traditional psychoanalysis should not be construed as an overall negative evaluation of psychotherapy. Psychotherapy as such does not refer to any specific way of interacting with patients. It includes any activity between patient and therapist that aids the patient's psychological functioning. For severely disturbed patients, empathic understanding and such supportive measures as teaching him what he needs to know about his disorder, assisting him with his life plans and advising him about work can be essential. Major psychiatric syndromes certainly require expert professional assistance, and supportive services will continue to be necessary in times of severe emotional crisis. We are hopeful that mental health professionals will study the interface between TM and psychotherapy and conduct research on how these approaches together can effectively contribute to the relief of suffering and the promotion of psychological growth.

The normalization process in TM also has parallels with systematic desensitization, a behavior therapy technique to help people paralyzed by fears and anxieties. A method of deep muscle relaxation was developed in the 1930s by Dr. Edmond Jacobsen. His popular book *You Must Relax* suggested that a wide range of psychosomatic illnesses and strains of living could be relieved through the practice of progressive relaxation.[129] Jacobsen trained his patients to systematically relax muscle groups throughout the body. In this relaxed state all sensory imagery would disappear, and at progressively deeper levels, inner kinesthetic imagery, recollection, thought processes and emotions would diminish as well.

Deep muscle relaxation became the foundation for Wolpe and Lazarus's work in systematic desensitization.[308] This technique is based on the concept of reciprocal inhibition, that relaxation inhibits anxiety. First, the patient is trained in Jacobsen's relaxation technique. Next, a list of anxiety-producing situations is compiled from the states, feelings and images which are most frightening to the patient. Then, while the patient practices the relaxation technique, each item, starting with the least anxiety-provoking, is presented and repeated until all anxiety is eliminated.

Daniel Goleman suggests that TM provides a more spontane-

ous and global desensitization than can be achieved through
Wolpe and Lazarus's technique.

> With the inward turning of attention in meditation, the medi-
> tator becomes keenly aware of the random chaos characteristic
> of thoughts in waking state. . . . The meditator witnesses the
> flow of psychic events. . . . The whole contents of the mind
> compose the meditator's "desensitization hierarchy." The con-
> tents of this hierarchy are organic to the life concerns of the
> meditator. . . . As in the desensitization paradigm, the "hier-
> archy" is presented coupled with the deep relaxation of deep
> meditation. Unlike the therapy, desensitization is not limited to
> those items which therapist and patient have identified as prob-
> lematic, though those are certainly included, but extends to all
> phases of experience. . . . It is natural, global self-desensitiza-
> tion. (106, p. 5)

The TM practitioner spontaneously experiences a very deep
level of rest in the first few minutes after he is taught the technique. Jacobsen's technique takes longer to learn than TM, and
some patients have difficulty achieving even a minimal state of
relaxation. Systematic desensitization requires the expertise of
a behavior therapist whereas TM is self-administered. While the
practice of TM is engaging and highly pleasurable, the therapist
and the patient often find systematic desensitization to be boring
and tedious. In the research project at the Institute of Living,
Dr. Glueck reported that patients trained in progressive relaxation demonstrated very little improvement and had a drop-out
rate close to seventy percent.[00] Most of them asked to stop by
the fourth week because, having seen considerably greater progress in their fellow patients who were meditating, they wanted
to switch to TM.

The relaxation achieved using Jacobsen's technique depends
on peripheral stimuli from the musculature, whereas TM engages the central nervous system directly. In systematic desensitization, signals from the musculature may act on the brain to
relax control processes, but by the time they reach the brain
they are third or fourth order effects and therefore very weak.
TM starts in the brain, where it directly reduces mental activity.
Such relaxation is achieved centrally and then extended to the

peripheral musculature. Instead of resting one muscle group at a time, the whole organism relaxes spontaneously.

The spontaneous desensitization accomplished by TM could explain the lessening of fears and worries so frequently reported by meditators. Leonce Boudreau documents a case study of a patient who failed to respond to systematic desensitization but who responded to treatment substituting TM as the agent of relaxation. He gives the following account:

> Mr. T., 18, a college student, expressed fears of enclosed places, elevators, being alone and examinations. His avoidance behavior to these situations was extreme, having started when he was 13. The physiological sensations he experienced gave him the additional fear of mental illness.
>
> At the beginning of treatment, systematic desensitization with relaxation as the inhibitor was tried . . . [but] no noticeable improvement was evidenced.
>
> At this point, the patient . . . [began] Transcendental Meditation. He was instructed to practice meditation following imagined phobic scenes for ½ hour every day and also at the actual appearance of fear-evoking situations. Marked improvement followed. Within one month, the avoidance behavior to enclosed places, being alone and elevators had all disappeared. Once his tension level had decreased, he did not experience abnormal physiological sensations and this reassured him as to his physical and mental state. (31, p. 97)

Ordinarily meditators are instructed to practice TM only twice daily. In this case, a therapist reports that a psychiatric patient gained relief from carefully supervised additional practice when incapacitated by fear or anxiety. Such use of TM as a technique for immediate desensitization has not been sufficiently studied. If such additional meditation is to be prescribed, therapist and patient should work closely with a specially trained TM instructor.

Psychologist Arnold A. Lazarus, one of the founders of systematic desensitization, has conducted follow-up studies which indicate that forty percent of the patients helped by this method experience relapses within one to three years after treatment.[166] Because the therapeutic effects of this method are so short-lived,

Lazarus has expanded his approach to include a more comprehensive program, dealing directly with the client's sensations, perceptions, emotions, cognitions, behaviors and interpersonal relations.[165] Since TM appears to promote improvement in each of these areas, it ought to complement the behavioral therapist's repertoire. Behavior therapy has been criticized as superficial and applicable only to a narrow range of problems. If it were combined with TM we would anticipate deeper and more durable results. Behavior therapy deals quickly and effectively with incapacitating sources of stress such as fear of highway driving, lack of assertiveness or sexual dysfunction, whereas TM promotes comprehensive psychological integration.

Other new therapies also aim at stress release. Gestalt techniques, bioenergetics, and primal scream therapy focus on what is most painful or distressing in a person's life. A person trains his awareness to go into the "here and now" and to rediscover his full range of feelings, bodily movements and life energy. These techniques seek to relieve the emotional and physical blocks which interfere with present awareness. People burst into laughter, screams and tears, as they relive past painful events, with all the physical and emotional intensity of the original experience. Freud called this process catharsis. These newer therapies aim at direct discharge of tension, and may bring temporary relief. Unfortunately they fail to provide the regenerative deep rest through which TM spontaneously normalizes and stabilizes the nervous system. Also, they lack the scientific validation which TM has received.

REINTEGRATION THROUGH TM

The interface between TM and other therapies offers great promise. While TM may prove some analytically oriented techniques unnecessary, it can significantly enrich the approaches to psychotherapy derived from the humanistic schools. We may now consider theoretical issues concerning TM as a psychotherapeutic technique.

Maharishi has explained that mental health may be understood as having a foundation in the integration of mind and body.[185] Mental illness reflects a breakdown in mind-body coordination. When a person becomes stressed, he loses access to his inner resources. His mind becomes weak, limiting the power and clarity of his thinking. He cannot provide a sufficient organizing force from within to engage in effective activity. He fails to fulfill his desires because he has lost direction. Each failure causes further stress. The breakdown of mind-body coordination is a vicious circle leading to increasing frustration, suffering and despair. How can someone trapped in the vicious circle of failure and increasing stress move out of it?

The techniques of modern psychotherapy attend to the mind or body (or both) in order to clarify thinking and strengthen the ability to fulfill desires. Analytically oriented therapies attempt to clarify thinking by freeing the mind from conflicts and repressions. Somatically oriented techniques undertake to free the body from stress, increase energy and improve mind-body integration. The mind-body system is so complicated, however, that it is questionable whether any technique aimed at effecting change in only one aspect of the system may prove very effective in improving overall integration.

TM provides an integrated approach to mind-body coordination, encouraging the body's self-healing processes through deep rest. Mind and body grow more energetic and are freed from stress. In addition, through the experience of pure awareness the individual gains access to the integrative nature of his inner self. TM provides the missing element for a suffering person, just as turning on a light transforms a dark room. Analysis of darkness in a dark room serves little purpose; similarly, analysis of the past experiences of a person who is beginning to grow in all aspects of life adds little—and may even inhibit progress. Once an individual gains access to his inner resources he sees opportunities for growth where before he had seen only tension-producing obstacles. When this transformation begins to take place, a psychiatric patient needs only support and encouragement to express himself in action. If his action leads to achievement and therefore fulfillment of even a small desire, he begins to step out of the cycle of increasing stress. Fulfillment then begins to grow stronger in his life.

Maharishi has also explained that TM is psychologically self-regulating in that the degree of normalization accomplished is roughly proportional to the degree of rest attained. Stress dissolves in proportion to the inner stability which an individual realizes. Growth through TM takes place naturally at its own rate, maximizing individual development while minimizing discomfort. By alternating the inner experience of TM with the outer experience of beginning to fulfill desires through activity, an individual begins to establish a rhythm of growth. Our experience suggests that this rhythm leads automatically to the patient's wanting to take more responsibility for himself. To facilitate this process, a patient needs only encouragement to meditate regularly and to engage in dynamic activity. Once a patient becomes established in this growth rhythm, his need for psychiatric care may diminish sharply. Perhaps the greatest promise of TM is the prospect of individuals continuing to grow on their own with minimal professional care.

TM FOR THERAPISTS

We recommend that psychotherapists interested in having their patients practice TM first learn the practice themselves, in order to become familiar with its principles. As they have received scientific reports of TM's values and have seen beneficial change in their colleagues and patients, many mental health professionals have begun TM. They report increased efficiency and more satisfaction in their work. A psychiatrist practicing TM for about one year informed us:

> I was a fairly happy person but unfortunately I absorbed a lot of my patients' problems. A day's work would leave me fatigued. I would sometimes carry the stresses from the office home with me and get into squabbles with my wife and children. I used to worry a lot about my clients and was unsuccessful in trying to unwind. Now meditating after my work day provides a kind of psychological housecleaning. I automatically process the material from my therapy sessions in a relaxed

fashion, and make intuitively better therapeutic responses these days. Listening attentively is coming easily, with less strain.

Psychologist Terry Lesh has demonstrated that therapists who practice meditation improve their empathy with clients.[170] Another account by a psychologist shows the changes in professional and personal life which may be expected by a therapist who learns TM:

> I decided to learn TM when I saw some remarkable changes in a client I had been treating. The results have far exceeded my expectations. During my years in training I had become an increasingly rigid person. I was always analyzing what people's "real" motivations were. I used to fear that I was an incompetent therapist; probably I wasn't very effective. Since practicing TM the last two years, I have become much more spontaneous and in touch with my feelings. All of my relationships have improved. My wife notes that I don't throw any more temper tantrums and that our sex life has improved. I feel more authentic, more human with my patients, but at the same time have more respect for my work as a therapist. I laugh and smile a lot more, in the office and at home.

The application of TM to the mental health problems of this country has been delayed by a lack of TM instructors trained to use TM in rehabilitative programs. When a person with a history of mental illness learns TM as a therapeutic technique, such a person requires careful supervision by a specially trained TM instructor. With the growing number of mental health workers becoming TM instructors, and with programs under way to train TM teachers as paramedical personnel, however, this situation is now being corrected. The Institute for Social Rehabilitation at Maharishi International University has begun training experienced TM instructors to work in all types of rehabilitative institutions including hospitals, mental hospitals, community mental health centers, nursing homes and prisons.

7

A PSYCHOLOGY
OF CREATIVE
INTELLIGENCE

TM did not emerge from Western science or culture but has come to us from the Vedic tradition of India. While the scientific evidence we have presented may seem to suggest that TM is simply a technique of improving health and relieving stress, the tradition of TM has been passed down for centuries as a means of gaining the highest goal of human life—fulfillment. Though Maharishi has translated ancient texts which offer insight into the overall purpose and meaning of TM,[184, 186] it is still necessary for us as Westerners to integrate the theory of TM into the perspective of Western understandings of human potentialities.

We have indicated that within every person there exists an unbounded reservoir of energy and intelligence which Maharishi has termed the source of creative intelligence. Transcendental Meditation systematically taps this vast resource as it normalizes the nervous system and unfolds the full potential of human life.

Responsibility for our ultimate values and goals has gradually passed from theologians to scientists. In recent times the principal paradigm of human nature has emerged from psychology. Today the function of answering such basic questions as the meaning and goal of life, and the sources of human values, has become the responsibility of psychologists. The development of psychology's current theories of self-actualization offers a theoretical stepping-stone to a psychology of creative intelligence. This theory provides a framework for understanding the impact that TM holds not only for restoring mental health but also for unfolding man's highest potentialities.

BEYOND THE STRUGGLE FOR PSYCHIC EXISTENCE

Modern psychotherapy owes its birth to the pioneering work of Sigmund Freud. When Freud began identifying the underlying structures of consciousness within a scientific framework, psychology gained independence from philosophy. Freud's work early in the twentieth century provided not only a dynamic theory of mind, but also a procedure for relieving the suffering of mental illness. Freud demonstrated the value of his theories through the results of his efforts at intervention with his patients. Though encouraging as the first scientific approach to helping the mentally ill, Freud's procedure of psychoanalysis itself proved only marginally effective.[26, 67] This limited efficacy of Freud's therapeutic approach suggests an underlying inadequacy in his theory.

Freud sought to explain the persistence of human suffering in the face of the mounting achievements of civilization. Therefore, he began with the axiomatic view that the psyche must essentially depend on conflict. At the basis of consciousness, he postulated an ongoing struggle between the instinctive drive for gratification through the reduction of tension—the pleasure principle—and the demand for survival in the environment—the reality principle. He argued that the essential impossibility of resolving these two principles governing human life not only denies man fulfillment but condemns him to suffering. Though Freud recognized that gratification provides a temporary pause in our battle with the environment, he insisted that out of every satisfaction of a desire emerges another desire which re-creates conflict with our environment. From this perspective, Freud argued that the most an individual can hope for is a life of the maximum satisfaction of instinctual desires with the minimum obstruction from the environment.

At the basis of mental life, Freud postulated an insatiable

pool of instinctual desires. He called this "cauldron of seething excitations," which operates only according to the pleasure principle, the id (82, p. 74). Opposing the id and representing the reality principle, Freud defined a mental mechanism which maintains coherent knowledge of the self and the world. Freud called this mechanism the ego. Consciousness, Freud argued, is a tool of the ego to resolve the conflict between instinct and environment. According to Freud, however, the demands of the id and of the environment are so opposed that the ego can never achieve lasting fulfillment.

Freud saw a further obstacle to individual fulfillment in the individual's relation to society. If the ego had only to meet the demands of the id and the environment, satisfaction might be possible. But the ego must also respect the demands of society. These demands, which operate in the psyche by means of what Freud called the superego, so complicate the possibility of satisfying the instinctual pressure for gratification that the ego must often deny instinctual demands through repression. Repression is a process of self-inhibition in the interest of society and at the cost of individual satisfaction.

Regarding this fundamental conflict in man's nature, Freud wrote:

> What decides the purpose of life is the pleasure principle . . . there can be no doubt about its efficacy, and yet its program is at loggerheads with the whole world . . . There is no possibility at all of its being carried through; all regulations of the universe run counter to it. One feels inclined to say that the intention that man should be happy is not included in the plan of "Creation." (81, p. 23)

Freud implied that life itself is a neurosis with no possible way for a man to reconcile his basic drives to social or environmental demands. War, pain, confusion and dissatisfaction are all part of civilization's cost. He found no evidence of any positive core within man's psyche which might give reason for optimism about man's future.

Nevertheless, some evidence suggests that Freud was partially familiar with the concept of pure awareness, which he described as the "oceanic feeling." He wrote:

> . . . There are many people in whose mental life this primary feeling has persisted . . . In that case, the ideational content appropriate to it would be precisely those of limitlessness and of a bond with the universe, the same ideas with which my friend elucidated the oceanic feeling. (81, p. 12)

He did not, however, view the oceanic experience of unbounded oneness positively. He described such experiences as regressive. Regression is a reflex return to an earlier developmental stage in reaction to overwhelming anxiety. For example, in an uncertain situation an older child may suck his thumb, or an adult may wish for a powerful parental figure for protection and care. Freud suggested that oceanic experience is a regression to an infantile state in which the ego is not differentiated from the rest of the world, and the pleasure principle is dominant. Freud thought that the mature ego could retain only a shrunken residue of its original, all-embracing unity with the world, and that this was as it should be. Freud was entirely pessimistic about man's ever being able to exist in a permanent state of oceanic bliss. He concluded his discussion of this experience on a sharp note of skepticism: "There is clearly no point in spinning our phantasy any further, for it leads to things which are unimaginable and even absurd." (81, p. 13)

Later interpreters of regression, chiefly Ernst Kris,[162] have noted that a highly valuable form of regression is characteristic of artists and geniuses. Such individuals showed an ability to delve into their deepest unconscious experiences, while retaining the highly refined, cognitive and communication skills of a mature person. Kris described this mature, useful form of regression as "regression in the service of the ego." Psychoanalyst Shafii has suggested that the experience of pure awareness in meditation may be understood in terms of this form of controlled beneficial regression to an earlier state of unity (251, p. 98). Meditators who have clearly experienced pure awareness might well question whether transcending is regressive. Nonetheless, Shafii's interpretation points up how recent developments in psychoanalytic theory have tended toward reexamination of Freud's original ideas which implied the impossibility of fulfillment. Freud saw little hope for a resolution of the fundamental conflict within the individual because he failed to appreciate the potentials of the deep psychic reservoir glimpsed through the oceanic feeling. In overlooking pure awareness, he neglected the pathway to resolving man's deepest psychic conflicts and thereby unfolding the possibility of fulfillment.

SELF-INTEGRATION IN PSYCHOANALYSIS

All theories of psychological integration are based on the notion of a center in the psyche which tends to evolve toward a state of perfect expression in human fulfillment. As a strict mechanist, Freud eschewed such teleological notions. But many of Freud's successors have felt that theories of the psyche without a concept of evolutionary development are not compatible with the evidence gathered from the centuries of man's spiritual development. Freud, like Marx and Darwin before him, tried to play down spiritual questions as rationalizations which obscured scientific progress. Freud's followers, on the other hand, tried to combine concepts of psychic purpose and development with Freud's rigorous observation and analysis.

Alfred Adler, originally one of Freud's most enthusiastic disciples, rejected his teacher's subordination of all mental processes to the level of instinctual conflicts. Such a notion, Adler argued, failed to recognize "that mysterious creative power of life which expresses itself in the desire to develop." Inside the psyche there "is the self which grows into life, which we recognize later on as the creative power" (2, p. 92). Yet Adler retained Freud's conflict metaphor. In his theory, suffering resulted from the irreconcilable opposition between the urge to perfection and humanity's fundamental inferiority before the world. This dualism may be interpreted as yet another form of Freud's theory of instinctual conflict. Nevertheless, Adler went beyond Freud in insisting on the necessity of tapping an inner creative impulse as a step toward fulfillment.

Carl Jung, Freud's other famous disciple who broke with the master, extended psychoanalytic theory toward an expanded vision of humanity's potential. He took the possibility of overcoming neurosis seriously and projected the possibility of growth toward a life of profound fulfillment. Instead of interpreting the unconscious as a "cauldron of seething excitation," Jung identified many layers of the unconscious deeper than those postulated by Freud. Within the unconscious, Jung saw not only desire for gratification, but also the possibility of self-realization. At the deepest unconscious layers, Jung found a universal intelligence with great creative energy: "The . . . unconscious contains the whole spiritual heritage of mankind's evolution, born anew in the brain structure of every individual. . . . The unconscious . . . is the source of the instinctual forces and the forms that regulate them" (135, p. 158).

Jung located suffering in conflict, but unlike Freud and Adler, discovered unity rather than duality at the root of the psyche. He therefore suggested that man might rise from suffering toward wholeness by growing to appreciate his unique inner nature, the self at the center of consciousness. He wrote: "The beginnings of our whole psychic life seem to be inextricably rooted in this point and all our highest and ultimate purposes seem to be shining toward it" (138, p. 238). This perspective on the origin and goal of human life constituted a radical departure from Freud. Jung asserted that the fundamental motivating principle of the psyche is not conflict, but pressure toward fulfillment. He defined fulfillment in terms of the realization of a primordial reservoir of creative energies, a primary wholeness underlying the diversity of conscious experience. At first rejected by most of the psychiatric community, this definition of man's possibility for fulfillment has attracted growing support since Jung first proposed it.

SELF-INTEGRATION AND GESTALT THERAPY

Freud's psychoanalytic theories center on the psyche. When the environment is mentioned at all, it appears as an obstacle to fulfillment. More recent theorists have taken the relation of the person to the environment as a starting point. The human organism needs the physical environment for air, food, water and shelter, and needs the social environment for emotional interchange and project collaborations. Gestalt psychologists have considered man as a whole in terms of his embeddedness in the environment. These analysts have shown that we do not so much "have" a lung and air to breathe, but rather are a system including lung and air. Because of this external-internal interdependence, they have argued that every organismic system constitutes a whole greater than the sum of its parts.

The first theorist to see the necessity for a psycho-physical-social theory of the organism was Kurt Goldstein.[104] He argued that consciousness arises from the interface between the organism and its environment. Consciousness, he suggested, focuses figures of interest against the organism-environment field. An object interests an organism when it relates to the organism's needs. Goldstein called this process Gestalt formation. This concept has provided a definition of consciousness equally suited to describing an amoeba seeking food as to describing a creative artist expressing his inner life. Gestalt formation follows a pattern which progressively expresses the emerging preferences of the organism. Through this process, the organism establishes its self.

Fritz Perls, also a psychoanalyst, expanded this concept into a system of psychotherapy which aims at increasing the immediacy of the organism-environment contact.[227] He defined maturation as a process of moving from a state of total dependence upon the environment to a state of self-sufficiency, independent of the immediate fluctuations of the environment. Neurosis could then be understood as a growth disorder resulting from a need to manipulate the environment in order to feel at home in it. Such manipulation artificially limits awareness. Perls believed that a person could begin to take care of himself, meet his needs, and actualize his potential, without exercising dictatorial control over the things and people around him. To explain this possibility, Perls postulated the self as a center of dynamic calm, the source of creative expression, the ground of consciousness and the basis of health. The purpose of Perls's Gestalt therapy is to help individuals regain contact with the self. Perls argued that identification with this center automatically sharpens awareness and fosters actualization of inner potential.

Perls described the process of growing to full appreciation of consciousness as centering:

> If you are centered in yourself, then you don't adjust any more . . . then you assimilate, you understand, you are related to whatever happens. . . . Without a center . . . there is no place from which to work. . . . Achieving a center, being grounded in oneself, is about the highest state a human being can achieve. (226, pp. 30, 37)

A centered individual can fully enjoy life. He is free from the continual need to adjust and modify himself to meet demands of his activity. Instead, he experiences an inner foundation from which he can fully assimilate, understand and work with the world. This platform of inner stability provides a basis for consistent successful action and growing fulfillment.

Perls added a further insight into the process of centering by identifying the relationship between centering and physiology: "If we are disturbed in our metabolism . . . we have no center from which we can live, we have to do something, to collect again the wellspring, the foundation of our being" (226, p. 64). The process of centering requires physiological integration.

SELF-ACTUALIZATION, PEAK EXPERIENCE AND TRANSCENDENCE

Psychology's most positive evaluation of human potential has emerged in the works of Abraham Maslow. Maslow's *Psychology of Being* offers the best theoretical stepping-stone to the formulation of a psychology of creative intelligence. Maslow's theory developed from the criticism that Freud's formulation of the pleasure principle as tension-reduction is inadequate to explain human motivation. The pleasure principle does not account for the spontaneous growth of children and for the activity of creative people. While Freud's theory suggested that gratification leads to rest and decreased motivation, recent studies cited by Maslow show that in healthy, fully functioning people, ". . . gratification breeds increased motivation; the appetite for growth is whetted rather than allayed by gratification. Growth is in itself a rewarding and exciting process" (196, p. 30).

Because of these observations, Maslow explained: "More and more psychologists have found themselves compelled to postulate some tendency to growth or self-perfection, to supplement the concepts of equilibrium, homeostasis, tension-reduction and other conserving motivations" (196, p. 23). Tension-reduction theory offers no insight as to why one desire should follow another, but self-actualization theory defines its organizing principle as "the tendency for new and higher needs to emerge as the lower needs fulfill themselves by being sufficiently gratified" (196, p. 155). Maslow argued that the need for beauty, truth and love are as biologically structured within people as are the survival needs for food, shelter and clothing. He insisted that many higher needs necessarily emerge after basic survival needs are met.

This principle of progressively emerging needs forms the basis of Maslow's theory of self-actualization. He described this goal of self-actualization as the fullest expression of Being:

> Man demonstrates in his own nature a pressure toward a fuller and fuller being, more and more perfect actualization of his humanness in exactly the same naturalistic scientific sense that an acorn may be said to be pressing toward an oak tree. (196, p. 160)

Maslow explained that the process of growth is the process of becoming a person, but that being a person is something different. Becoming implies striving, while Being describes fulfillment. The perfect expression of Being is simply a state free from striving. Maslow suggested that the nature of Being can be directly perceived in what he calls the "peak experience." Generally occurring spontaneously, a peak experience is

. . . an episode, or a spurt in which the powers of the person come together in a particularly efficient and intensely enjoyable way, and in which he is more integrated and less split, more open for experience, more idiosyncratic, more perfectly expressive or spontaneous, or fully functioning, more creative, more humorous, more ego-transcending, more independent of his lower needs, etc. He becomes in these episodes more truly himself, more perfectly actualizing his potentialities, closer to the core of his being. (196, p. 89)

Maslow studied the peak experience in great detail. He asked artists, students, engineers, social scientists, performers, politicians and workers to talk about experiences which best expressed their deepest sense of self. The peak experiences which they reported showed remarkable similarities, including appreciation of a quiet inner center and a sense of self-validating fulfillment. At the core of peak experiences Maslow described something like what we have called pure awareness.

Maslow asserted that this experience is the primary defining characteristic of all healthy, fully realized persons. People who have had regular peak experiences exhibit all the highest ideals of humanity, including creativity, love of truth, sensitivity, self-sufficiency, and valuing others for their intrinsic worth. Peak experiences also seem to have therapeutic effects, in that those who have had such experiences tend to become more fully functioning, less anxious and more in touch with their feelings. Such changes are lasting.

Comparing Maslow's accounts of peak experience and meditators' reports of personal growth through TM, we are struck by their similarity. We might hypothesize that meditation greatly facilitates both the frequency and receptivity of individuals to peak experiences. The research studies evaluating the effects of meditation on personality repeatedly show the growth of characteristics described by Maslow as indices of self-actualization.

Maslow labeled the perception which occurs during peak experiences "Being-cognition." During those moments, awareness is closest to pure, unbounded, unneedful perception of an object or the self. Is the experience of transcending during meditation a peak experience? In his later work, Maslow differentiated two kinds of Being-cognition. The most common peak experience is a dramatic, exciting, orgasmic moment of undifferentiated unity, an intense form of what Shelly, whose work we described in chapters 3 and 5, called an exciting pleasure. In contrast to this experience, Maslow identified the "plateau experience," characterized by serene and contemplative Being-cognitions, similar to what Shelly called quiet enjoyments. The plateau experience is so named because it is sustained for long periods of time:

> . . . the serene and calm, rather than poignantly emotional, climactic, automatic response to the miraculous, the awesome, the sacralized, the Unitive, the B-Values. . . . It is far more voluntary than peak experiences are. One can learn to see in this Unitive way almost at will. It then becomes a witnessing, an appreciation, what one might call a serene, cognitive blissfulness which can, however, have a quality of casualness and lounging about it. . . . The less intense plateau-experience is more often experienced as pure enjoyment and happiness, as let's say, a mother sitting quietly looking, by the hour, at her baby playing and marveling, wondering, philosophizing, not quite believing. . . . (192, p. 88)

This contrast between peak and plateau experience will serve as a basis for distinguishing TM from peak experiences.

The experience of transcending in TM is perceived when the attention comes to rest in pure awareness, a state of inner wakefulness without an object of perception. The experiencer experiences his innermost identity as unbounded awareness; that is, awareness not bound by a thought or emotion. This experience is characterized by profound physical and mental relaxation. Transcending, then, differs profoundly from the peak experience which Maslow described as predominantly or even "purely and exclusively emotional" (192, p. 88). As Maslow commented, peak experiences may in fact not constitute a cognition of Being, but rather an enhanced or heightened appreciation of Being-in-the-world, of the organism and environment's integrated and continuous nature. Compared with transcending in TM, the peak experience can be described as an intensification of the quality of perceptual processing during activity in the waking state of consciousness. Transcending in meditation is the final stage in a progression toward minimized metabolic activity, while maintaining inner wakefulness.

The quieter nature of plateau experiences suggests some correlation with the experience of TM. However, differences are obvious. Maslow described the plateau experience as a voluntary state especially accessible to him in museums, pastoral milieus or tranquil situations.[161] The experience is essentially cognitive and rich in imagery, though not willfully produced. On the other hand, the experience of pure consciousness involves neither imagery nor will. We conclude that plateau experiences, being a product of the "compression of a thousand experiences" (161, p. 117), are simply a distillation of the peak experience's clear cognition of Being-in-the-world. Yet, the notion that the integrated individual can experience such a sustained cognition of Being suggests the possibility that an adequately developed individual might be able to sustain the experience of pure awareness. This possibility is central to the psychology of creative intelligence.

It is important to remember that the experience of pure awareness and its effects occurs only during a specific physiological state. Although peak and plateau experiences may be of tremendous benefit to some individuals, they do not necessarily provide the neurophysiological integration which must underlie all significant human development. As a result, peak and plateau experiences may, in fact, not lead to any kind of integration at all, but may instead be confined to short-lived moods. Maslow remarked,

> My attention was called to this partly by the fact that if you witness heaven in a peak experience, why isn't everybody getting better all the time? We should soon turn into a race of angels. Well, very obviously I was able to get reports of peak experiences from extremely sick people. (161, p. 115)

Nonetheless, though peak and plateau experiences may or may not lead to growth, they remain a characterizing expression of the self-actualizing tendencies of human nature.

TOWARD A PSYCHOLOGY OF FULFILLMENT

Out of the evolution of psychological theories from Freud to Maslow, two basic concepts have emerged with self-actualization theory. First, desire is progressive; man's aspirations for achieving his highest ideals are structured in the satisfaction of his basic needs. Second, the psyche has a foundation; human awareness is grounded in a largely untapped center of potential which exists within every individual. These two ideas suggest tremendous possibilities for human growth in energy, intelligence and satisfaction. Yet new techniques and therapies to foster self-actualization have appeared regularly since Perls and Maslow first published their work. The human potential movement in psychology is still searching for an effective program to unfold man's untapped resources.

TM research has provoked considerable interest in this simple mental process as a technique for unfolding man's full potential. The impact of regular TM practice on individual health, mental stability and performance has been so profound that traditional theories of the mind have simply been inadequate to explain the data. Explanations of TM's effects suggest the elaboration of a new psychological paradigm which treats creative intelligence as a resource at the basis of the psyche.

Concerned specifically with unfolding human potential, the psychology of creative intelligence may be developed from the two hypotheses most important to self-actualization theory. Despite these common underlying principles, however, the psychology of creative intelligence differs significantly from self-actualization theory. To identify this primary difference we have only to examine how these psychological theories interrelate the basic principles that desire is progressive and the psyche has a foundation. The difference between the two psychologies lies not in a difference between their two basic premises but in how the two theories relate these basic ideas.

Both theories recognize a primary interdependence between

the two ideas. Maslow gives a key to his notion of their interaction when he writes:

> . . . growth forward . . . takes place in little steps, and each step forward is made possible by the feeling of being safe . . . We may use as a paradigm the toddler venturing away from his mother's knee into strange surroundings. Characteristically he first clings to his mother as he explores the room with his eyes. Then he dares a little excursion, continuously assuring himself that the mother security is intact. These excursions get more and more extensive. In this way, the child can explore a dangerous and unknown world. If suddenly the mother were to disappear, he would be thrown into anxiety, would cease to be interested in exploring the world, would wish only the return to safety, and might even lose his abilities, e.g., instead of daring to walk, he might creep. (196, p. 46–47)

To express the urge toward growth, even an adult requires a minimum level of safety. When a man meets a threatening situation, he naturally becomes increasingly conservative in his actions until he feels safe enough to risk extending himself in hope of expanding his achievements and accelerating his progress. The tendency to minimize change in the face of danger is as apparent in a general confronted by an overwhelming enemy attack as it is in a child who has lost sight of his mother.

Though self-actualization theory and the psychology of creative intelligence both recognize the wisdom of conservatism in the face of danger and the importance of safety to growth, they differ in their interpretation of what constitutes the ground of safety. Maslow argued that the basis of safety and therefore of the urge toward growth lies in satisfaction of what he calls survival needs (196, p. 49). In the light of his need hierarchy, he suggested that the satisfaction of the basic needs for food and shelter and a modicum of love and trust leads naturally forward to the need for friendship, creative expression, and ultimately toward the highest need for actualizing the full potential of the inner self. The psychology of creative intelligence, on the other hand, identifies the ultimate ground of safety in the direct experience of the inner potential of the self, pure creative intelligence.

Close examination of the mechanics of self-expression under threatening circumstances reveals why the psychology of creative intelligence insists that the experience of the self is the foundation for, rather than the final expression of, the urge toward growth. When a child loses sight of his mother, no amount of food or shelter will assuage his panic and withdrawal. The child gained confidence necessary for self-expression from his knowledge of his mother's being. Only finding his mother or perhaps another adult who can supply a similar quality of being will restore the child's confidence and permit his return to exploratory play. The confidence which a child derives from his mother's presence does not simply arise from the knowledge that food and shelter are available, but rather from the support of an uncaused, loving, energizing presence, his mother. Similarly, when a man faces a threatening circumstance, food and shelter are not the prerequisites for activity to meet the danger. On the contrary, a person must find within his own being a stability, energy and intelligence in which he feels confident enough to undertake activity. The very effort demanded of a hungry, cold and physically weakened man to find the food and warmth necessary to continue living can only arise from an inner experience of the self as energetic, intelligent and somehow invincible in the face of catastrophe. Perls suggested the idea that a center deep within the psyche is the prerequisite to effective interaction with ourselves, others and environment when he wrote, "In the absence of such a center, we wish only to collect ourselves to regain contact with our innermost being" (226, p. 64).

The psychology of creative intelligence, therefore, differs from self-actualization theory in the way it identifies the relation of the urge toward growth and the experience of the innermost self. While self-actualization theory defines the experience of the self as a final expression of the urge toward growth, the psychology of creative intelligence holds that the experience of the self is prerequisite to the urge to grow. In fact, whereas self-actualization theory holds that the degree to which a person can experience his self is directly proportional to his satisfaction of survival needs, the psychology of creative intelligence states that the degree to which a person can fulfill his desire to grow is directly proportional to his experience of his self.

In outlining self-actualization theory, Maslow and his colleagues always began with a discussion of motivation. They discussed the urge to grow as the key to expressing our highest values. In outlining the psychology of creative intelligence, however, we must begin with a discussion of the self. From the perspective of the psychology of creative intelligence, the key to expressing our highest values lies in experiencing the self and thereby gaining the capability of fully expressing the urge to grow.

THE CENTER OF LIFE:
PURE CREATIVE INTELLIGENCE

The fundamental premise of the psychology of fulfillment is that within every person exists a seemingly inexhaustible center of energy, intelligence and satisfaction. Because this center stands at the origin of all thinking and acting but remains distinct from the boundaries of both thought and action, it has been identified as pure creative intelligence. Purity refers to the independence of this center from thinking and acting. Creativity refers to the energetic and generative values displayed by this center. And intelligence implies the role which this center plays as the ordering principle of awareness and behavior. To the extent that our behavior depends on the degree of energy and intelligence available to us, this center of pure creative intelligence may be described as that resource which gives direction to all that we experience, think and do.

Unless we investigate this concept closely, both analytically and experientially, we might easily dismiss it as pure speculative fancy. Therefore, let us begin by examining experience. Do we find any indication of the existence of a reservoir of energy and intelligence at the basis of the mind? We have all experienced innumerable thoughts, each of which exhibits qualities of energy in its flow and intelligence in its directedness. Can we take responsibility for the creation of these thoughts? Close observation of the thinking process reveals that we cannot try to think. Thought arises spontaneously from some center within us.

Further observation of the thinking process reveals that energy and intelligence increase as we experience quieter levels of the thinking process. Our most potent ideas arise when the mind is quiet. A person may struggle with a problem for days until finally he sits down to relax and notes a powerful solution bubbling up as a thought. A general plans a battle in the quiet of the rear guard, not on the front lines; a philosopher develops his insights in the quiet of his study, not in his classroom; an architect designs his buildings in the quiet studio, not amidst the activity of the construction site. The closer a person comes to experiencing the most quiet aspect of the thinking process, the more energy and intelligence he finds embodied in his thinking.

TM is a systematic technique for gaining access to the quieter levels of thought and to the experience of pure awareness. If individuals practicing TM find increasing energy, intelligence and satisfaction in their lives, such evidence constitutes further proof that pure creative intelligence lies at the quietest level of the mind. Research offers strong support to this argument.

But the existence of pure creative intelligence must ultimately be validated through direct experience. As long as our awareness is limited to the surface of the mind, that is, to the level of being conscious of something, we will necessarily label pure creative intelligence an abstract concept. During TM, however, a person experiences quieter levels of the thinking process by engaging an object of perception less and less distinctly, naturally transcends conscious thought and gains pure awareness, the experience of creative intelligence. By virtue of this state, meditators recognize that a boundless field underlies and upholds all awareness of objects. When an individual returns from this state to activity with increased energy, intelligence and happiness, he understands that the field of boundless awareness which he has contacted is a reservoir of these qualities.

Analysis of the thinking process, the effects of TM, and the direct experience of transcending constitute the primary evidence for the existence of pure creative intelligence. Is this experience of transcending mystical, and therefore not subject to scientific analysis or logical description? No. We have shown in chapter 4 that this experience has unique physiological correlates. Now we will show that the experience of transcending itself may be logically explained. Maharishi has described the process of transcending:

> Proceeding toward the subtler layers of the expression of creative intelligence within the mind, we experience a tender field of feeling. Deep within the tenderness of feeling we experience the "myness" of feeling. We say, "I feel like this," "I feel." "*I* feel *my* feelings." So the I in the seat of all my myness is more tenderly located within the feeling. Deep within the I is a more tender level of creative intelligence which is "I-ness." The "I-ness" is almost the abstract value of individual existence, intelligence. And deep within, that individual "I-ness" is boundless —the unmanifest, non-changing, immortal, eternal reality. (186: XIX)

The boundless reality unfolded in the most intimate experience of "I" is pure creative intelligence.

Analysis of this experience reveals that it is very simple in nature despite the possible obscurity of terms such as "I-ness." In chapter 2 we noted that transcending is an automatic process like diving. The mind follows the experience of the mantra to quieter levels of mental activity, charmed by the increasing satisfaction associated with quieter mental activity. This process takes place in four stages. First the mind begins experiencing a thought. Second, this thought begins to fade, as the mind passes through various levels of feelings and thinking. Third, the thought fades, leaving the mind alone with itself in the state of "I-ness." Maharishi describes this state as the mind holding ". . . its individuality in the void—the abstract fullness around it—because there is nothing for it to experience. It remains undisturbed, aware in itself" (184, p. 422). Finally, from this level of inner serenity, the mind is charmed by unbounded pure consciousness. The mind transcends even the experience of its own bounded individuality and gains the status of pure creative intelligence. This final step of transcending, Maharishi states,

. . . begins with the expansion of individuality, and when this happens the intellect, losing its individuality, begins to gain the unbounded status of pure creative intelligence. While merging into pure creative intelligence, it cognizes pure creative intelligence as its own self and gains bliss consciousness . . . (184, p. 423)

Maharishi implies that experiencing pure creative intelligence significantly affects a person's sense of identity. The term identity generally refers to the synthesis of roles and images which a person gathers through social interaction as he grows from infancy to adulthood (66, p. 211). Identity also implies the assurance a person feels about himself as the meaningful center of awareness in his environment. Under present world conditions, the environment is subject to continuous and accelerating change. The prospects of finding a stable basis for identity are not favorable. As Marzetta, Benson and Wallace have suggested in an important article on TM,

One must find a source of inner stability independent of institutions and relationships that are subject to change. Having a solid base separate from the life around him, one becomes free to adapt to circumstances without threatening his integrity. (190, p. 13)

How is it possible that a person's identity formation might be liberated from externally determined roles and self-images? The Indian philosophical text, the Bhagavad-Gita, presents an argument concerning the basis of identity: because our body and experience change continuously, the identity by which a person knows himself to be the same throughout life could not depend on either his body or any particular set of experiences (184, p. 47). Thus the ultimate basis of identity must lie in the boundless inner field of pure creative intelligence, the only aspect of ourselves which, as we experience it while transcending, is truly unchanging.

Experience determines identity formation. As long as the individual experiences himself only in relation to his activities, he knows himself only in terms of his actions, feelings, responsibilities and roles. Until the self has been experienced as separate from activity, the self necessarily seems unstable and limited. In order for an individual to appreciate his unbounded status, he must systematically experience a level of the self which is more basic than any activity, even the activity of thinking.

Through the regular experience of pure creative intelligence, the individual ego, or "I," spontaneously becomes associated with unboundedness. All the objective changes which take place through practicing TM regularly—increased energy, intelligence and happiness—are accompanied by a corresponding subjective change. Maharishi has explained this change in terms of the direct experience of creative intelligence:

> When pure honey comes on the tongue, the taste of great sweetness surpasses in degree all the sweet tastes experienced up to then. If the tongue continues to cherish the taste of honey, then there will be no chance for a previous sweet taste to recur. (184, p. 285)

The repeated experience of unbounded energy, intelligence and satisfaction at the depth of the mind is so profoundly significant that this experience gradually supplants all previous identity formations.

The discovery that experiencing pure awareness enriches every aspect of a person's life constitutes a major advance in psychology. Previous theories of psychological development, even the farsighted work of Maslow and Perls, prescribed techniques to resolve—one at a time—the conflicts which trouble a person and limit his self-expression. The psychology of creative intelligence, on the other hand, prescribes the experience of pure creative intelligence as a means of transforming identity and thereby achieving global improvement in all aspects of a person's psychology. Instead of prescribing techniques to integrate repressed parts of the personality by separately coming to grips with each uncomfortable past experience, the psychology of creative intelligence insists on the holistic value of gaining an identity grounded in pure creative intelligence. When a person discovers tremendous satisfaction within himself, he naturally begins to reintegrate lost parts of his personality spontaneously and comprehensively.

THE IMPULSE TO FULFILLMENT

The central theme in Maslow's self-actualization theory developed from consideration of why the gratification of desire often whets the appetite for further gratification. Investigation of this question revealed that growth takes place in steps of increasing satisfaction. Moreover, the quality of satisfaction achieved at each stage of growth reflects a higher order of value than previous stages. This observation suggested that growth may be interpreted as a process through which organisms actualize their intrinsic potentialities. Maslow argues that our highest needs are biologically structured within the human nervous system and emerge as soon as the basic needs for safety are satisfied. Maslow's theory suggests a definition of the essential motivating factor in all life which is fundamental to the psychology of creative intelligence. Regarding this issue, Maharishi has stated,

> What is the nature of life? When we look around, we find that everything is growing, evolving, progressing. Progress, evolution, and growth are the nature of life. . . . This same tendency can be found in man's life. It is our experience that the natural tendency of the mind is to go to a field of greater happiness. Everyone wants more power, more happiness, and this desire expresses the tendency of life. (186: I)

Our desire is so intimate to us that we overlook its fundamentally progressive character. Despite the fact that our basic needs must be satisfied repeatedly, once a desire of higher order has been satisfied, desires of an identical quality no longer lead to satisfaction. Instead, a desire of greater promise emerges to motivate our action. Having learned to ride a bicycle in the driveway, a child is not satisfied to ride just in the driveway. He wants to ride all over the neighborhood. Having become an assistant vice-president in a company, a man naturally wants to become a president.

This theory may be taken to imply that desire leads to a spiral of growing demands for satisfaction. If so, we might well interpret the crisis of modern life as an expression of this principle.

People demand more and more satisfaction at an increasing rate, unwittingly creating stress, interpersonal difficulties and social fragmentation. Does each new desire simply aim at an expansion of happiness irrespective of the biological conditions of life? Or can the sequence of emerging desires be integrated with the best interests of our biological condition to sustain some optimum level of fulfillment? Is life merely the explosion of increasing desires, or does it have a goal?

Self-actualization theory and the psychology of creative intelligence identify a very specific goal and meaning for life. Maslow explained the goal of life as the possibility of living a state of Being, actualizing one's fullest, unique potentials. This end does not point to an interminable spiral of increasing demands. On the contrary, Maslow saw life as gaining increasing integration through the progression of fulfilled desires. For example, having satisfied the desire for food, a person may then feel the desire for friendship. Similarly, having found friends, a person might then ask for a stronger expression of intimacy in marriage. Each stage of fulfilled desire leads to a higher stage. Maharishi refers to this process in terms of progressive refinement of desire. According to Maslow, this progression reaches completion with the fully functioning human being. Maharishi describes the goal of life in even more glowing terms:

> Because the play of creative intelligence is in the direction of greater happiness, greater knowledge and greater achievement, it becomes obvious that life desires to be lived in the state of fulfillment, where everything would be of maximum value: maximum knowledge . . . achievement . . . strength . . . power . . . fulfillment. Life aspires to be lived on the level of abundance, on the level of affluence. To live infinity in life—that is life's natural tendency, and if the infinite value of life would become a living reality, that natural tendency would be satisfied. (186: I)

In such a state of full development, life reveals its ultimate meaning. We may understand this goal of life in terms of values. When a person rises to a state of living full creative intelligence, he expresses man's highest ideals. Maslow listed some of these universal values as discerned in the personalities of self-actualizing people: wholeness, perfection, orderliness, spontaneity, richness, goodness, effortlessness, playfulness and self-sufficiency (196, p. 83). Similarly, the psychology of creative intelligence holds that our highest values are structured as inherent qualities of creative intelligence. In the fully actualized individual, Maharishi has explained that the progressive, integrative, discriminative, self-sufficient and invincible nature of creative intelligence is expressed in every aspect of a person's awareness (186:V).

Such realizations of man's highest values, however, are not limited to subjective experience. Maharishi has argued that full personal development must include life's inner and outer aspects, that the goal of life is the realization of "two fullnesses" or "200% of life."[187] In other words, the inner fulfillment resulting from increasing identification with pure creative intelligence supports the individual's expression of his full potential. It is reasonable, therefore, to expect that regular practice of TM will foster the growth of fulfillment not only internally but also externally in every aspect of a person's activity. The research findings reported in previous chapters as well as in numerous reports from meditators, strongly support this conclusion. However, to make the full significance of this growth explicit, we must describe in some detail an encompassing change consistently reported in both internal and external experience by long-term meditators.

NORMAL LIFE: THE DAWN OF FULFILLMENT

Though pure creative intelligence exists as a limitless resource of energy and intelligence within every individual, the degree to which a person taps this resource varies from person to person and, within a particular person, from time to time. The difference in energy and intelligence which a person expresses while sleeping, dreaming and waking, well illustrates the variability of people's access to pure creative intelligence. Through the practice of TM, however, a person gains direct access to pure creative intelligence in the experience of a fourth state of consciousness, distinctly different from waking, sleeping and dreaming. Research has indicated that regularly experiencing this fourth state improves the regenerative values of sleep and dreaming, while enhancing every aspect of a person's wakeful life.

Research on the physiological effects of TM has defined the mechanism of growth through TM in terms of stress reduction and corresponding brain integration. This research has not, however, found any evidence that the fourth state actually structurally or functionally develops the nervous system itself. Consequently, the effects of the fourth state have been consistently discussed as normalization. Contrary to the popular belief that excessive stress is a normal and even necessary part of life, research on the physiological effects of TM suggests that the body seeks to throw off stress as naturally as the body seeks to recover from disease through deep rest. In other words, despite the fact that almost everyone suffers from stress and the debilitating effects of stress have reached crisis proportions in most industrial nations, stress is no more normal to the body than cancer.

The holistic growth resulting from systematically experiencing the fourth state arises from normalizing the nervous system. Because regular experience of the fourth state not only reduces stress but also increases resistance to stress by improving autonomic stability, the long-term regular practice of TM should eventually normalize the nervous system completely.[213] What effect does complete integration of the nervous system have on the quality of subjective experience? Furthermore, what effect will a completely normalized nervous system have upon a person's activity and interpersonal skills? The impact of TM on the quality of the subjective and objective aspects of people's experience is so global as to necessitate discussion of the end result of regularly practicing TM in terms of a fifth state of consciousness physiologically distinct from waking, sleeping, dreaming and the fourth state.

Initially, however, this transformation is not always noticeable. We can explain the subtlety of this development with an analogy. Imagine that consciousness illuminates the objects of our perception like a flashlight beam illuminating various objects. If the light is dim, we have difficulty seeing and therefore dealing with whatever we examine. Now imagine that we are able to increase the intensity of the light gradually. This increase in intensity corresponds to heightening our awareness by making more creative intelligence available to the mind through TM. As the intensity of the light grows, we begin to notice that everything we see is more visible than before. We also find improvement in our ability to work with the objects under the light. Because we are depending on light to see, however, we don't at first notice the changes in terms of the light. Instead, we become aware of our greater ability to function effectively with what we see. Similarly, meditators do not at first discern the benefits of their meditation in terms of the improved quality of their subjective experience. Instead they experience how much more effectively and enjoyably they accomplish their everyday tasks than before learning to meditate. Eventually, however, with the steadily increasing light and growing ability to see and work with objects under the light, a person discerns the change in the light itself. Similarly, with regular daily practice of TM, meditators begin to notice a fundamental and charming change in the overall quality of their subjective experience. They begin to appreciate their own consciousness as unbounded pure unchanging bliss which illuminates all that they perceive.

The experience of personal identity as unbounded pure awareness grows gradually. As Maharishi explains, at first a meditator simply experiences the mind quieting down in meditation until the mind simply remains wide awake with no thoughts or objects of perception.[187] With regular practice, the clarity of this state increases and the mind enjoys lucid inner wakefulness. Further practice of TM normalizes the nervous system sufficiently to enable an individual to experience his own consciousness clearly established in the infinite field of pure creative intelligence. As this clarity of inner experience during meditation grows, the benefits of TM become increasingly apparent during activity. With continued practice of TM, ability to sustain unbounded awareness along with mental activity of thinking or feeling increases. Thereafter, a meditator may be walking down the street or engaged in conversation when he again experiences that same unboundedness which he had previously known only during meditation. Such experiences do not conflict with his activity. On the contrary, they inspire lively and attentive participation in whatever activity is at hand because the individual sustains maximum alertness and comprehension. These glimpses of the fundamental basis of consciousness, the unbounded field of pure creative intelligence, become increasingly frequent and profound.

Maharishi has explained that this gradual expansion of the ability to experience pure awareness outside of meditation is the result of the systematic alternation of Transcendental Meditation and activity (184, p. 314). Each session of TM infuses the mind with the qualities of creative intelligence, and each period of activity after TM stabilizes this effect. Maharishi holds that the significant effect of this alternation of TM and activity is to make awareness of pure creative intelligence permanent. He explains this development in terms of an analogy.[187] In India, for a cloth to become colorfast, each dipping in dye is followed by exposure of the cloth to sunlight. Though the sun bleaches the color, whatever color remains is colorfast. Through repetition of this cycle, deep color is made finally permanent. Similarly, repeated TM followed by daily activity is necessary for the nervous system to become capable of continuously sustaining awareness of pure creative intelligence.

Throughout this process, the energy, intelligence and satisfaction experienced in the fourth state of consciousness enrich the other three states of consciousness. The activities of the day improve, sleep becomes deeper and more restful, dreaming better serves to normalize stress gathered during daily activity. Stress is more and more completely eliminated and the body becomes more and more integrated. As Maharishi explains, regular practice of TM eventually completely normalizes the nervous system (180:XXIII). At this point, the meditator achieves perfect psychophysiological integration. This objective change in the body results in a distinct change in awareness. Free from stresses which had inhibited their conscious access to full creative intelligence, practitioners of TM become permanently established in unbounded awareness.

When a meditator gains permanent conscious access to full creative intelligence, he maintains pure awareness at all times, throughout the natural alternation of waking, dreaming and sleeping. Whether awake, dreaming or asleep he uninterruptedly reflects intimate familiarity with the full range of the mind's possible experience. He continuously expresses the unbounded energy, intelligence and satisfaction of the source field in which his consciousness is grounded. Maharishi has called this expansion of awareness "cosmic consciousness" (184, pp. 136–37). The term "cosmic" refers to the all-inclusive status of this development: "Energy, intelligence and creativity rise to their limitless value and the limited individual gains the status of unlimited cosmic existence."[187] Maharishi holds this to be the normal state of human life.

The ease, naturalness and universality of TM suggests that cosmic consciousness is everyone's birthright. Maharishi has explained this universality in terms of the inherent ability of the human nervous system to simultaneously maintain conscious contact with the pure field of creative intelligence while expressing its qualities in activity. Maharishi has written: "The human nervous system is an instrument, a creation of creative intelligence, which is capable of incorporating the whole range of creative intelligence: the unmanifest value and the fully developed manifest value" (180:VII). Maharishi has further explained that the natural, spontaneously actualized goal of life is the attainment of the ability to enjoy continuous awareness of creative intelligence. The only seeming obstacle is stress. Just as the body spontaneously heals a wound if given proper rest, so the whole nervous system is structured to throw off stress and realize the full value of cosmic consciousness. It is only the lack of physiological integration which withholds anyone from this state of lasting fulfillment. Through the deep rest gained during the practice of TM, however, anyone can systematically reintegrate his nervous system and spontaneously achieve the full value of normal life.

The rise to cosmic consciousness is therefore in no sense the result of intellectual understanding or emotional commitment. In fact the process is purely physiological. Any attempts to induce this state by simulating the mood of "bliss consciousness" or trying to live in terms of fulfillment will at best be of little value and may result in personality distortion. Similarly, the attempt to maintain experiences enjoyed during meditation when returning to activity will not contribute to growth and may retard progress. The growth of consciousness is not fostered by will. On the contrary, creative intelligence grows spontaneously in a person's life at the maximum possible rate through the regular practice of TM. Once a person has systematically eliminated all stress from his nervous system, he simply *is* more creatively intelligent and doesn't need to *try* to be.

LIFE IN FULFILLMENT

What is it like to live continuously grounded in pure creative intelligence? When a meditator gains full creative intelligence, what changes take place in his everyday activities, relationships, goals and achievements? We can best answer these questions in terms of freedom. Grounded in unboundedness, a cosmically conscious person is free to appreciate his surroundings fully. He is free from perceptual distortions which restrict creative interaction with the environment. He is free from negative impressions from past experience to enjoy an easy and rich involvement with everything and everyone around him. Never overshadowed by any aspect of what he needs or what is required of him, he is free to act with complete success and spontaneous altruism.

On what basis can such freedom be attained? Because the pure field of creative intelligence is the source of all our thinking and acting, it is independent of all thought and action. Once pure awareness is maintained continuously, an individual's self is established as separate from his experience and his activity. His unbounded identity supports a natural independence from life's vicissitudes.

One of Maharishi's analogies, reminiscent of Plato's cave, elucidates the unfoldment of such freedom in terms of the relation of consciousness to objects of experience.[187] Imagine a person who has always been confined in a totally darkened movie theater, with nothing visible but the movie on the screen. Knowing only the movie, this person assumes that his experience is inextricably bound to the events on the screen, and that he is utterly determined by them. Whenever the projector is turned off, there is no experience: he is asleep. During the darkness, he sometimes becomes dimly aware and creates illusory movies; he is dreaming. When he begins TM, he begins to enjoy a new experience; he is able to leave the projector on but fade the image on the screen until the surface upon which the image is projected becomes visible. He then begins to realize the nature of the theater. Repeating this experience twice daily, he ultimately becomes so familiar with the theater that he always perceives the screen, even during the movie. As a result, not only does he understand and enjoy the theater, but for the first time, he can sit back and really enjoy the movie. The content of the film which previously dominated him, and also the formal properties of the projected image on the screen become a source of delight.

This analogy is not intended to imply that the unfoldment of cosmic consciousness reveals life to be unreal, any more than understanding that a movie is only a movie prevents a person from becoming involved in it. The analogy only serves to distinguish between the reality of awareness itself and its manifestation in our experience of the world. Our experience becomes lively through our awareness, but awareness is prior to and therefore independent of experience. Appreciating this independence of awareness as an all-time reality, a person can enjoy his activity without being overshadowed by it. Just as understanding the real nature of movies enhances a person's enjoyment of every movie, so full knowledge of the self in cosmic consciousness provides a stable basis for full participation in life.

Such independence of the self from activity is in no sense a state of dissociated detachment. As Maharishi explains,

> When, through the practice of Transcendental Meditation, cosmic consciousness has been gained . . . the mind automatically functions from the level of its full potentiality, and the senses,

having reached their maximum development, function at their highest capacity. . . . That is why the senses, acting from their raised level, experience objects more completely, resulting in even greater appreciation of objects, thus providing an experience of greater happiness on the sensory level. The objects of sense are enjoyed more thoroughly than before, but . . . fail to capture the mind. The enlightened man thus naturally remains in a state where the senses continue to experience their objects while he remains free. (184, p. 343)

Psychologists have studied and described the stereotyped and rubricized relationships which characterize the experience of most adults. Charles Tart points out that people generally "substitute abstract cognition patterns for . . . raw sensory experience" (273, p. 486). Thus people lose the ability to notice the places they daily pass on their way to work, rigidify their social relationships and perceive others only through stereotyped preconceptions. Lamenting this general tendency to perceive the world only in terms of rigid perceptual patterns, Ornstein describes the limiting aspect of "linear modes of consciousness" which impoverish the experience of reality (220, pp. 41-46). Erich Fromm describes how a threefold filter of language, logic and societally acceptable concepts eliminates richness and uniqueness from life (87, pp. 99-104). This process of closing ourselves to experience may be described as automatization.

We can understand the freedom of cosmic consciousness as complete deautomatization. In cosmic consciousness, individuals report great openness to experience—a freshness, even innocence, through which they become sensitized to the novelty of every situation, even though it has occurred hundreds of times before. As one five-year meditator remarked:

> I can appreciate fully now. I'm just engrossed in whatever my awareness falls upon. I feel I'm naturally seeing it for what it is. I remember looking at a tree and feeling so much more how fully alive it was—it wasn't just wood, it was living. I could see the beauty of its creation in every shimmering pine needle, every piece of bark. I had passed by that tree many times in the past, but now it's a fresh perception every time I take a minute to look at it.

Individuals in cosmic consciousness report a state of balance and integration in which they enjoy stable, centered richness at all times. Secure in an unlimited flow of energy, intelligence and satisfaction, which liberates them from the uncertainties of life, they have no need to defend themselves with rigid perceptual expectations. One practitioner of TM who seems to be approaching this experience explained.

> After having meditated for six years, I've noticed that everything inside of me has become so much calmer that I interfere less with the larger pattern of whatever is going on around me. I used to have so much inner noise, either emotional turmoil or intense thinking, that I wasn't able to appreciate the larger developments taking shape all around me. As a result, I feel my participation in life now is more an appreciation of what happens in *and* around my life, instead of trying to make this or that happen. I call it "participatory alertness." You find you're maintaining a balance between keeping up active participation to the fullest possible extent and having this continual alertness to a larger awareness of developing situations and patterns so that you aren't caught up in trivia, you aren't forcing things to happen, but you're able to see more clearly at every moment what you can be doing that's most significant.

An essential component of the rise to cosmic consciousness is dissolving the influence of negative impressions from the past. We naturally interpret every new situation in terms of previous experience, and process and respond to new sensory data through categories and tendencies associated with similar previous impressions. Therefore, the costs of negative impressions in limiting our ability to perceive the world lucidly and to enjoy interacting positively with our environment are great. Imprinting from the past leads people to read causes for anxiety or anger into benign situations. A twenty-nine-year-old teacher of TM who has been meditating for four years reminisced about this problem:

> I can remember being thrown off balance by overwhelming circumstances, but now I'm just not affected. I can feel what is happening, I experience emotions and subtleties more fully, but it's not unsettling or overshadowing, as it sometimes used to be. I just do what's to be done and keep going. I don't feel any

kind of carryover from heavy experiences anymore. Other people's problems used to really get to me, I'd feel for them so much I'd lose my equilibrium, but now I feel for them much more because I can help, if possible, without losing my own stability. . . .

The memory of previous stresses is not washed away. Like the peel of an orange, the bitter part is always there, it's just that you know how to always get the good part. And because the mind knows about how to get the good, you don't even think about the bad, you just go straight through it. It's just a matter of starting to make the right connections. All the memory is there; in a person who is stressed, all the wrong connections get made all the time. As one evolves, the connections become very purposeful, oriented toward progress, toward supporting both your own and everyone's evolution. . . .

It's still a pinch to look around and see people suffer. But there's a difference between a pinch and a sledge hammer. It's like the difference of tasting honey in the analogy Maharishi uses. Once you've tasted honey, or once you're established in some non-changing field, fine, you know that value and you know it as an all-time reality. At the same time change keeps going on. Lesser values are always present. You don't lose a lesser value just because you've gained a greater value. Things keep going on in the world, but the beauty is, when one person is unshakable, then he's better able to stabilize everything else around him just by being who he is, and then his action just augments his being, just increases the effect of that stability by expanding it, by making it available to the environment.

Maharishi has discussed the elimination of the negative imprinting from the past primarily as the result of experiencing pure awareness which suffuses every experience, past and present, with the unbounded satisfaction of pure creative intelligence. He has stated that the principal effect of unfolding cosmic consciousness is that a person gains an identity grounded in "bliss consciousness." He continues: "Then a man realizes that his self is different from the mind which is engaged with thoughts and desires. It is now his experience that the mind, which had been identified with thoughts and desires, is mainly identified with the Self" (184, pp. 150–151). In other words, negative past impressions are not annihilated with the rise to cosmic consciousness but they do become wholly secondary to the great satisfaction intrinsic to this state.

This grounding of mental processes in pure satisfaction which characterizes the rise to cosmic consciousness explains changes taking place deep within the psyche. In cosmic consciousness, a person

> . . . experiences the desires of the mind as lying outside of himself, whereas he used to experience himself as completely involved with desires. On the surface of the mind, desires certainly continue, but deep within the mind they no longer exist, for the depths of the mind are transformed into the nature of the Self. All the desires which were present in the mind have been thrown upward, as it were—they have gone to the surface, and within the mind the finest intellect gains an unshakable, immovable status. (184, p. 151)

With this rise to cosmic consciousness our finest faculty of discrimination, the intellect, is freed from obsession with desires. Liberated from desires at the depth of the mind, a person experiences the unbounded status of his own Self and enjoys "bliss consciousness."

This liberation from desire through the infusion of the mind with bliss, however, does not have the effect of diminishing a person's involvement in life:

> It is quite wrong to think that one who has gained this state remains slumped in inertia and does not engage in action. This state of life is such that it maintains the freedom of the . . . inner self, and at the same time deals with all actions most efficiently and successfully. (184, p. 151)

Though a person has gained fulfillment, the nature of existence forces him to continue to perform action. In a completely fulfilled person, the desire for such action is different from the desire of a person seeking contentment. Supported by maximum creative intelligence, the resulting action is expressive rather than manipulative. No longer worried about personal limitations, the cosmically conscious person naturally enjoys success.

Further, the cosmically conscious person's constant alertness and openness to the external world allows him to make right decisions spontaneously. Here is a description of this experience from a twenty-six-year-old, five-year meditator:

> I find that I'm really able to do what I have to do quickly. When I want something or need it, I don't have to wait around trying to decide what to do, or to be consistent with my tastes or interests or whatever. Because that harmony is there, I find that every moment, the best opportunity is right there. So it's not a matter of deciding how to take best advantage of the situation. The best situation is always at hand and one is able to use it to maximum advantage for himself and for others. What happens in this spontaneous way is a function of both what's right for the individual who's initiating the action as well as right for everyone else around him in the environment. So the two are happily working together. Whatever I'm doing has to do with the whole of the environment.

Sustaining maximum inner freedom, the person in cosmic consciousness can make decisions according to ultimate values rather than shortsighted needs. It may well be that whatever work a cosmically conscious person undertakes, a spontaneous altruism will structure his objectives in terms of achieving humanity's best interest. Sustained unbounded awareness enables such an individual to realize a natural sense of morality, justice, beauty and truth, the values projected by Maslow as the deepest level of man's nature (196, p. 83). Living perfect inner fulfillment, the cosmically conscious person engages in activity to elevate his changing environment to the level of the stabilized perfection which he experiences within.

THE PHYSIOLOGY OF COSMIC CONSCIOUSNESS

Every state of consciousness depends on a corresponding state of the nervous system. This psychophysiological principle which guided our discussion of the first four states of consciousness— waking, sleeping, dreaming and the transcendental—applies to cosmic consciousness as well. As Maharishi has described it, the rise to cosmic consciousness is the natural result of regularly alternating the restful alertness gained during TM with normal daily activity until all stress is systematically eliminated from the nervous system. Cosmic consciousness then emerges as a unique state of psychophysiological integration. Because of its apparent distinction from all other states of consciousness, Maharishi has explicitly identified cosmic consciousness as the fifth state of consciousness.

Investigation of higher states of consciousness is one of the more exciting frontiers of psychophysiological research. R. K. Wallace, whose ground-breaking studies of TM have established the fourth state,[286,289] suggested to the authors that the psychophysiological description of the fifth state is the next great challenge for researchers concerned with the physical basis of human awareness. In their efforts to delineate the characteristics of cosmic consciousness, researchers must initially determine where to look for the physical effects of the fifth state of consciousness. MIU neurobiologist John Farrow offered this insight in a conversation with the authors:

> I expect that future research into higher states of consciousness will reveal increasing synchrony of all bodily rhythms. EEG studies have already demonstrated highly significant synchronous activity during Transcendental Meditation. We may well find a similar stabilizing integration in the harmonious interplay of other rhythms, including Circadian rhythms. My personal opinion is that physiological research into cosmic consciousness may well reveal significant changes in hormonal rhythms as well as brain-wave activity.

Banquet[18, 19] and Glueck[99] have already reported dramatic increases in the coherence of the electrical activity of various areas of the brain during the practice of TM. In advanced meditators the frequency spectrum of their EEGs develops persistent narrow peaks simultaneously in the theta and beta regions, along with phase coherence between the back and front of the brain and between the left and right cerebral hemispheres.[19] Such hypersynchrony is unique in EEG studies and appears to be a physiological correlate of the experience of expanded awareness. We may hypothesize from these early findings that the continuous unbounded awareness of cosmic consciousness would appear as complete temporal and spatial wave coherence of the entire electrophysiological system of the brain.

Maharishi's claim that a person in cosmic consciousness sustains unbounded pure awareness throughout waking, dreaming and sleeping offers another promising area for investigation (184, p. 183). We may hypothesize that distinct EEG patterns should appear during the sleep of a cosmically conscious man. Banquet has accumulated some as yet unpublished data from sleep studies of long-time practitioners of TM. He found that during long periods of sleep, alpha waves, usually characteristic of relaxed wakefulness, are superimposed on large delta waves characteristic of deep sleep. If substantiated through further studies, this finding may well give physiological confirmation of these meditators' reports of awareness during sleep.

The restful effects of experiencing pure awareness during activity provides another target for researchers investigating the physiology of the fifth state. A twenty-eight-year-old, seven-year mediator reported: "I rest more than I did before, but I stay in bed less. The rest is the greatest rest I've ever known, in fact, all the time, twenty-four hours a day." Such persons also claim that their daily output of energy considerably surpasses their previous abilities. Such an increase of energy and stamina should be measurable in terms of metabolic rate and biochemical assays. According to Maharishi, this unrestricted flow of energy results from the elimination of all previously accumulated stress and high resistance to accumulating further stress. The stress reaction is physiologically measurable. The studies by Orme-Johnson and Thomas Routt,[213, 239] which demonstrated greater autonomic stability in practitioners of TM, suggest still another means of delineating the fifth state.

Maharishi has offered further insight into the physiological changes accompanying the rise to cosmic consciousness in discussing the necessary integration of the fourth state of consciousness with waking, dreaming and sleeping:

> Transcendental consciousness corresponds to a certain specific state of the nervous system which transcends any activity and

is therefore completely different from that state of the nervous system which corresponds to the waking state of consciousness.

Now, for transcendental consciousness to become permanent and to co-exist with the waking state of consciousness, it is necessary that the two states of the nervous system corresponding to these two states of consciousness should co-exist. This is brought about by the mind gaining alternately transcendental consciousness and the waking state of consciousness, passing from one to the other. This gradual and systematic culture of the physical nervous system creates a physiological situation in which the two states of consciousness exist together simultaneously. It is well known that there exist in the nervous system many autonomous levels of function, between which a system of coordination also exists. In the state of cosmic consciousness, two different levels of organization in the nervous system function simultaneously while maintaining . . . separation of function. . . . In the early stages of the practice of transcendental meditation, these two levels of function in the nervous system are unable to occur at the same time; the function of the one inhibits the function of the other. That is why, at this stage, either transcendental consciousness or the waking state of consciousness is experienced. The practice of the mind passing from one to another gradually overcomes this physiological inhibition, and the two levels begin to function perfectly at the same time without inhibiting each other and still maintaining their separate identities. (184, pp. 314-315)

In this discussion, Maharishi presents several insights into the physiological changes resulting from daily TM practice. Two interesting ideas significant to further research are: first, cosmic consciousness involves the simultaneous functioning of two different aspects of the nervous system; and second, that these processes are at first inhibited by one another.

One final possibility for research into the physiology of cosmic consciousness deserves mention. The Vedas, ancient Indian texts, contain frequent references to a compound called soma (184, pp. 9-17). Many verses, especially in the Rig Veda, are devoted to poetic description of the ritual preparation of this substance and to praise of its marvelous qualities. Where certain commentators have inferred that this material may have been a ritual food or hallucinogenic drug, Maharishi has explained that soma is a natural metabolic compound which is produced via digestive refinement in cosmically conscious individuals. Maharishi indicated that this substance is a chemical and should be measurable. In conversation with medical scientists, he has suggested that research must discover whether soma is a new chemical produced within the body only after the onset of cosmic consciousness, or whether it is a new use of an existing chemical like serotonin, a compound found in the stomach and brain which is known to affect significantly states of awareness.[20] Maharishi has explained the value of soma as an essential physiological component of further refinements in awareness after an individual has gained cosmic consciousness.[187]

FURTHER HORIZONS OF CONSCIOUSNESS

Cosmic consciousness is not the final stage of human development unfolded through the systematic practice of TM. Once cosmic consciousness has been attained, Maharishi holds that two higher states, refined cosmic consciousness and unity consciousness, emerge successively. These states of awareness express the meditator's increasing realization of the full value of the pure field of creative intelligence. Maharishi has described these states as the sixth and seventh states of consciousness, and has indicated that they are as physiologically distinct from each other and from cosmic consciousness as they are from waking, dreaming and sleeping. Though no research has been completed to verify these claims, Maharishi's systematic description of the development of these states has been supported by the reports of persons who have been practicing TM for ten years or more (186: XXIII). As increasing numbers of meditators reach this plateau, scientific study will presumably substantiate Maharishi's description of higher states just as it has substantiated his description of the fourth state.

According to Maharishi, developments of awareness beyond cosmic consciousness occur primarily in terms of the individual's experience of his world. The sixth state, refined cosmic consciousness, unfolds with the spontaneous perception of finer aspects of reality in a person's immediate environment. Just as science has shown that matter may be analyzed on molecular, atomic and subatomic levels, a parallel expansion of perceptual ability occurs with the rise to the sixth state. Maharishi has explained that the ability to perceive finer aspects of things emerges through the full development of appreciation and love.[187] To one extent or another, everyone is familiar with the effect of mood on perception: when we feel good, things appear beautiful; when we are depressed, everything seems flat and gray. When we are in love with a person, a work of art, or an ideal, we perceive in the beloved object fine qualities which are invisible to persons lacking similar loving feelings. Maharishi has explained the sixth state as a profound expansion of the "heart" through which a person is drawn into loving engagement with everything he experiences (186: XXIII). Relationships of devotion to a marriage partner, family, parents, or intellectual ideal further this development.

The growing charm of love draws a person who has risen to the sixth state into discovering quieter, more intimate aspects of what he perceives. Maharishi has explained that just as a person experiences the thought process at increasingly refined levels through the practice of TM, so persons enjoying the sixth state perceive finer levels of the objects of their experience while engaging in daily life. As he refines cosmic consciousness, a person begins to perceive aspects of the external world, which reflect his experience of pure creative intelligence.

This perception of refined levels of reality on the basis of heightened universal love provides a stepping-stone to an even higher degree of perceptual acuity. This transformation unfolds the seventh state, unity consciousness. Just as the mantra leads a person inward through quieter states of thought to the field of pure creative intelligence, so perception of finer levels of external reality leads a man in the sixth state to begin discerning the field of pure creative intelligence underlying everything he sees:

> In this further development, the liveliness of the infinite is cognized on the bed of the finite. This is only possible when the

conscious mind has become vibrant with the infinite value and the perception has become so refined as to spontaneously cognize the finest relative values. In this situation, the finest relative perception rises to the level of the infinite value of perception. (186:XXIII)

Maharishi has reported that in unity consciousness, the same pure creative intelligence which has been the basis of the self from the first attainment of cosmic consciousness, is perceived as the underlying essence of everything in the environment. This quality of perception results in a complete dissolution of separation between the individual and his world. Maharishi has reported that a person enjoying this state experiences every object as being as dear to him as he is to himself:

> In this unified state of consciousness, the experiencer and the object of experience have both been brought to the same level of infinite value, and this encompasses the entire phenomenon of perception and action as well. The gulf between the knower and the object of his knowing has been bridged. (186:XXIII)

Thus the unifying force of love, which initiated the ultimate integration of the individual and his world by unfolding perception of finer levels of relative existence, completes the process by uniting the subject and his object on the level of absolute pure creative intelligence.

This state of unity consciousness is of an altogether different nature than states described by psychologists, in which a person loses his ability to differentiate himself from the objects of his experience. Freud alluded to a primal unity in which the infant is unable to distinguish himself from his world (81, p. 12). Jung described a "participation mystique," through which cultural traditions impart to primitive peoples a lasting sense of oneness with each other and nature at the expense of all individuality.[136] R. D. Laing has described terrifying psychotic experiences involving the dissolution of ego boundaries and complete identification with whatever is seen or heard.[163] Ernst Kris has pointed out that artists and creative people often enjoy productive regressive experiences in which they feel at-one-ment with the objects of their perception.[162] All of these experiences are achieved at the cost of the uniqueness and stability of the subject's individuality. The subject becomes lost in the object of perception.

Maharishi has explained that unity consciousness unfolds on the basis of cosmic consciousness (186: XXIII). In the fifth state, individual awareness is immovably established in pure creative intelligence. Grounded in an unchanging center within the individual, unity consciousness enhances rather than diminishes individuality. The seventh state is neither a regressive nondifferentiation between the individual and his environment nor a state in which the individual is in any way overshadowed by the objects of his experience. Instead it involves a unification of the subject and object in terms of the highest value of the subject. The internal value of unbounded creative intelligence which characterizes the experiencer is found to characterize the object, and therefore to unite the subject with the object. Such an ability to perceive the underlying unity of all existence directly on the level of the self allows a person in the seventh state of consciousness to understand all he sees deeply. More importantly, it produces a state of life in which the value of unbounded bliss consciousness is lived fully in both the internal and external aspects of life.

THE GOAL OF LIFE

Everything we undertake has not only an immediate but also an ultimate goal. Though we are engaged in continually varying activities emerging from a changing fabric of desires, the subjective inner goal of all people is fulfillment. This statement of ultimate purpose does not imply that everyone ought to, could or ever will become the same. Every person is unique, and, in fact, the progress of civilization depends on the differentiation of human ability. In the course of human development, however, every person needs and actively seeks to express his innermost potentialities fully, his full measure of energy and intelligence, to achieve his own highest possible fulfillment. If every individual were somehow able to achieve this goal, we might envision a resolution of the constellation of crises burdening modern life.

Our primary thesis may be stated simply: the human nervous system can experience unbounded creative intelligence uninterruptedly. Thus, as a person gains access to his unlimited inner potential and begins reflecting the values of creative intelligence in the activities of daily life, his awareness expands. We may identify the degree to which an individual has tapped the value of this unlimited resource by examining his state of consciousness.

We have outlined seven states of consciousness which identify seven major transitions, from the most limited possibility of human experience to the most expansive state of fulfillment:

sleeping

dreaming

waking

pure awareness or transcendental consciousness

cosmic consciousness

refined cosmic consciousness

unity consciousness

Maharishi has defined these seven states of consciousness as major stages of growth characterized by distinct levels of subjective and physiological change. Sleeping, dreaming and waking are familiar and well-defined physiologically. TM introduces the regular experience of pure awareness. Evidence suggests that this state of restful alertness is distinct from the first three states and necessary to their full expression. Systematic exposure to the fourth state results in the fifth state, man's normal condition in which the perfectly integrated nervous system fully expresses creative intelligence. An individual in the state of cosmic consciousness enjoys sustained pure awareness along with waking, dreaming and sleeping. The physiological integration of the fifth state makes possible further development of awareness. The enrichment of emotional abilities on the basis of perfect psychophysiological integration refines the faculties of perception to provide an experience of subtler levels of objective existence in the sixth state. Finally, the seventh state completes this development by unfolding direct perception of the absolute field of pure creative intelligence not only within the individual but also in the world. Thus the individual expresses the full dignity of life on the basis of lasting and unbounded fulfillment in everything he does.

8

TOWARD
A FULFILLED SOCIETY

We are standing before the dawn of what is to be one of the greatest transformations in human history. Accelerating into the future, we are privileged to have witnessed several decades of cultural and economic change which exceed in magnitude and significance historical shifts which, in the past, have taken place over centuries. Very few people in early nineteenth-century Europe recognized the significance of textile mills and rising urban populations, at the dawn of what we now call the Industrial Revolution. Fewer still appreciated the importance of Copernicus's new method of approaching astronomy or Gutenberg's revolutionary method of printing at the dawn of the Renaissance. We may justifiably doubt whether anyone foresaw the impact of Christianity on the Roman Empire at the time of Christ. And we can be quite certain that no one grasped the impact of the new tools emerging with the discovery of how to extract iron from ore. With the technological revolution, however, the whole world has witnessed information processing develop from mechanical calculators to vast computer systems over four decades, watched communication networks encircle the globe with means of instantaneous audio and video exchange within twenty-five years, and stood amazed at our transformation from earthbound to space travelers in a mere fifteen years. Changes of such magnitude are taking place so rapidly that we may be the first generation ever to appreciate the dawn of a new era in one lifetime.

Though the spectacular feats of technological achievement continue to attract attention as the primary sign of a new post-industrial society, these achievements have little continuing revolutionary significance. While the recent shortages of energy and resources foreshadow significant industrial reorganization, they represent only an extension of the Industrial Revolution's achievements and problems. Today's great historical change is going on quietly behind the scenes, almost as unnoticed as the great historical transformations of the past. The most significant changes of our time are not taking place outwardly but inwardly through a rapidly growing number of individuals who are becoming sensitive to a new set of values, a new quality of awareness, a new way of being.

In light of the failure of highly optimistic liberal and highly vocal revolutionary efforts to address the problems of technological society, the early 1970s have brought much reflection on what lies before us. Most critics agree that the change under way begins with the individual reassessment of personal values and potentialities. This change gathers momentum as the individual discovers increased personal capability for growth and fulfillment. It takes on social significance when the individual begins to apply his new appreciation for the wider horizons of consciousness within his social milieu. Social visionaries including Buckminster Fuller,[90, 92] Abraham Maslow,[196] R. D. Laing,[163] Carl Rogers,[236] Norman O. Brown,[38] Dennis Gabor,[94] Willis Harman,[114] George B. Leonard,[169] Theodore Roszak,[238] Charles Reich,[230] and William Irwin Thompson[276] all quietly insist on our reappraising our innermost values. They concur on humanity's tremendous untapped inner potential, and project the dawning of the social application of this potential. They agree that this effort will be collective but not political, a coordinated growth arising not on the basis of alliances or agreement but out of a fundamentally shared view of man and his unfolding possibilities.

REAPPRAISING THE INDIVIDUAL

None of today's social visionaries propose a specific program through which the great societal transformation of which they speak is to be achieved. Certainly, some offer a broad vision of steps to be taken, but none prescribe a specific method to accelerate the unfoldment of human potentials.[90, 92, 238] Similarly, social planners responsible for solving the problems of crime and poverty seem to be taking a conservative stance after watching the only marginal success of the liberal social prescriptions of the 1960s.[277] In the face of such difficulties in addressing large-scale social problems, many sociologists are reconsidering the nature of fundamental problems in our society. Yale sociologist Wendell Bell explained: "There's a feeling that traditional social engineering doesn't really matter. Whatever it does—curriculum planning, neighborhood studies, compensatory social factoring—doesn't really work" (277, p. 81).

As S. M. Miller has pointed out, many sociologists are now saying that social problems remain insoluble "because they have their roots in immutable individual characteristics."[277] In any case, both social visionaries and social pragmatists seem to recognize that the change under way in our society is not occurring through an all-encompassing plan for social reorganization, but through fundamental changes within the individual.

To some social critics, the prospect of change dependent upon individual growth is a reason for pessimism. Though they recognize that we cannot simply legislate away the problems confronting our society, they have little confidence that we can achieve solutions by depending on individual growth. As Henry Kissinger recently stated:

> We have tended to suppose that every problem must have a solution and that good intentions somehow guarantee good results. Utopia was seen not as a dream but as a logical destination if only we travelled the right road. Our generation's the first to find that the road is endless and that in travelling it we find not Utopia but ourselves. (277, p. 81)

Kissinger implies that in discovering ourselves we reveal only an interminable source of problems. Those individuals throughout society who are truly discovering themselves, however, are finding within themselves vast, unanticipated reservoirs of energy, intelligence and satisfaction. If we believe we have discovered ourselves by simply accepting the apparently interminable individual and social problems which history records, we do great injustice to the concept of self-discovery. All of us are familiar with the extent to which our society reflects individual dishonesty, manipulation, fear, anger, frustration, prejudice and hatred. The clear indication of the evidence presented in this book, however, is that these characteristics result from individual stress and are not intrinsic to the self.

Transcendental Meditation allows the individual to tap a deep inner resource of creative intelligence and unfold the spontaneous expression of full human capacities. Contrary to the long-held belief that people must be ever restricted to conditioned personalities and confined to suffering, mounting evidence suggests that fulfillment is everyone's birthright. If we fail to appreciate the energy and intelligence inherent in the human nervous system because we lack a means to tap our full potential, our vision of social change must remain dim.

That social change must begin with the individual is an age-old thesis dating from the Vedic tradition in the East and at least from the time of Plato in the West. Yet, few practical people have been able to take this thesis seriously because of the apparent impossibility of fostering significant change in the individual. No matter what the economic or political structure, individuals seem to have remained essentially the same throughout history. What they have remained is not very encouraging. As Konrad Lorenz points out, man's instinctual aggressive nature has not changed throughout history.[175] R. D. Laing laments that selfish, destructive tendencies have led men to kill "perhaps 100,000,000 of their fellow men in the last fifty years" (163, p. 28).

The visionaries who discern a great social transformation now in progress reject the idea that individuals must remain mired in their selfish destructive personalities. More importantly, a large number of individuals have already begun to experience and express significant positive changes in all aspects of their behavior. For example, over one-half million people practice TM, which alleviates stress, promotes full physical and mental health, enriches human relationships and unfolds full creative intelligence. All of these changes in the individual suggest corresponding effects on society. *The collective result of many people all over the world practicing TM promises more than just many people feeling healthy and functioning effectively. A global qualitative improvement in all aspects of individual life must lead to a parallel improvement in all aspects of the social environment, including the design of social institutions.*

The social effects of TM are taking place in two ways. First, individual meditators inspire change in those around them. As meditators find stress, anxiety and hostility diminishing within themselves, they dampen tension and defensiveness in others.[207, 213] Meditators' energy, optimism, acceptance and love catalyze positive feelings in others, including nonmeditators.[70, 71] When nonmeditators observe changes in their friends who start TM, they generally take up the practice. This effect is responsible for the sustained growth of the TM movement, which has more than doubled its size each year.

Until recently, the major social impact of the TM movement has emerged from such one-to-one interactions. Within the past two years, however, a second channel has opened for TM to catalyze significant positive social change. A number of social institutions have begun incorporating TM into their daily operations. Medical and rehabilitative institutions are discovering the therapeutic value of TM. Business and government are finding that TM may be the most effective personnel enrichment program available. Educational institutions are beginning to find that Science of Creative Intelligence courses not only inspire students, but improve learning ability to such an extent that students show significant improvements in performance.

The prospect of unfolding full creative intelligence in every individual gives substance to the vision of great transformation current among our most insightful social critics. By tapping his full measure of creative intelligence, an individual may begin to reflect humanity's highest ideals in his daily life. The prospect of our whole society rising to express these ideals through the growth of individuals is no longer an outlandish dream, but a significant process now ongoing in our society.

The great transformation of our society is silently in progress. TM is spreading extremely quickly but also very quietly. Though we sounded a note of cultural crisis in our first chapter, we have shown that the practice of TM has positive influence on all areas of life affected by the psychophysiological challenge of technology. We have presented scientific evidence that through TM people can find relief from stress, can lead meaningful lives and can rise to fulfillment. Such individual development offers the key to solving modern man's social problems.

We cannot, however, forecast specific changes which will result in social institutions from the widespread practice of TM, for any specific political or economic projections would stand as prescriptions for social change similar, by their prescriptive nature, to the many social prescriptions which have failed in the past. With the widespread unfoldment of individual creative intelligence, our social institutions will not change suddenly, but rather will grow with individual insights into how we can better achieve our highest material and spiritual objectives. Though such change will not occur suddenly, it may well take place quickly because of the accelerated pace of technological society. While the significance of the Industrial Revolution took a century to become apparent, the significance of TM may become clear within one or two decades. We can already report the preliminary results of TM's application in various institutions and the logistics of a plan which Maharishi has developed to make TM available to everyone on earth.

TM AND PRISON REFORM

Of all the current social problems troubling our nation, crime is among the most malignant, threatening and intractable. No matter how much money local, state and federal agencies spend on crime prevention, the crime rate continues to rise.

To deal with crime, we must identify its roots. Sociologists and psychologists have gathered abundant data on the mental, social and environmental factors which apparently contribute to criminal behavior. Poverty, poor family life and drug abuse are the three most frequently cited causes of crime. Despite these analyses, however, an effective method of reducing crime is not as yet forthcoming. The failure of all current methods in widespread use indicates either that treatment programs do not resolve the problems to which they are addressed or else that the analyses of the crime problem have failed to identify its real root.

Maharishi has offered a simple but incisive analysis of criminal behavior which suggests that not only has the root of crime not yet been identified but also that treatment programs have not effectively addressed the problems they were intended to correct. Regardless of the contribution of social or psychological factors to criminal attitudes, antisocial behavior may be explained in terms of one cause—individual weakness. Maharishi writes:

> Crime is evidently a shortcut to satisfy a craving—a shortcut which goes beyond normal and legal means. . . . Crime, delinquency and the different patterns of anti-social behavior arise from deep discontent of . . . a weak mind. (185, p. 322)

Although innumerable environmental influences may weaken an individual, the cause of crime lies in an individual's inability to fulfill personal needs through acceptable behavior. To attack crime directly we must find a method of strengthening the individual's ability to fulfill his natural and legitimate desires through legal means.

Because TM strengthens the individual emotionally, physically and intellectually, penologists have begun exploring its possible value in abating the cause of criminal behavior. Whether or not TM can strengthen a criminal sufficiently to relieve his need to commit crimes must be resolved through controlled experiment. Toward this end, researchers have completed several pilot studies of TM in prisons and several other studies are currently under way.

An inmate population provides a perfect situation for testing the value of TM in reducing criminal behavior. Though state and federal correctional agencies have made great efforts within their limited budgets to develop programs which will rehabilitate prisoners, abundant evidence discloses the failure of these programs to relieve the inmates' need to commit crime. The problem of recidivism is clearly described in this extract from the 1971 Congressional Record:

> Two thirds of the 200,000 inmates currently incarcerated in our federal and state prisons are "alumni" of other institutions. Of the 100,000 prisoners released from confinement each year and returned to society, seventy-five percent again commit crimes and return to confinement. (16, p. 2)

Why are current penal rehabilitation programs so ineffective? The success of any rehabilitation program is dependent on the motivation of the participant to make changes within himself. If an individual has a positive attitude toward his own development, then any regimen he follows is likely to be effective; if not, nothing will bring improvement. As one prisoner put it, "Treatment is unnecessary, because if I want to change, I will; if not, I won't."

It is difficult to motivate prison inmates because they experience any rehabilitation program through the same complex of attitudes which motivated their former maladaptive life-styles. Whatever misguided belief or inner tension previously prevented an inmate from creating a useful life in relation to his world will continue to operate during his exposure to rehabilitation programs. The problem of rehabilitation remains what it has always been: to facilitate without coercion the development of attitudes and values within the individual which are life-supporting and which lead to behavior that is fulfilling. But change of such fundamental attitudes has proven almost impossible. Resentment and despair characterize our prisons.

Given such a situation, the practice of TM might well be useful in triggering inmates' motivation for self-improvement, especially their acceptance of programs of job training and education which would be useful to them upon their release from prison. Unlike other programs which attempt to solve a specific problem or develop a limited skill, the practice of TM produces a constellation of effects which markedly facilitate learning and promote general psychological well-being. Because these effects are physiological, resulting from individual practice of the technique rather than verbal communication, they are felt immediately. The resulting experience of an increase in personal satisfaction through TM whets the inmate's appetite for self-esteem and further satisfaction. Such growth can be achieved only through positive behavior. Having grown in ability through the normalizing effects of TM, a prisoner finds he easily achieves of his own volition what he had found difficult or even impossible in conventional rehabilitation programs.

Because TM is extremely easy to learn and to practice, it takes considerably less time to implement than other rehabilitation programs. Furthermore, TM programs designed specifically for rehabilitation are inexpensive and easy to introduce into any prison setting. Nevertheless, any new program requires support from prison officials, particularly in its early stages. It may be a necessary prerequisite for TM rehabilitation programs that some members of the staff actually learn TM. At Haney Correctional Center near Vancouver, four SIMS teachers instructed sixteen inmates. However, prison officials did not allow the instructors to maintain a proper follow-up program. Despite these major drawbacks, half the prisoners are still meditating.

At the Federal Correctional Institution in Lompoc, California, nearly fifty men and several staff members have learned TM. Under the direction of Monty Cunningham, Instructional Systems Developer for the Bureau of Prisons, the program has generated considerable interest and some intriguing data. Due to lack of funding, Cunningham was able to supervise the program only in his spare time. Though the program was not initially designed as an experiment, several tests were administered in order to quantify certain effects of TM in the prison setting. Cunningham used the State Trait Anxiety Inventory (STAI) as the major test instrument. It was administered a month before and a month after the inmates began TM. A control group, whose members became interested in starting TM through hearsay from the experimental subjects, also took the test. The scores of both groups were virtually the same beforehand, with norms close to the statewide norm and no significant statistical difference between the two groups. After three months Cunningham found several highly significant differences between the groups, and established a clear relationship between regular TM practice and improved STAI scores.[51] Nearly all of the meditating subjects showed less anxiety than the nonmeditating controls. Regular meditators were the least anxious and the average number of missed meditations was directly reflected in the STAI scores.

The inmates also took a self-evaluation test in which they were asked to rate words that described changes in their lives since the beginning of the test period. Of the forty items on the scale, the practitioners of TM ranked highest decrease in nervousness, irritability, restlessness, boredom, depression, desire for drugs and use of nonprescribed drugs; and increase in physical health, improvement in emotional stability, overall harmony and happiness. The correlation between a high score on this scale and the regularity of practice of TM was very significant.

After only three weeks of practicing TM, meditating inmates were pleased with the results of the technique. This statement exemplifies their reaction:

> The program should be continued for obvious reasons: this is a stress-filled environment. So is the world of cities and human habitation (outside), but here stress is more concentrated and definitely more blatant. I have noticed, in myself and others instructed about the same time, a decided decline in the adverse effect tension can have on me. Little by little I myself am becoming less tense, experiencing a little more peace, quiet, rest and relaxation, but the finest possible quality that meditation has allowed me to see the possibility of is an autonomy; living in a world full of clatter, absurdity, and tension as a peaceful human. This feeling should be going around.

The administration is also pleased with the program. Dr. Scott Moss, Coordinator of Mental Health, is now supervising the ongoing program with the cooperation of the Education Department. Plans are being implemented to make TM available to the entire inmate population.

Scientific reports of TM's general effects and the availability of funds for new approaches to rehabilitation have led some prison officials to design programs specifically aimed at measuring the rehabilitative value of TM for inmates. Orme-Johnson studied the effects of meditation on prisoners at the La Tuna Federal Penitentiary in Texas.[219] In this project, twelve addict-prisoners were taught TM and were compared to a control group. Orme-Johnson found that the meditating group decreased their level of stress as measured by spontaneous Galvanic Skin Response (G.S.R.) (Chart 23). Although the group which began TM started with a higher stress level than the controls, after two months of regular practice the meditators' stress level was considerably lower than the level of the controls. The meditating prisoners also showed reduced stress levels as measured by the Minnesota Multiphasic Personality Inventory. Abnormal values on the MMPI for psychasthenia and social introversion, factors strongly connected with criminal behavior, showed normalization after two months of TM (Chart 23). The more regular their meditations, the greater their physiological and psychological improvement.

Anthropologist David Ballou[16] recently completed a twelve-month pilot program at the Stillwater State Prison, a maximum security institution in Minnesota. Ballou collected psychological and behavioral data on sixty-four inmates who were instructed in TM. During the first several months Ballou spent considerable time acquainting himself with the activities, problems and viewpoints of nonmeditating inmates through informal daily contact and personal and written interviews. The inmate population readily accepted TM. Initially, implementation of the project was limited by the prison administration to a special cell block containing 125 prisoners already under treatment for problems of drug dependency or emotional disturbance. Seventy-five of these men elected to attend an introductory lecture in

TM, and of these, fifty signed up to begin the practice. Each inmate instructed was required to:

1) Have at least one more year of his sentence to serve.
2) Agree to full participation in the course of instruction and follow-up program, and to cooperate in the data-gathering procedures.
3) Refrain from the use of nonprescription drugs for at least fifteen days prior to personal instruction.
4) Pay a course fee of $1.00.

Initially, thirty men were trained in TM. Separate control groups were formed of both those desiring to begin the practice and of those who had no wish to learn meditation. By the time the project had been under way for two months, however, over a hundred inmates located in other cell block areas had requested to begin the practice. As a result, the prison administration agreed to permit TM courses for the whole inmate population. TM instructors conducted four other courses and trained a total of sixty-four inmates during the year. Questionnaires and inmate files revealed no particular distinguishing traits among those who desired to participate in the TM program in terms of age, education, socioeconomic background, race, IQ or crime.

The instructors conducted group meetings on a regular basis for the meditating inmates: every night for the first month after instruction, then weekly for the next three months, then biweekly for the duration of the project. During these sessions the teachers provided checking, group meditation, advanced lectures and discussion. Despite noisy, confusing conditions, inadequate facilities for group meetings, and a wide variety of distracting circumstances, about eighty-five percent of the sixty-four inmates who completed the course (seven started but did not complete it) continued to meditate regularly.

Shortly before the end of the project, each meditator was asked to evaluate the practice of TM in a written questionnaire. Although data were not collected from about half the project participants who had been paroled or transferred to other institutions, virtually all those responding indicated the following:

1. Extremely favorable general reactions to the TM program: "I was turned on to the program by a friend that said it was a trip to find oneself. You couldn't buy it or take it from me now."

2. Better understanding and communication with self and others, less loneliness and depression and more sociability: "I find that I relate to others better because I seem to communicate more and understand more of others as I learn and understand more of myself. . . . Relationships on a positive level are fantastic for me because I have never cared about others or for anything but me."

3. A 200% increase in participation in sports, educational and other voluntary activities.

4. Effective participation in programs like group therapy or drug dependency classes through a new openness to knowledge.
   "The difference is a difference in myself due to TM. I have found a lever and the *want* to betterment. . . . In the therapy group meetings it has made an accomplishment because I notice . . . a willingness which I never had or cared to have. . . . I have accomplished a lot in my program, but TM found it and the piece was placed!"

5. Greater work efficiency and effectiveness.
   "I take an interest and pride in my work now, before I just didn't care."

6. Sharp decrease in the use of nonprescription hallucinogenic, opiate and barbiturate drugs, and alcohol and cigarettes. A similar reduction in the use of prescribed medication, particularly sedatives and tranquilizers.
   "Because of my addiction problem I had a hard time communicating with others, but with meditation I have gained an insight of myself and found I wasn't so bad. One of the main reasons I used drugs was because they gave me self-confidence to do things, and made me feel like someone. Now I have these things without the use of chemicals."

7. Better physical health and fewer days of illness in the months after starting TM.[16]

Such glowing reports might be suspect in a prison population, where prisoners quickly learn to say whatever the staff wants to hear, but other measures substantiate alleged changes. Observation and interviews, conversations with inmate meditators, nonmeditators and prison staff over a period of several months led Ballou to conclude that meditating inmates adapted more easily and successfully to prison life than nonmeditating inmates. Data from two psychological tests also supported these findings. On the State Trait Anxiety Inventory, anxiety in the meditating group as compared to control group was found to decrease quickly during the initial two-week period after TM instruction. Thereafter, meditators' anxiety maintained a new, low level. Results from the other questionnaire, a measure of attitudes developed specifically for the Stillwater project, indicated that TM helped inmates to relieve some of the negative emotions generated by the prison environment and to reinterpret unpleasant experiences so that they were less disturbing.

One inmate counselor reported an almost complete cessation of violent outbursts in a patient who started meditation. Although evidence was not conclusive on this point, there was a distinct decrease in the number of disciplinary write-ups earned by some meditators. No meditator showed an increase in disciplinary write-ups during the course of the project as compared to the previous year. In view of the high correlation which has been found between number of disciplinary write-ups and recidivism, one might reasonably predict a lowering of recidivism among meditating prisoners. More long-term research to test this hypothesis is now being planned.

An important lesson learned from these studies is the absolute necessity for a strong follow-up program for the inmates after their initial instruction in order to assure their continued practice of the technique. Though some prison administrators originally feared that a TM program might disrupt the daily routine, the data suggest that TM programs encourage prisoners to respect prison routine. Because a TM program requires only a place for prisoners to meditate twice daily and meet regularly with a TM instructor, the program does not violate security procedures or require unusual attention from prisoners or staff. In addition, TM programs may be designed for staff as well as prisoners, allowing for a generalized reduction of tension between the two groups. Anecdotal reports about improved inmate-staff relations again suggest that where TM is introduced to prisoners it should also be made available to staff.[16, 51]

On the basis of this pilot data, several studies are scheduled to begin at other penal institutions. A state funded one year project to involve 100 inmates at the Men's Correctional Facility in Somers, Connecticut, was planned for November 1974. At the California Men's Colony in San Luis Obispo, two staff psychologists have begun TM and are seeking funding for a proposed TM program. At the Terminal Island Federal Correctional Institution in Los Angeles, the Narcotic Addicts Rehabilitation Act (NARA) in-care staff have taken a TM course and are planning to introduce TM to the inmates as soon as possible. The NARA after-care programs at the Suicide Prevention Center and Center for the Study of Self-Destructive Behavior in Los Angeles will provide data over a ten-year period to compare meditating and nonmeditating ex-narcotics addicts. This program will provide interesting long-term physiological data on various indices, including hormonal changes, blood chemistry and behavioral patterns. Other programs are being considered by several state penal systems.

TM AND EDUCATION

Because America's education system is our central agency for human development, TM may have its greatest social impact through application in our schools. In the search for new methods of making learning meaningful, college and secondary school educators have begun incorporating credit courses on the practice, theory and implications of TM in their curriculums. Generally called the Science of Creative Intelligence (SCI), such courses have been offered at over thirty colleges. Over two dozen public and private high schools now offer similar courses designed specifically for high-school students. Research projects are under way in high schools and colleges to measure the impact of Science of Creative Intelligence courses on students' academic performance, social relationships, psychological health, creativity and intelligence.

Unlike courses which aim at developing competence in one branch of knowledge or a specific skill, SCI courses develop the individual's capacity to learn and his ability to interrelate knowledge from various fields. The need for an interdisciplinary approach to learning has long been recognized in the face of rising criticisms from students that the knowledge they absorb is irrelevant. Teachers have voiced similar criticisms about the futility apparently inherent in the knowledge explosion: no person can keep abreast of developments in his own field, let alone in unrelated disciplines. While technological society certainly requires people equipped with specialized skills, the continued progress of our society depends upon individuals grounded in comprehensive knowledge which enables them to see coherence in, and give direction to, modern life.

From the time of Plato, Western educators have projected two fundamental goals: the integration of all knowledge and the full development of the individual student. The achievement of these goals has never been more crucial than it is today, when the knowledge explosion not only threatens to fragment all learning but demands unprecedented learning capacities from every student. Almost thirty years ago Ortega y Gasset eloquently described this challenge:

> It has come to be an imminent problem, one which mankind can no longer evade, to invent a technique adequate to cope with the accumulation of knowledge now in our possession. Unless some practicable way is found to master this exuberant growth, man will eventually become its victim. (221, pp. 90–91)

Such a practicable way is now available through SCI, which locates the integrative basis of knowledge in intelligence itself. SCI is the theoretical and applied study of intelligence as the potentiality which facilitates man's increasing comprehension of all fields of knowledge. As Seymour Migdal, Dean of the College of Arts and Sciences at MIU, points out, however, what makes SCI the supremely feasible way to master the exponential growth of knowledge is its practical aspect, TM. Through TM the student becomes intimately familiar with those basic laws which govern and structure every field of knowledge within the structure of his own consciousness.[201]

Many educational experiments have aimed at integrating knowledge and increasing learning capacity, but none has realized more than limited success. On elementary, secondary and college levels, these experiments have concentrated primarily on modifying such external aspects of the teaching process as classroom scheduling, teaching styles, methods of presenting material and physical school design. While many colleges and some high schools now encourage interdisciplinary and independent study, only a small minority of students have proven capable of successfully taking advantage of these programs. The general limitations of these approaches to revitalizing the educational process have led researchers like Douglas Heath of Haverford College to look within the student for the key to fulfilling the highest ideals of education.

> My understanding of man tells me the deepest source of the creative-aesthetic impulse is in our less conscious and more primitive inner world, and that we make contact with it through a receptive meditative attitude. Not until we learn how to reach and touch and then channel and witness our inner voices will we be truly educable. If a youth learns how to develop such accessibility to his inner powers and integrates such forces and insights with more social modes of communication, then I have no fear for him. He will have developed a capacity for resiliency and autonomy that will enable him to cure his estrangements and create his own adaptations to his unknown society of the future. He will come into control of his growth. . . . Within a few years, schools and colleges will be offering courses on meditation. Fanciful? Not at all. One of the exciting frontiers of psychological research is the demonstration that man can secure much greater access to and control over his consciousness through meditation than most of us have thought possible. (117, pp. 365–367)

Sidney Reisberg, a dean of the State University of New York at Albany, voiced similar feelings about where we should look for the most powerful means of revitalizing education:

There have been countless attempts to improve the quality of education in America, which have resulted in many important changes, innovations and improvements. Yet the billions of dollars spent by private foundations and public agencies in the last twenty-five years appear to leave a great many teachers and students unfulfilled. Teachers as well as students find themselves overwhelmed with a mass of information, knowledge and thoughts for which they can find no connections. The Science of Creative Intelligence suggests that the unifying process exists within each individual and that each person can learn how to be in touch with that process within himself. Thus, the Science of Creative Intelligence seems able to provide a missing ingredient that can give focus and meaning to education. (242, p. 854)

Because the Science of Creative Intelligence offers a means of expanding learning capacity through its practical aspect, TM, it differs substantially from previous efforts at reforming education. SCI begins by addressing the student's need to unfold his full measure of energy, intelligence, creativity and satisfaction. From this experiential foundation, SCI provides a coherent framework for the individual, society and knowledge itself. The basic premise of SCI is that *knowledge is structured in consciousness*. This simple principle reflects the point that the nature of a person's awareness determines both what he experiences in the world around him and what he can know. As an individual grounds his awareness in the field of pure creative intelligence within himself, he gains access to that level within his consciousness on which all knowledge is integrated. Thereby, he develops an intuitive grasp of what he knows in its most fundamental form and begins to perceive subtle interrelationships between different disciplines.

The first academic courses in SCI resulted from the demands of meditating students who sought a coherent theoretical framework for their changing appraisal of life's possibilities. Meditators have reported a growing disenchantment with the various negative assumptions of many modern world views. Such assumptions, they explain, are incompatible with their own increasingly positive experience. Simultaneously, meditating students enjoy an increased ability to understand and assimilate what they learn. The following statement by a twenty-year-old student who was instrumental in setting up an SCI course at Yale is typical:

> TM has provided a unification and direction of my studies. It has given me an integration of myself. It also provides a philosophical and practical context into which I can fit all my different studies. I can take a philosophy course and I can see that Heidegger was probably aware of consciousness expansion, or I have the direct experience of what is mentioned in a poetry class about Blake. Which is really amazing, it never used to happen.

The first course in the Science of Creative Intelligence was given by Jerry Jarvis at Stanford University in 1970 and attracted the largest undergraduate enrollment of any new course ever taught there. Subsequently, many similar programs have been offered at such schools as the University of Colorado, Universities of California at Sacramento, Los Angeles and Humboldt, University of Massachusetts, Goddard, Colby, Columbia, Harvard and Yale. SCI courses have been offered in adult education as well. One three-month extension course at the University of California at Santa Barbara reversed a reported characteristic attrition rate of 75 percent by doubling its enrollment while in progress.

College level SCI courses have presented TM and its effects in a highly interdisciplinary context. One of the authors, Michael Cain, taught the course at Yale which brought medical researchers, psychologists, philosophers, political scientists, astronomers, biologists, art historians and artists together into an interactive exploration of creative intelligence and its practical applications. The primary goal of this course was to integrate a wide range of knowledge through a model of consciousness derived from the experience and theory of TM. On this basis the students were able to formulate a systematic description of the pure field of creative intelligence in relation to a variety of academic disciplines.

Students in such courses tend to enjoy their work and do it well. They report that SCI offers a positive framework for their knowledge and a meaningful alternative to the reductive assumptions underlying other aspects of their curriculum. Students have also evidenced the development of internalized learning goals which they pursued effectively, often through ingenious uses of the specialized resources of the university. An increased sense of meaning and resulting fascination with academic subjects is reflected in statements by students who took the Yale course.

One junior, somewhat disenchanted with school, who began TM while taking the course, said:

> Since I began meditating, my whole perspective on school has changed. I was thinking of dropping out, but now I am beginning to see the purpose of being here in terms of my own growth toward fulfillment. The relationships of material in this course have made me think seriously of switching into pre-med.

Another student, a sophomore who had been meditating for several months prior to taking the course, commented:

> This course in SCI has added a whole new dimension to my academic life. Though I found TM helpful right from the beginning, this course has really opened a new horizon of knowledge for me. I'm seeing relationships between my courses which I never saw before. And yesterday, I proposed an independent study project in English based on some principles of SCI. My professor really liked my idea.

Teachers of college-level courses in SCI corroborate these reports. This report from a thirty-six-year-old English professor from University of California at Humboldt, who was a four-year meditator, is typical:

> Teaching SCI has provided a tremendously educational experience, of having to think through one's discipline and rediscover its relevance. You have to rethink your field. The classroom experience was tremendous. Meditating students want to learn. They rightfully consider everything they learn relevant to their own evolution. It's very satisfying to the teacher to teach an integrative course which relates the profound experience of meditation to his field. Such teaching helps one's own growth, helps the students and enlivens one's discipline. The only problem is that the students are so lively, so intelligent that you have to be fantastically prepared.

Interest in the Science of Creative Intelligence grew so rapidly between 1969 and 1972 that during the summer of 1971 an international university was established to offer a complete program of higher education based on SCI. Incorporated in early 1972, Maharishi International University (MIU) is now offering bachelors and masters degree programs at the main Fairfield, Iowa, campus as well as throughout many U.S. cities and foreign countries. MIU professors, most of whom left teaching positions with schools from all over the U.S. and Europe to join the MIU staff, believe that SCI gives a foundation to education which makes learning meaningful and successful. A thirty-five-year-old MIU literature professor, meditating three years, describes this experience:

> SCI puts the basis back into education. The experience of teaching here at MIU fulfills the ideal I had in mind when I became a teacher. The whole process of education, grounded in the experience of evolving awareness, rises to its full glory. You can see the purpose for everything. The involvement and tremendous success of the students makes every aspect of the program extraordinary, and its integrative aspect insures that none of the learning that goes on here will be inert, but that instead it will serve toward the real intellectual and personal growth of the student.

Similarly, an MIU professor of mathematics, a thirty-eight-year-old, who has been meditating four years, recounts:

> I've been teaching for a while, I taught at Harvard and I've taught here, and in terms of education, I feel that what I've been able to do here with SCI is extremely useful. Extremely subtle concepts of mathematics can be effectively presented to beginning students. Very abstract ideas and recent mathematical developments like mathematical logical and set theory can be presented in a readily intelligible way to meditating students through SCI. Without having any background in mathematics, they can master the most abstract principles, and through this integrative vision, understand these principles in a way that even mathematicians don't understand them. And all this knowledge is so lively to them that I think they will find rich ways of applying it.

Students enrolled at MIU are very enthusiastic about their program. For example, one twenty-five-year-old student who has been meditating three years says:

> I majored in sociology at Brandeis, but I wasted my time while there. Studying SCI at MIU has been a tremendous experience. I feel that I've gained in a few weeks all the value I had hoped to gain from four years of college, not only in terms of knowledge but also in terms of being able to think. The experience of TM is essential to this process since in order to know anything intelligence is necessary. The more available intelligence there is, the more meaning there is in any field one is studying. And, by taking each subject in the light of the unfolding subtleties of intelligence itself, one really sees how the same basic laws which are applicable to one's personal experience are being manifested in creation and expressed in different fields. What I'm learning seems to be completely integrated into my whole life.

MIU has developed an innovative college curriculum. Along with learning TM, the first year begins with a month-long, in-depth examination of Maharishi's video-taped SCI course as an introduction to the basic principles of consciousness and knowledge. This course provides an integrative focus for the rest of the first year curriculum involving the study of twenty-four fields of knowledge in intensive one-week courses. In addition, students participate in four one-month advanced courses and become certified TM teachers by the end of the first year. Each student begins his second and third year with a two-month period of field work. Along with more advanced courses in personal experience, the second year consists of month-long, in-depth courses in physics, mathematics, biology, psychology, literature, and organization and administration. Thereafter students choose any of a variety of majors from the physical or social sciences, humanities or arts. Undergraduate reaction to this new program has been extremely favorable.

To test the innumerable glowing reports of enhanced academic performance through SCI, Roy W. Collier of the University of Hawaii studied the grade point averages of college students before and after they began TM.[47] He derived his data from the records of past student bodies at the University of Hawaii. Since the study was based on past records, in that it was conducted after the data were complete, students' performances were not affected by the study in any way. Out of twenty-nine subjects contacted, only seven met the criterion of having been in college for a full semester or more preceding and three semesters following their instruction in TM.

Using a grade point average on the standard four-point scales (4 = A, 3 = B, 2 = C, 1 = D), Collier charted students' mean cumulative grade point ratio (Chart 25). Collier notes, "Historical experience indicates that with the omission of the first semester's work the average of [college] students' grades remains essentially level throughout the academic experience." In his data, however, the mean rose 0.17 points in the first semester after the start of TM, leveled in the second semester and continued to rise for the third semester. On the basis of a similar study at several American universities, Orme-Johnson and Heaton have reported an even greater improvement in grade point average among meditating students (Chart 25).[117a]

The use of TM in high schools has been given a significant boost by the widely publicized effects of TM on decreased drug use. Maharishi has formulated a syllabus for teaching SCI in junior and senior high schools. At the University of California at Humboldt in August 1972, 130 high-school teachers attended a one-month course designed to train them to teach SCI to their students. Half of them received stipends from a $21,000 grant from the National Institute of Mental Health which was interested in exploring the application of TM to schools. After returning to their jobs, these teachers reported an improved ability to teach, increased creativity in their work and greater patience. They also confirmed that students who take up TM tend to decrease their drug use drastically.

Several school systems, including the York School System in Toronto and the Dade County School System in Miami, and many individual schools, have adopted pilot programs in SCI and TM. One ambitious program of introducing TM into a school system came in the suburban town of Eastchester, New York. Superintendent of Schools Francis Driscoll has written about his experience, providing several useful guidelines for other schools contemplating this step.[63] After hearing about TM and research about its effects from a TM teacher, Driscoll became convinced that it would be useful for high school students. Also, he found that it was administratively feasible to introduce TM into the school, as it involved no religious or philosophic beliefs. However, anticipating that such an innovative program might encounter community resistance, he began with an extensive public information program.

For six months, teachers of TM talked to community clubs, the PTA and parents' groups. Afterward, in January 1971, an introductory lecture was presented to the student body. By this time most of the community was aware of the nature of TM and its relevance to the school. Four teachers were available to students for a day after the lecture to answer their questions on a one-to-one basis. Another lecture was presented to the faculty and their spouses; in a short period twelve percent of the faculty received TM instruction. Many students followed suit. Classrooms were made available to TM teachers after school for follow-up sessions. TM was also introduced into adult education classes. The use of school space for TM programs and lectures continues, with many community members learning to meditate. Superintendent Driscoll has observed that "meditating students experience improved relationships with families, teachers, and friends, and often improve their grades as well."[63]

In response to the highly favorable reports of TM's value for high-school students, four high schools in the Hartford, Connecticut, area began offering an SCI course for credit in February 1974. This program was designed as a research project and funded by a local Hartford foundation. The project will run for two years and involves a range of student populations from an inner-city school to one of the most prestigious private schools in Connecticut. Researchers responsible for evaluating the effect of the SCI courses are measuring changes in academic performance, attendance, teachers' evaluation of the students' behavior, parents' evaluation of the students' behavior, and students' self-evaluation. Data gathered after students completed a one semester SCI course showed a significant improvement in grade point average and a significant reduction in anxiety levels. Grade point averages and anxiety levels for the control group remained unchanged. Further data on this project will be available in mid-1975.

TM courses have also been prepared for primary-level students and implemented by a few teachers. Though no systematic results have been published to date, anecdotal reports indicate that this program improves creativity. In one instance, a teacher of TM asked a group of young children to make drawings. They were then taught the children's technique of meditation. After learning the technique, the group was given a second opportunity to make a series of pictures. The contrast between the first series of constricted though varied images and the later series of expansive and colorful patterns suggested a quantum increase in the students' ability to apply their creative resources. This report suggests that child psychologists should investigate the effect of the children's technique of TM on early cognitive development and creativity.

One of the most forceful recognitions of the value of SCI for education came from a resolution of the Illinois House of Representatives, passed in May 1972:

> That all educational institutions, especially those under State of Illinois jurisdiction, be strongly encouraged to study the feasibility of courses in Transcendental Meditation and the Science of Creative Intelligence on their campuses and their facilities; and be it further . . . resolved that a copy of this resolution be sent to: the Superintendent of Public Instruction, the deans of all state universities, the Department of Mental Health, State of Illinois, to inform them of the great promise of the program herein mentioned.[129]

Further indication of the widespread recognition of TM came when Maharishi was invited to address the 28th Annual Conference of the American Association for Higher Education in Chicago in March 1973. Increasing enthusiasm reflects the promise that TM holds as an educational tool to improve human performance and the quality of human life. In the near future, we may expect many educational institutions to follow the leadership of MIU and those forward-looking schools presently teaching SCI.

TM AND BUSINESS

The health of any business firm and the well-being of our society as a whole depend upon growth. Implicit in this demand are two unavoidable personnel needs. First, with the complex of individual, environmental and social demands pressuring business firms from all sides, the need for vital, foresighted and creative executive leadership has never been greater than it is today. The notion of realizing one's full potential, both personally and professionally, is in common parlance among business leadership. Second, with the accelerating rate of technological development throughout business, the need for employees who can find meaning and success in adapting to repeated changes in their jobs has never been greater in history.

Although discussion of these needs is occupying more and more pages of business journals, few programs have proven successful in fulfilling these needs and none has achieved more than limited success in a relatively small number of firms. Nevertheless, business professionals admit the possibility of strengthening their organizations by encouraging individual growth. The insight that corporate expansion depends upon the quality of individual performance is indisputable. In complex organizations executives often find the pressures and stress of demanding responsibility limiting to their productivity and satisfaction. The inherent stress of organizational life has gained recognition as the enemy of executive health, intelligence, creativity and effective action. Correspondingly, the boredom felt by a vast majority of white- and blue-collar workers in our increasingly technological society is recognized as the enemy of productivity. Unless a method is found to make work more meaningful, management will face increasing absenteeism and job turnover as well as decreasing productivity and quality of performance.

To improve executive achievement and decrease organizational stress, management science has concentrated on the interaction between members of an executive team as an avenue for growth. Chris Argyris of Harvard Business School used the term "interpersonal competence" to describe the goal of his program of T-groups, whereby members of an executive team become aware of how they go about achieving a task together.[11] By becoming aware of their working relationships, executives develop competence in working with each other as well as their subordinates and overcome interpersonal habits which destroy effective working relationships. To improve employee performance and return meaning to work, Frederick Herzberg, Western Reserve psychologist, developed what he calls job enrichment, whereby jobs are redesigned by managers to give employees more responsibility and opportunity for achievement.[119] While these two approaches to individual growth in organizations have become popular enough to dominate the field of organizational development, great difficulties have arisen in applying these organizational growth programs. Only a small fraction of those interventions where T-groups or job enrichment programs were applied in business firms have proven successful. Organizations seem almost impervious to efforts to change their basic operating assumptions.

The Science of Creative Intelligence offers a unique approach to developing individuals in organizations. In 1973, well over 200 executives from the northeastern United States attended a symposium on "Transcendental Meditation and Management Enrichment" held at Rensselaer Polytechnic Institute in Hartford, Connecticut. Hans Laue, senior management scientist at Stanford Research Institute, summarized the unique value of SCI:

> Six of the most significant problems facing management today are mounting grievances, job alienation, increasing absenteeism, reduced productivity, lower quality of output, and lack of in-

novation. In searching for solutions to these "people problems" management has investigated them in detail. But these problems are only symptoms; they are not causes. They are symptoms of an underlying cause—the lack of full development of each individual working in an economic environment. To eliminate these problems we should attend to the cause, not merely the symptoms. The most effective treatment is to enable each individual to realize his dynamic potential; to maximize and make most intelligent use of his creative energies by practicing the methods of the Science of Creative Intelligence.

The complex of "people problems" facing business today may be traced to the lack of full individual development. Psychologists estimate that an average person uses no more than 5 percent of his full mental potential. SCI's approach to organizational development is to provide each member of the firm with a technique to tap unused inner resources of energy, intelligence, creativity and satisfaction.

Although management style may need improvement and jobs may need to be redesigned, the success of any effort to change an individual or his environment depends upon the degree of creative intelligence expressed through insightful thinking and efficient action. By making more creative intelligence directly available to the individual, problems with interpersonal relations and organizational stress decrease while clear thinking and comprehensive vision grow.

A personal account by Bill Hillman, an executive and meditator who began an extremely successful manufacturing firm, illustrates the reason why TM is growing in popularity among executives:

> Soon after I began meditating I noticed a clarity of mind that was, obviously, an asset in business situations where the responsibility of decision requires the careful weighing of many factors. Also of the utmost importance was the development of a reliable confidence in myself. In times of intensified emotional stress previous to meditation, I would often become stubborn and inflexible. This inflexibility was an asset in that it was one of the factors that allowed me to stand firm under criticism, and helped carry me along the paths that I thought to be the best, but it stemmed from a lesser state of personal

development. I now have the same or more determination but the roots are grounded in satisfaction and inner freedom. The feeling of reacting against has left, and in its place stands a firmness, growing inner peace and harmony.

Some of the immediately applicable changes I've felt include:

1. Increased organizational ability—capacity to take in ever larger amounts of data and carry more in the memory store.

2. Ease of concentration—my mind is developing more and more to its full capacity, one aspect being the ability to focus, or return to the rhythms of the present.

3. Speed of thought—the ability to draw quickly from accumulated knowledge, and piece connections in rapid-fire order benefits greatly and adds to the development of confidence.

4. Diminishing of the sense of working to get a shiny new set of wheels—watching this fade has its own brand of nostalgia, but the pleasure derived from work as its own reward supplants any desire to turn back. It is a pleasure to watch the business expand and provide a real service.

Overall, TM for me is of paramount importance in developing a fine state of personal tuning. This is of benefit in business and also in areas of deeply personal import.

Hillman's evaluation of TM has been seconded by executives all over the country. Alexander M. Poniotoff, founder and Chairman of the Board Emeritus of Ampex Corporation has stated:

Realizing that stress has a destructive effect on human life, the Foundation for Nutrition and Stress Research has studied various methods to relieve stress and tension. The methods we found in the past were very complicated and required extensive amounts of time. For this reason we found these methods inefficient in resolving the problem of human stress.

Recently as a technical director of the A.M.P. Bio-Research Institute, I became acquainted with and began practicing Transcendental Meditation. Even after a few months of practicing, I am convinced that TM could not only effectively and efficiently solve the problem of stress but could also help to develop many other positive qualities in human nature.

Over thirty executives at Arthur D. Little, one of the most creative management consulting firms, practice TM regularly and have set aside a room for meditation. Among the many large firms where executives practice TM are: Ampex, Monsanto, General Motors, Travelers Insurance, Sprague Electric, Westinghouse, Aetna Insurance, IBM, Kodak and Xerox. TM has recently become so popular that every major firm in the country may well have at least a few meditators in executive positions.

The American Foundation for the Science of Creative Intelligence offers SCI programs to business and government and teaches basic and advanced SCI courses for executives. These courses are offered through business schools and in firms directly. The Upper Avenue National Bank in Chicago, AT&T, Crocker National Bank in San Francisco, General Foods, St. Joe Mineral Co. in Pittsburgh, Tilley-Lewis Food Co. in California, the Detroit Engineering Society and Rensselaer Polytechnic Institute of Connecticut are among the organizations which have taken advantage of this course. Until SCI was formally presented to the business world through a series of symposiums throughout the United States in the spring of 1974, the SCI course for executives was offered only on a limited basis. Nevertheless, Dr. Francis Barrett, President of Management Concepts, Ltd., Canada, predicted as early as 1972 that "within 10 years the Science of Creative Intelligence will be taught in over 50% of North American executive training programs."

Until recently, evaluation of SCI in business was available only in relation to executive performance. Recent programs where SCI was introduced to employees have also offered the first evidence of the value of SCI in improving productivity, reducing absenteeism and decreasing job turnover. David Frew, director of the MBA program at Gannon College, has published a preliminary study on TM, productivity and job satisfaction.[84] He gave questionnaires to over one hundred regular meditators, to a control group and to both groups' supervisors and co-workers. Frew included supervisors and co-workers in order to evaluate not only meditators' self-report data but also how others at work saw them. His study is thus able to report not only subjective experience, but also on-the-job performance.

The meditators reported that they were more satisfied with their jobs, performed them better, felt less desire to change them, enjoyed better personal relationships and had more interest in rising to higher positions in the organization. Their data were significantly different from those furnished by a control group, and agreed generally with the reports of supervisors and co-workers. The close correspondence between the self-report by the meditators and their evaluation by supervisors lends strong support to the thesis that TM improves employee performance. His findings are summarized in Charts 26 and 27.

Frew produced interesting data concerning the type of organization and job in which people improve most upon the introduction of TM. People higher up in the organizational hierarchy, particularly in management levels, experience greater gains through TM. Also, the more democratically an organization is structured, the greater the gains which individuals experience from TM, particularly in the area of increased personal relationships and decreased job turnover. In a democratic structure, especially at upper levels, there are more opportunities for an individual to express himself through his work. The implication is not that people who work at lower levels of an organization do not change as a result of TM, but rather that their personal gains are not reflected as fully in their work because of the lack of opportunity to express new abilities. On the basis of this finding, Frew suggests that organizations need to tap the creative potential of lower-level employees.

One of the first projects formally introducing SCI to employees at the company's request took place in the summer of 1973 in a Connecticut bank. The First Federal Savings and Loan Association of Meriden began making TM available to their employees in June 1973. The project began at the request of the personnel director and executive vice-president, both of whom learned TM individually and found the technique very rewarding. Because this bank's assets doubled between 1970 and 1973 and are expected to double again by 1976, a need for personnel from within the bank's ranks capable of taking managerial responsibility is critical. The bank became interested in TM as a means of improving productivity and developing employees' ability to take responsibility. Of the one hundred employees at the bank, a group of twenty decided to enroll in the first course. Several weeks later, a course for management was also offered. All but one of the management team enrolled in the course.

Though the Board of Directors were originally quite skeptical about the value of a TM program, after evaluating it over a five-month period they granted approval to continue the program indefinitely. The mediators showed increased productivity, improved working relationships, decreased absenteeism and a general reduction in tension and anxiety. Many of the mediators reported improvement in their personal and family lives, often noting these benefits as the most rewarding gains from TM. In response to a request from the employees, the bank facilitated employees' spouses learning TM, and future courses in TM at the bank will be open to husbands and wives of bank employees.

The First Federal's program is continuing as part of their personnel development program and is under the direction of the personnel director. The bank's president, who became a meditator several weeks after the program began, fully supports the use of TM. He has said that the money spent on the TM program may be their "most well-spent personnel development dollars." Having completely eliminated a migraine headache which had plagued him for years before he learned TM, the president never misses morning and evening meditation. The bank's board of directors has several meditating members and may soon have a majority of meditators.

A similar case report of TM's value for improving productivity and working relationships comes from a large packaging company in Columbia, Tennessee. Rick Polk, chairman of the board of P. A. Medical Corporation, began TM in late 1972. After his first ten months of meditation he reported "less tension and stress and a greater clarity of mind . . . enabling more effective and intelligent decisions." He also found that his relations with other executives improved. As a result, he introduced TM to the management and employees of his company. As of September 1973 he reported:

> At the present time 50% of my administrative staff of one plant and 100% of the other (over 50 people) are practicing TM. We have found that the executives and the employees are working together more effectively and accomplishing greater productivity with significantly decreased absenteeism. The general atmosphere of the plant has markedly improved and the working conditions seem to be more pleasant and acceptable.

Polk does not hesitate to recommend TM as a management tool for increasing productivity and improving performance generally.

The number of large and small firms all over the country requesting SCI programs is growing rapidly because SCI offers a promising approach to unfolding latent potential. Wherever business finds an important resource ninety-five percent unused, time will not be wasted in tapping that resource. The ninety-five percent of untapped human potential is the most important resource available to any business firm.

A WORLD PLAN

On January 8, 1972 in Majorca, Spain, Maharishi inaugurated a World Plan to make SCI and TM available to everyone on earth. In a five-hour presentation of this plan before an audience of 2,000 prospective teachers of TM, Maharishi cited two fundamental reasons for his willingness to structure a program aimed at making TM universally available. First, the psychophysiological effects of TM have received such acclaim from the scientific community as to validate TM as a promising solution to the problems of modern life. Second, the steadily rising number of meditators interested in becoming teachers of TM and SCI suggests the possibility of training enough teachers to instruct everyone in the world.

Ever since the first substantial research on TM was published by Wallace in 1970, the scientific community has shown increasing respect for TM as a technique of deep rest. Only after the publication of over a dozen applied studies, however, have researchers felt comfortable with an understanding of TM as more than a relaxation technique. The significant improvements in meditators' physiological and psychological well-being and performance lend strong support to the thesis that TM is a means of gaining access to a great internal resource of creative intelligence. Because the process by which meditators discover inner resources of energy and intelligence unimaginable before starting TM is entirely definable physiologically, researchers have begun discussing TM as a scientific technique for both unfolding and studying man's full potential.[60, 68, 216]

Because TM must be taught on a person-to-person basis, the project of making TM available to 3.6 billion people presents staggering logistical problems. Though Maharishi has consistently projected the growth of TM in terms of the whole world's population, he has only begun insisting on the feasibility of world-wide practice of TM since it became apparent in 1972 that enough teachers could be trained to make TM universally available. At the beginning of 1972, 1,000 teachers of TM had been trained and another 2,000 were in training. In addition, an international university had been established which could formalize a program to begin training thousands of teachers all over the globe. Finally, video-tape technology had advanced sufficiently for the inexpensive mass production of easily used cassette video-taped instructional material.

The World Plan may be understood initially as a teacher-training program but also as encompassing the structure to make TM and SCI available to every individual on earth. Maharishi estimates that one teacher of SCI for every 1,000 people will be sufficient to insure the universal availability of TM. With the world's population presently at 3.6 billion, the World Plan calls for training 3.6 million teachers of SCI. To achieve this end, teacher-training centers are being established throughout the world, one World Plan center for each population area of one million people. Plans are now in progress for the establishment of 3,600 World Plan centers under the auspices of the World Plan Executive Council. Each teacher-training center will train 1,000 teachers of SCI, thereby fulfilling the goal of one SCI teacher for every one thousand people in each population area of one million people.

Though now primarily a program to train SCI teachers, the World Plan has seven goals which guide the application of SCI to social problems. These objectives are:

1. To develop the full potential of the individual.
2. To improve governmental achievements.
3. To realize the highest ideal of education.
4. To solve the problems of crime and all behavior that brings unhappiness to the family of man.
5. To maximize the intelligent use of the environment.
6. To bring fulfillment to the economic aspirations of the individual and society.
7. To achieve the spiritual goals of mankind in this generation.

These objectives stand among the ideals of innumerable social movements throughout history, yet they remain to be attained. Consequently, some critics refuse to take the World Plan seriously, lumping the growing social interest in the Science of Creative Intelligence with utopian political or religious movements of the past. Both the design and the achievements of the World Plan suggest that such critics fail to perceive the unique value of SCI and the unprecedented strategy of the World Plan.

To achieve these seven goals, Maharishi prescribes neither an ideology nor a moral system. He insists only that individuals experience pure creative intelligence through TM and understand that experience by means of critical scientific scrutiny. Never before in world history has any social movement aimed at providing a fundamentally identical experience to every man, much less the experience of a limitless inner reservoir of energy, intelligence and satisfaction. Every effort to give a new course to history in the past has depended on some system of belief, whether moral, religious, economic or political. Such movements have often turned to violence or coercion to uphold their beliefs. Transcendental Meditation, on the other hand, spreads by word of mouth. Meditators share their delight with their friends, whose interest in the technique naturally grows. When meditators begin to notice profound personal growth, they seek to study and understand this growth using the methods of modern science. The history of academic interest in TM, which gave rise to the formulation of its basic principles as a Science of Creative Intelligence, reflects just this growth pattern.

Many scholars and researchers first became interested in studying TM because of changes they observed in themselves or others through the practice. With the significance of these changes becoming increasingly apparent, the demand arose to understand how TM can have such a broad range of overwhelmingly positive effects on the individual. Growing interest in TM among professors from universities all over the world led to a series of thirteen international symposiums on SCI which were attended by over 10,000 individuals. Among the contributors to these symposia have been psychologist Frank Barron, engineer Harvey Brooks, Nobel Laureate chemist Melvin Calvin, political scientist Robert Dahl, environmental designer Buckminster Fuller, psychiatrist Bernard Glueck, physicist Gerson Goldhaber, educator Willis H. Harman, literary scholar Erika Lorenz, humanist Marshall McLuhan, astronomer Lloyd Motz, physiologist Hans Selye, biologist Robert Sinsheimer, school superintendent Dr. Francis Driscoll, Nobel Laureate William Glazer, General Franklin Davis, East Asian expert Alfred Jenkins, and Dr. Jonas Salk. These men were invited to discuss in terms of their own field, Maharishi's working definition of creative intelligence—"that impelling life force which manifests itself in the evolutionary process through creation of new forms and new relationships in the universe." The following interchange was typical:

> Dr. Calvin—Maharishi has recently said: "The whole of individual and cosmic life is fundamentally creative because it goes on and on; it is progressive, evolutionary; and the whole of life is fundamentally intelligent because it proceeds systematically, containing its own order and *unfolding in an overall orderly way.*" . . . This seemed to focus my attention on that part of our more recent work in which we were concerned with the processes of chemical evolution. . . .
>
> The important idea here is that the structure of an atom is

such that if one has those atoms present under the proper conditions (in the laboratory or in the primeval earth) with an energy input, they will combine in only certain kinds of ways. . . . Therefore there must be a molecular mechanism to decide which molecules are dominant over other ones. This requires the concept of stereospecific autocatalysis, [which] means that molecules are capable of inducing their own generation in a highly geometrically specific fashion.

Maharishi—It's so beautiful. One expression of an outstanding scientist innocently reveals the essential nature of creative intelligence. . . . The functioning of creative intelligence is such that under similar circumstances, similar results occur. Just this phenomenon explains why there is harmony in creation, not chaos. The apple tree grows only into apple fruit; it doesn't produce guavas. But if the circumstances changed, grafting could produce guavas. The infinite flexibility of creative intelligence maintains its stereospecific quality.

There is something definite: nothing is random, and it is this specific value of creative intelligence which automatically carries out evolution everywhere. (188, p. 31)

The first International Symposium on SCI ran for two weeks during July 1971 at the University of Massachusetts, Amherst. Perhaps the greatest achievement of this symposium was the formulation of initial plans to found a university which would examine every traditional academic discipline in light of SCI. Only eight months later, Maharishi International University was incorporated in California. Now offering an undergraduate and graduate degree program, MIU may be regarded as the key to the World Plan. To train millions of teachers of SCI on an international scale, a formal educational organization is necessary. MIU provides a structure in which individuals can study the pure theoretical aspect of the Science of Creative Intelligence in depth, as well as the relation of SCI to all fields of knowledge. One of the few truly international universities, MIU aims at making its core academic program available through extension centers throughout the world.

Impressive steps toward this end have already been achieved. Residential campuses are now operating in Fairfield, Iowa, and Seelisburg, Switzerland. Over 20,000 students have completed

Maharishi's video-taped SCI course since it first became available in the fall of 1972. And by the end of 1974, Maharishi had personally trained over 8,000 teachers of TM. Of these, 5,600 are from the United States. SCI courses are now taught in over 300 centers in the United States alone. Distinguished faculty members from MIU have prepared video-taped courses which present their fields of knowledge from the perspective of SCI. In the fall of 1973, more than a hundred specially trained and certified college-level teachers began to offer these videotaped academic courses in World Plan centers around the globe. To maximize the availability of all MIU programs, negotiations are currently under way to establish TV stations in the most highly populated areas of the United States. The first such station will start televising soon in the greater Los Angeles area. These stations will assure the availability of SCI to the vast majority of Americans. Local MIU teachers will work closely with individuals wishing to earn their degrees at home through televised MIU programs. For the developing nations, Maharishi envisions a global television system involving microwave TV transmitters located in every major population area of the world. Early in 1974, MIU formally proposed an "Alliance for Knowledge"[5] to governments all over the world, whereby MIU would provide knowledge through broadcast material and national governments resources to establish global television in their countries.

Because MIU holds the seven goals of the World Plan as its primary objective, MIU will offer more programs than standard graduate and undergraduate courses. A complete curriculum for primary and secondary schools as well as adult education programs are planned. In addition, six MIU institutes have been established to address specific social problems through SCI programs. For example, the Institute for Social Rehabilitation (ISR) will offer advanced training to teachers wishing to apply TM to problems of mental health or crime and will assist local hospitals and correctional institutions desiring to explore the clinical value of SCI. The Institute for Environmental Development (IED) will apply SCI to the most critical ecological problems facing industrial nations and encourage sound ecological planning based on principles of SCI in developing nations. Other institutes have been established to coordinate SCI programs for governmental officials, military professionals, businessmen, educators and the retired. Each of these institutes addresses one of the seven World Plan goals. The International Center for Scientific Research (ICSR) coordinates and facilitates scientific research on SCI. A central research information office has become necessary, since projects studying the physiological, psychological and sociological implications of TM are already under way at over a hundred fifty research institutions throughout the world.

The academic research and training development program of MIU together with the field activities of SIMS, IMS, SRM, and AFSCI are all coordinated through the World Plan Executive Council. This council was established to guide the integrated expansion of the entire TM-SCI movement. In a recent interview Jerry Jarvis, President of the World Plan Executive Council, said, "For the first time in history we have available Maharishi, the knowledge, technique, plan and organization to fulfill the intrinsic purpose of human life, not only in this generation but as an ongoing reality for all generations to come." The World Plan is gaining a remarkable momentum. In November of 1973, World Plan weeks were declared in major cities in Canada and the United States. During this same period, Maharishi accepted invitations to address the legislatures of Illinois, Iowa, New Hampshire and Michigan. Nearly twenty state and local governments, including Illinois, California and Cincinnati, have passed resolutions calling for feasibility studies of introducing SCI programs through municipal or state agencies. During National World Plan Week in the fall of 1973, day-long symposiums in many cities all across the country introduced SCI to local community leaders in cities where the World Plan had just got under way.

World Plan centers are now active in over 200 cities in the United States, thereby providing one center for each one million people. Internationally, the World Plan is also gaining momentum. Record numbers of individuals are learning TM in Great

Britain, Germany, France and the Scandinavian countries. Saskatchewan education officials decided to introduce SCI courses throughout their school system by the fall of 1974. In Africa, the Ethiopian government has sanctioned the development of SCI for the secondary school system. In addition, an SCI-TM teacher-training course was held in Ethiopia during the summer of 1973. SCI is now being taught throughout India and in the educational system of several Indian provinces. In January of 1973, Maharishi inaugurated the World Plan in São Paulo, where officials promised assistance in establishing ninety-eight World Plan centers in Brazil. Because of the slow pace of progress in the developing nations, Maharishi has called on several hundred SCI teachers from the United States to spend a year abroad working to implement the World Plan in those nations outside of Europe, Canada and the United States. This program will result in establishment of 1,900 World Plan centers in developing nations around the globe at the present time.

In addition to the 3,600 centers to be established in major cities around the globe, the World Plan calls for the establishment of a residential facility, popularly known as a forest academy, in the countryside around each major city. Plans are under way to establish ten such facilities in the United States at the present time. Since the spring of 1973, similar academies are in progress or planning in Israel, Great Britain, Venezuela, Germany and many other countries. These facilities will not only provide for extended residence and SCI courses, but also make full-time MIU graduate and undergraduate programs available on a local basis, and to serve as rural cultural centers for the world's meditating population.

By the end of 1975, more than a million people will be practicing TM. Over 10,000 individuals are beginning TM every month in the United States alone. This rate is double the number starting the practice a year ago. Since 1966, the number of meditators has grown by an average rate of 130 percent per year. But this rate of growth appears to be only the beginning of the World Plan. Despite the achievements of the World Plan nationally and internationally, most people continue to start TM because their friends enjoy it and not because social institutions are encouraging it. Yet, the rapidly growing number of educational, business and governmental institutions currently applying the practical value of SCI to resolve the manifold problems which they face promises a reintegration on many levels of society. With his World Plan, Maharishi challenges us to realize a momentous possibility:

> The solutions to the pressing problems that concern our world can be found quickly and easily when every man is living the full potential of life. The knowledge is available to unfold the complete glory of humanity. The validation of the effectiveness of that knowledge has been sufficiently established for everyone to see its truly unlimited capacity to universally raise the quality of life on this planet. All that remains is for every responsible and interested citizen to lead or follow in this challenge—to bring lasting fulfillment to the highest aspirations of civilization in our generation. (181a, p. 25)

MAJOR
WORLD PLAN
CENTERS IN
THE UNITED STATES

THERE ARE 205 WORLD PLAN CENTERS IN THE UNITED STATES OFFERING COURSES IN THE SCIENCE OF CREATIVE INTELLIGENCE AND TRANSCENDENTAL MEDITATION

ATLANTA
3615 North Stratford Road N.E.
Atlanta, Georgia 30342
phone 404 262-2902

BERKELEY
2716 Derby Street
Berkeley, Calif. 94705
phone 415 548-1144

BOSTON
73 Newbury Street
Boston, Mass. 02116
phone 617 266-3770

CAMBRIDGE
33 Garden Street
Cambridge, Mass. 02138
phone 617 876-4581

CHARLOTTE
1724 East Seventh Street
Charlotte, N.C. 28204
phone 704 332-6694

CHICAGO
604 Davis Street
Evanston, Ill. 60201
phone 312 864-1810

CINCINNATI
3960 Winding Way
Cincinnati, Ohio 45229
phone 513 281-5296

COLUMBUS
1818 W. Lane Ave.
Columbus, Ohio 43221
phone 614 486-9298

DENVER
240 St. Paul
Suite 102
Denver, Colorado 80206
phone 303 320-4007

DES MOINES
1311 34th Street
Des Moines, Iowa 50311
phone 515 255-1547

DETROIT
Colonial Federal Bldg.
63 Kercheval, Suite 204
Grosse Pointe, Mich. 48263
phone 313 882-7211

HARTFORD
5 Lincoln Street
Hartford, Conn. 05106
phone 203 247-6733

HONOLULU
227 S. King Street
Honolulu, Hawaii 96813
phone 808 533-2335

HOUSTON
2518 Drexel
Houston, Texas 77027
phone 713 627 7500

KANSAS CITY
6301 Main Street
Kansas City, Mo. 64113
phone 816 523-5777

LOS ANGELES
1015 Gayley Avenue
Los Angeles, Calif. 90024
phone 213 478-1569

MIAMI
4th Floor Suite
2929 S.W. 3rd Ave.
Miami, Florida 33129
phone 305 854-7850

MILWAUKEE
400 E. Silver Spring
Whitefish Bay, Wisconsin 53217
phone 414 962-2300

MINNEAPOLIS
720 Washington Ave. S.E.
Suite 200
Minneapolis, Minn. 55414
phone 612 331-9135

NEW HAVEN
1974 Yale Station
New Haven, Conn. 06520
phone 203 776-5784

NEW YORK
Wentworth Building
59 W. 46th Street
New York, N.Y. 10036
phone 212 586-3331

PHILADELPHIA
1712 Locust Street
Philadelphia, Penn. 19103
phone 215 732-9220

PORTLAND
7743 S.W. Capitol Highway
Portland, Oregon 97219
phone 503 244-9377

SACRAMENTO
2015 J Street
Suite 32
Sacramento, Calif. 95814
phone 916 443-4895

ST. LOUIS
742 Emerson Road
St. Louis, Mo. 63141
phone 314 569-0020

SAN FRANCISCO
218 11th Avenue
San Francisco, Calif. 94118
phone 415 387-0223

SEATTLE
P.O. Box 21051
Seattle, Washington 98111
phone 206 322-1800

WASHINGTON, D.C.
2127 Leroy Place N.W.
Washington, D.C. 20008
phone 202 387-5050

CHART

1

CHANGE IN METABOLIC RATE

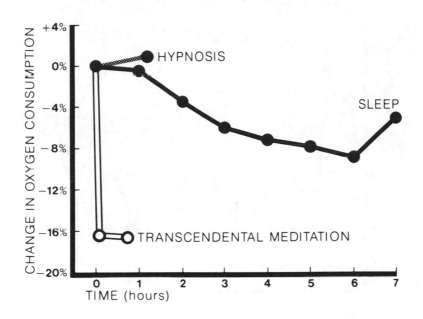

CHART

2

NATURAL CHANGE IN BREATH RATE

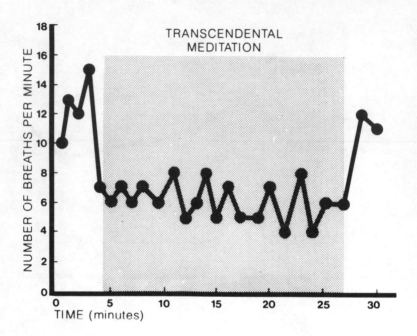

Reference: Allison, J., "Respiratory Changes During the Practice of the Technique of Transcendental Meditation," *Lancet,* No. 7651, pp. 833–34, April, 1970.

CHART

3

CHANGE IN SKIN RESISTANCE

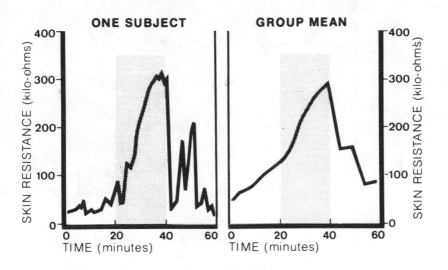

ONE SUBJECT

GROUP MEAN

Reference: Wallace, R. K., and H. Benson, *Physiology of Medita-tion.* Copyright © 1972 by Scientific American, Inc. All rights reserved.

CHART

4

BIOCHEMICAL CHANGES

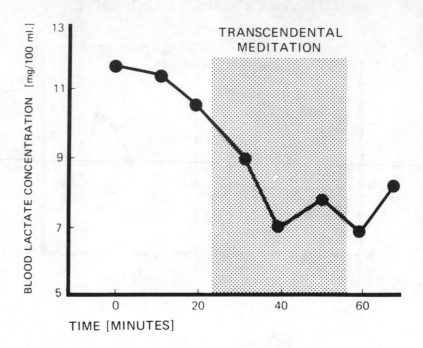

CHART

5

BRAIN WAVE SYNCHRONY

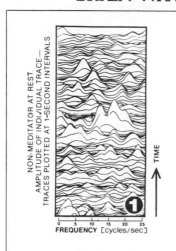

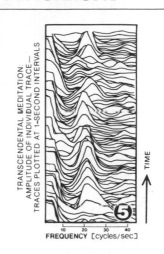

1. NON-MEDITATORS	5. MEDITATOR
Wakefulness with de-synchronized EEG of mental activation; mixed, incoherent frequencies.	TRANSCENDENTAL MEDITATION: a time series of spectra showing a beta wave (22 cycles per second) of very constant frequency and background of constant slow waves. This pattern is seen during deep meditation.

COMPARING 1 WITH 5

Ordinary waking consciousness is represented by random, inconsistent, mixed waves (1) with dominant fast frequencies. During TRANSCENDENTAL MEDITATION, orderliness increases (5); organized coherent waves of constant fast frequency.

Reference: Banquet, J. P., "EEG and Meditation," *Electroencephalography and Clinical Neurophysiology,* Vol. 33, pp. 449–458, 1972; Banquet, J. P., "Spectral Analysis of the EEG in Meditation," op. cit., Vol. 35, pp. 143–151, 1973. As adapted by MIU Press— "Results of Scientific Research on Transcendental Meditation," 1973.

Chart 5 (continued)

2. NON-MEDITATOR

Drifting from relaxed wakefulness (alpha waves, 8 cycles per second) to drowsiness (slow frequencies—mixed theta, 4 cycles per second, and delta, 2 cycles per second).

6. MEDITATOR

A shift from theta (5 cycles per second) in deeper meditation, to alpha (10 cycles per second) towards the end of meditation.

COMPARING 2 WITH 6

Just as the transition from wakefulness to sleep, as indicated by the shift from alpha to slower waves (2), is a natural progressive change, so the transition from meditation to the waking state, as indicated by the shift from theta to alpha waves (6), is a natural progressive change—gradual and effortless.

Chart 5 (continued)

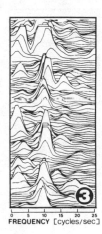 

3. NON-MEDITATOR	7. MEDITATOR
Drowsiness: alternating bursts of alpha and mixed, slow frequencies (delta and theta).	TRANSCENDENTAL MEDITATION: a typical time series of spectra showing persistent alpha (12 cycles per second) and theta (5 cycles per second) waves simultaneously and continuously.

COMPARING 3 WITH 7

TRANSCENDENTAL MEDITATION is a new form of rest, clearly distinct from drowsiness or sleep. Drowsiness is characterized by alertness alternating with light sleep (3) whereas TRANSCENDENTAL MEDITATION brings experience of deepest physical rest simultaneously with expanded alertness (7).

Chart 5 (continued)

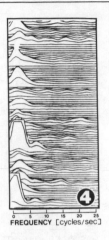 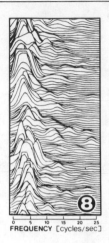

4. NON-MEDITATOR	8. MEDITATOR
Light sleep: disappearance of alpha, presence of mixed, slow, intermittent waves (dominant low and high amplitude delta).	TRANSCENDENTAL MEDITATION: a typical time series of spectra showing a long period of pure, high amplitude, single frequency theta waves (5 cycles per second).

COMPARING 4 WITH 8

TRANSCENDENTAL MEDITATION is clearly distinct from sleep (4). A click stimulus presented during meditation blocked the theta for 1 to 3 seconds whereupon it spontaneously reappeared. However, during drowsiness in non-meditators, the click caused an arousal reaction with no return to theta.

CHART
6

SYNCHRONY OF ELECTRICAL WAVES IN THE FRONT AND BACK BRAIN DURING TRANSCENDENTAL MEDITATION

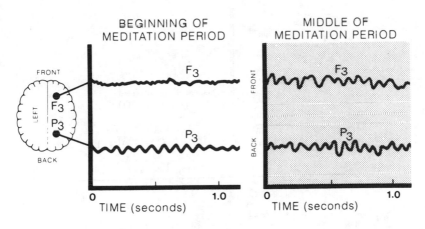

Reference: Banquet, J. P., "EEG and Meditation," *Electroencephalography and Clinical Neurophysiology*, Vol. 33, pp. 449–458, 1972; Banquet, J. P., "Spectral Analysis of the EEG in Meditation," op. cit. Vol. 35, pp. 143–151, 1973.

CHART

7

SYNCHRONY OF ELECTRICAL ACTIVITY OF THE BRAIN HEMISPHERES

NON-MEDITATOR DURING REST

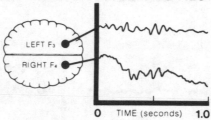

0   TIME (seconds)   **1.0**

MEDITATOR DURING TM SHOWING LARGE BETA SPINDLE CORRELATED AMONG ALL LEADS

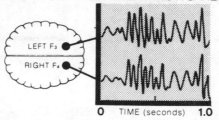

0   TIME (seconds)   **1.0**

Reference: Banquet, J. P., "EEG and Meditation," *Electroencephalography and Clinical Neurophysiology*, Vol. 33, pp. 449–458, 1972; Banquet, J. P., "Spectral Analysis of the EEG in Meditation," op. cit., Vol. 35, pp. 143–151, 1973.

CHART

8

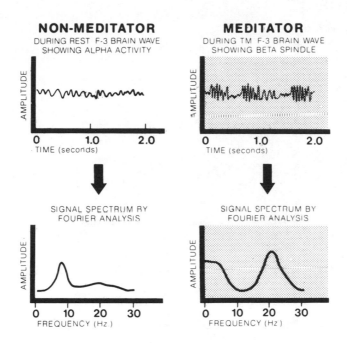

NON-MEDITATOR
DURING REST F-3 BRAIN WAVE
SHOWING ALPHA ACTIVITY

MEDITATOR
DURING TM F-3 BRAIN WAVE
SHOWING BETA SPINDLE

SIGNAL SPECTRUM BY
FOURIER ANALYSIS

SIGNAL SPECTRUM BY
FOURIER ANALYSIS

Reference: Banquet, J. P., "EEG and Meditation," *Electroencephalography and Clinical Neurophysiology*, Vol. 33, pp. 449–458, 1972; Banquet, J. P., "Spectral Analysis of the EEG in Meditation," op. cit., Vol. 35, pp. 143–151, 1973.

CHART

9

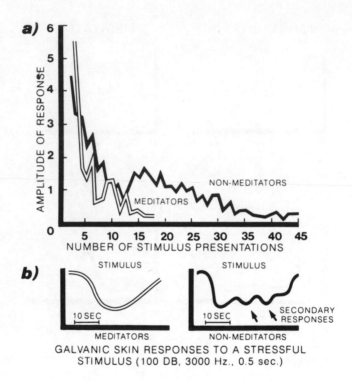

a)

AMPLITUDE OF RESPONSE

NON-MEDITATORS

MEDITATORS

NUMBER OF STIMULUS PRESENTATIONS

b)

STIMULUS

STIMULUS

10 SEC

10 SEC

SECONDARY
RESPONSES

MEDITATORS

NON-MEDITATORS

GALVANIC SKIN RESPONSES TO A STRESSFUL
STIMULUS (100 DB, 3000 Hz., 0.5 sec.)

Reference: Orme-Johnson, D. W., "Autonomic Stability and Transcendental Meditation," *Psychosomatic Medicine*, Vol. 35, No. 4, pp. 341–349, July–August, 1973.

CHART

10

FEWER SPONTANEOUS GALVANIC SKIN RESPONSES

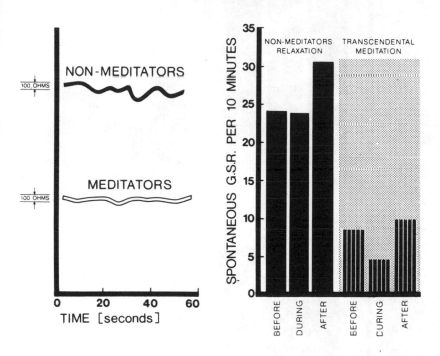

Reference: Orme-Johnson, D. W., "Autonomic Stability and Transcendental Meditation," *Psychosomatic Medicine,* Vol. 35, No. 4, pp. 341–349, July–August, 1973.

CHARTS

11, 12

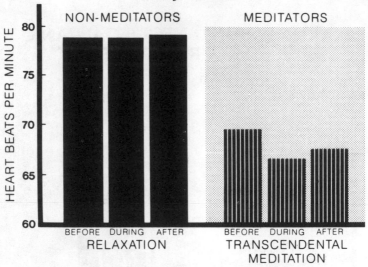

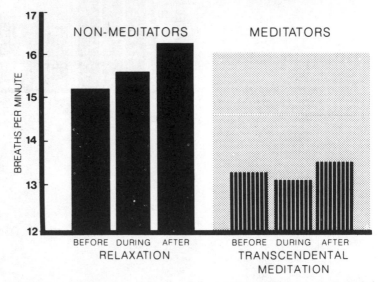

Reference: Routt, T., "Transcendental Meditation and Relaxed States: A Pilot Study Comparing Physiological Parameters," Huxley College of Environmental Studies, Western Washington State University, Bellingham, September, 1973.

CHART
13

DECREASED BLOOD PRESSURE IN
HYPERTENSIVE PATIENTS

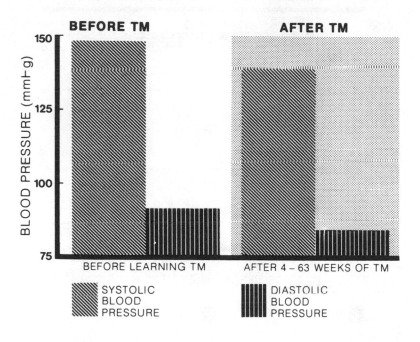

Benson, H. and R. K. Wallace, "Decreased Blood Pressure in Hypertensive Subjects Who Practiced Meditation," Supplement II to *Circulation*, Vols. XLV and XLVI, October, 1972.

CHART

14

DEVELOPMENT OF PERSONALITY

PERSONAL ORIENTATION INVENTORY

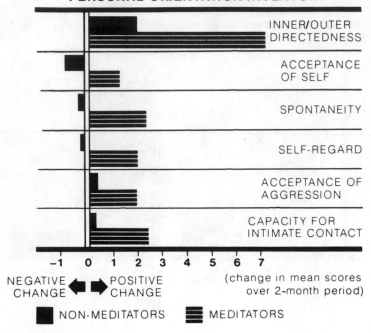

NEGATIVE ◀ ▶ POSITIVE
CHANGE   CHANGE

(change in mean scores over 2-month period)

■ NON-MEDITATORS   ☰ MEDITATORS

Reference: Seeman, W., S. Nidich, and T. Banta, "The Influence of Transcendental Meditation on a Measure of Self-Actualization," *Journal of Counseling Psychology,* Vol. 19, No. 3, pp. 184–187, 1972.

CHART

15

DECREASED ANXIETY

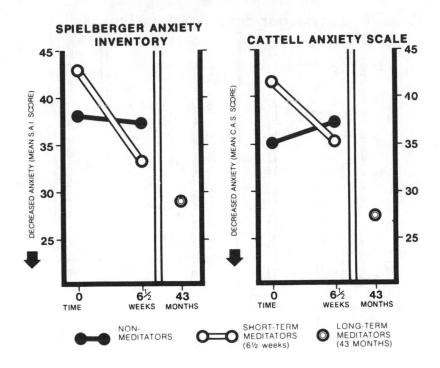

Reference: Ferguson, P. C., and J. Gowan, "The Influence of Transcendental Meditation on Anxiety, Depression, Aggression, Neuroticism and Self-Actualization," School of Education, California State University at Northridge, California, 1973.

CHART

16

INCREASED PSYCHOLOGICAL HEALTH

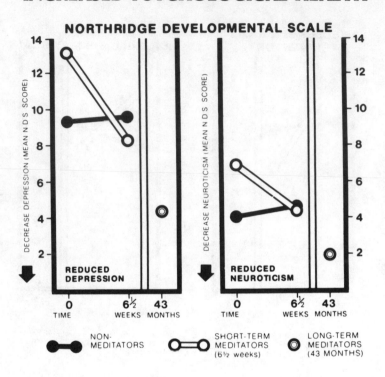

NORTHRIDGE DEVELOPMENTAL SCALE

REDUCED DEPRESSION

REDUCED NEUROTICISM

NON-MEDITATORS

SHORT-TERM MEDITATORS (6½ weeks)

LONG-TERM MEDITATORS (43 MONTHS)

Reference: Ferguson, P. C., and J. Gowan, "The Influence of Transcendental Meditation on Anxiety, Depression, Aggression, Neuroticism and Self-Actualization," *Journal of Humanistic Psychology,* in press, 1974.

CHART

17

INCREASED SELF-ACTUALIZATION

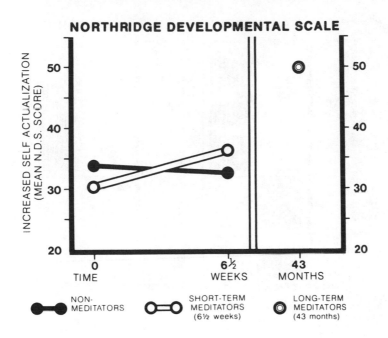

Reference: Ferguson, P. C., and J. Gowan, "The Influence of Transcendental Meditation on Anxiety, Depression, Aggression, Neuroticism and Self-Actualization," *Journal of Humanistic Psychology*, in press, 1974.

CHART
18

INCREASED PERCEPTUAL ABILITY

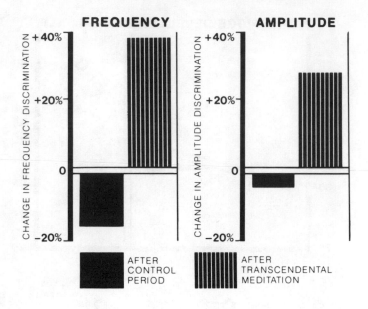

Reference: Graham, J., "Auditory Discrimination in Meditators," *Scientific Research on Transcendental Meditation: Collected Papers,* D. W. Orme-Johnson, L. H. Domash and J. T. Farrow (eds.), Vol. 1, Los Angeles, MIU Press, 1974.

CHART
19

FASTER REACTION TIME

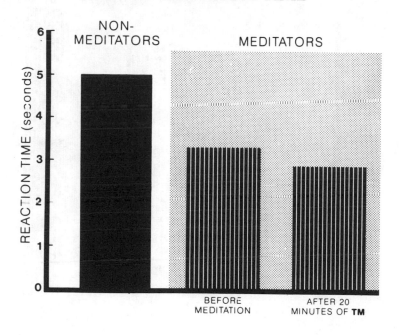

Reference: Shaw, R., and D. Kolb, "One-Point Reaction Time Involving Meditators and Non-Meditators," *Scientific Research on Transcendental Meditation: Collected Papers,* D. W. Orme-Johnson, L. H. Domash and J. T. Farrow (eds.), Vol. 1, Los Angeles, MIU Press, 1974.

CHART

20

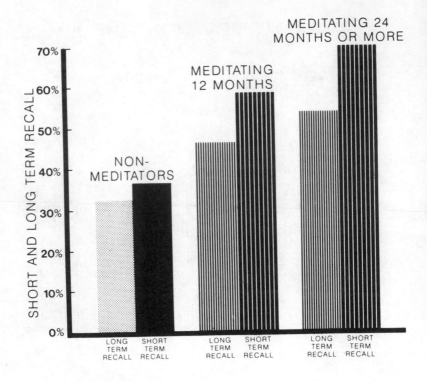

Reference: Abrams, A. I., "Paired Associate Learning and Recall: A Pilot Study Comparing Transcendental Meditators with Non-Meditators," *Scientific Research on Transcendental Meditation: Collected Papers*, D. W. Orme-Johnson, L. H. Domash and J. T. Farrow (eds.), Vol. I, Los Angeles, MIU Press, 1974.

CHART

21

REDUCED USE OF NON-PRESCRIBED DRUGS

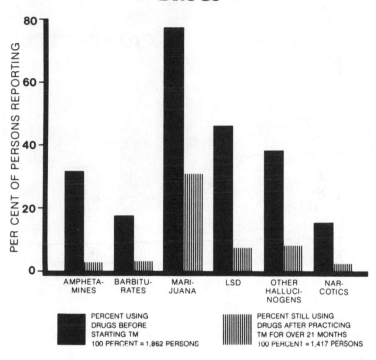

Reference: Benson, H., and R. K. Wallace, *Drug Abuse Proceedings of the International Conference,* Philadelphia, Pennsylvania, Lea and Febiger, pp. 369–376, 1972. *Congressional Record,* Serial Number 92-1 (United States Government Printing Office, Washington, D.C., 1971).

CHART

22

REDUCED USE OF ALCOHOL AND CIGARETTES

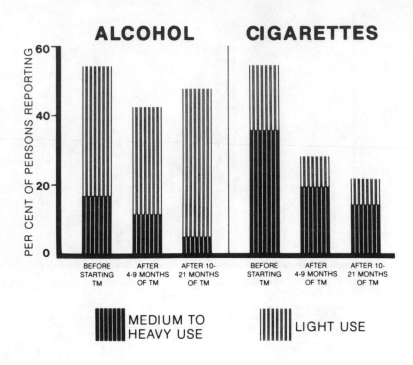

Reference: Benson, H., and R. K. Wallace, *Drug Abuse Proceedings of the International Conference,* Philadelphia, Pennsylvania, Lea and Febiger, pp. 369–376, 1972. *Congressional Record,* Serial Number 92-1 (United States Government Printing Office, Washington, D.C., 1971).

CHART

23

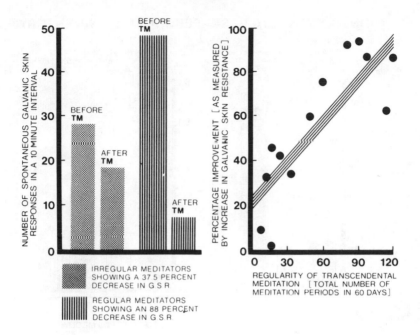

NUMBER OF SPONTANEOUS GALVANIC SKIN RESPONSES IN A 10 MINUTE INTERVAL

BEFORE TM

BEFORE TM

AFTER TM

BEFORE TM

AFTER TM

IRREGULAR MEDITATORS SHOWING A 37.5 PERCENT DECREASE IN G.S.R.

REGULAR MEDITATORS SHOWING AN 88 PERCENT DECREASE IN G.S.R.

PERCENTAGE IMPROVEMENT [AS MEASURED BY INCREASE IN GALVANIC SKIN RESISTANCE]

REGULARITY OF TRANSCENDENTAL MEDITATION [TOTAL NUMBER OF MEDITATION PERIODS IN 60 DAYS]

Reference: Orme-Johnson, D. W., J. Kiehlbauch, R. Moore and J. Bristol, "Personality and Autonomic Changes in Meditating Prisoners," La Tuna Federal Penitentiary, Texas, August, 1972.

CHART
24

MINNESOTA MULTIPHASIC PERSONALITY INVENTORY

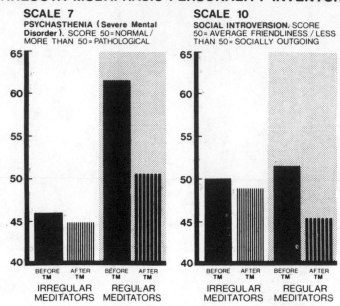

SCALE 7
PSYCHASTHENIA (Severe Mental
Disorder). SCORE 50=NORMAL/
MORE THAN 50=PATHOLOGICAL

SCALE 10
SOCIAL INTROVERSION. SCORE
50= AVERAGE FRIENDLINESS / LESS
THAN 50= SOCIALLY OUTGOING

BEFORE TM / AFTER TM — IRREGULAR MEDITATORS
BEFORE TM / AFTER TM — REGULAR MEDITATORS

Reference: Orme-Johnson, D. W., J. Kiehlbauch, R. Moore, and J. Bristol, "Personality and Autonomic Changes in Meditating Prisoners," La Tuna Federal Penitentiary, Texas, August 1972.

CHART

25

IMPROVED ACADEMIC PERFORMANCE

**Student Grade Point Average Improves After
Starting TRANSCENDENTAL MEDITATION**

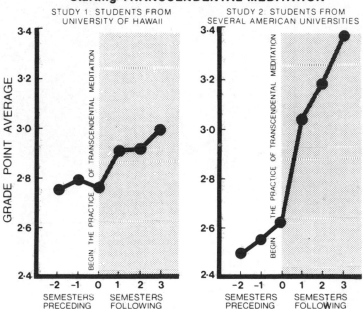

STUDY 1: STUDENTS FROM
UNIVERSITY OF HAWAII

STUDY 2: STUDENTS FROM
SEVERAL AMERICAN UNIVERSITIES

Reference: Collier, R. W., "The Effect of Transcendental Medita-
tion upon University Academic Attainment," *Proceedings of the
Pacific Northwest Conference on Foreign Languages, Seattle, Wash-
ington,* in press, 1974, and Heaton, O. P., and D. W. Orme-Johnson,
"Influence of Transcendental Meditation on Grade Point Average:
Initial Findings," *Scientific Research on Transcendental Medita-
tion: Collected Papers,* D. W. Orme-Johnson, L. H. Domash and
J. T. Farrow (eds.), Los Angeles, MIU Press, 1974.

CHART

25A

University of Hawaii Student Grade Point Ratio Preceding
and Following the Practice of Transcendental Meditation

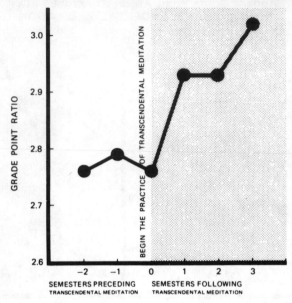

CHART

26

INCREASED PRODUCTIVITY

Comparing Meditating High Level Executives with Meditating Employees

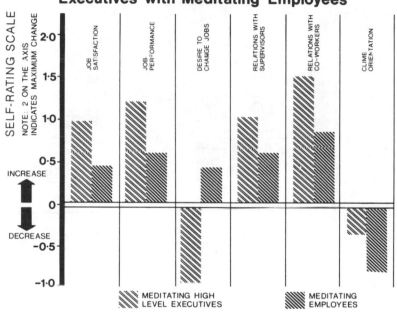

Reference: Frew, D. R., "Transcendental Meditation and Productivity," *Academy of Management Journal*, in press, 1974.

CHART

27

Comparing Meditators with Non-Meditators

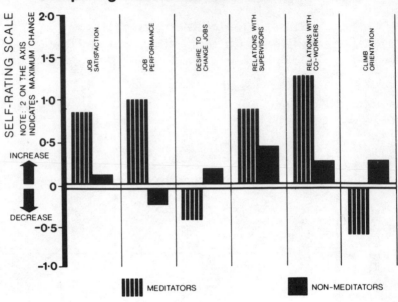

Reference: Frew, D. R., "Transcendental Meditation and Productivity," *Academy of Management Journal*, in press, 1974.

BIBLIOGRAPHY

1 ABRAMS, A. I. "Paired Associate Learning and Recall." *Scientific Research on Transcendental Meditation: Collected Papers*, D. W. Orme-Johnson, L. H. Domash, and J. T. Farrow (eds.), Los Angeles, MIU Press, 1974.

1a ACKERMAN, S. II. and E. J. Sachar. "The Lactate Theory of Anxiety: A Review and Reevaluation." *Psychosomatic Medicine*, Vol. 36, No. 1, January-February, 1974, pp. 69–79.

2 ADLER, A. *The Individual Psychology of Alfred Adler*. Ansbacher and Ansbacher (eds.), New York, Harper Torch Books, 1967.

3 AKISHIGE, Y. "A Historical Survey of the Psychological Studies in Zen." *Kyushu Psychological Studies*, Akishige (ed.), Bulletin of the Faculty of Literature of Kyushu University, Number 77, Kyushu University, Fukuska, Japan, 1968, pp. 1–56.

4 ALLEN, C. "Possible Psychological and Physiological Effects of Transcendental Meditation on Aphasic Patients." University of Michigan, 1973.

5 *Alliance for Knowledge*. MIU Press, Seelisburg, Switzerland, 1974.

6 ALLISON, J. "Respiratory Changes During Transcendental Meditation." *Lancet*, No. 7651, London, April 18, 1970, pp. 833–834.

7 ANAND, B. K., G. S. Chhina and B. Singh. "Some Aspects of Electroencephalographic Studies in Yogis." *Altered States of Consciousness*, C. T. Tart (ed.), New York, John Wiley & Sons Inc., 1969, pp. 503–506.

8 ANAND, B. K., G. S. Chhina and B. Singh. "Studies on Sri Ramanand Yogi During His Stay in an Air-Tight Box." *The Indian Journal of Medical Research*, Vol. 49, No. 1, 1961, pp. 82–89.

9 ANONYMOUS. "Meditation May Find Use in Medical Practice." *Journal of the American Medical Association*, Vol. 219, No. 3, January 17, 1972, pp. 295–299.

10 ANONYMOUS. "TM, Some Results." Students' International Meditation Society, 1969.

11 ARGYRIS, C. *Interpersonal Competence and Organizational Effectiveness*. Homewood, Illinois, Irwin-Dorsey, 1962.

12 ASERINSKY, E., and N. Kleitman. "Regularly Occurring Periods of

Eye Motility and Concomitant Phenomena During Sleep." *Science*, Vol. 118, 1953, pp. 273–274.

13 ASSAGIOLI, R. *Psychosynthesis*. New York, Hobbs, Corman, 1965.

14 BAGCHI, B. K., and M. A. Wenger. "Electrophysiological Correlates of Some Yogi Exercises." *Electroencephalography and Clinical Neurophysiology*, Vol. 9, Supplement 7, 1957, pp. 132–149.

15 BAGCHI, B. K., and M. A. Wenger. "Simultaneous EEG and Other Recordings During Some Yogic Practices." *Electroencephalography and Clinical Neurophysiology*, Vol. 10, 1958, p. 1963.

16 BALLOU, D. "Transcendental Meditation Research at Stillwater State Prison." Stillwater State Prison, Minnesota, October 1973.

17 BANQUET, J. P. "Comparative Study of the EEG Spectral Analysis During Sleep and Yoga Meditation." *First European Congress on Sleep Research*, October 1972.

18 BANQUET, J. P. "EEG and Meditation." *Electroencephalography and Clinical Neurophysiology*, Vol. 33, 1972, pp. 449–458.

19 BANQUET, J. P. "Spectral Analysis of the EEG in Meditation." *Electroencephalography and Clinical Neurophysiology*, Vol. 35, 1973, pp. 143–151.

20 BARCHAS, J. *Serotonin and Behavior*, E. Usdin (ed.), New York, Academic Press, 1973.

21 BATTOZZI, A. A., and G. Luce. "Physiological Effects of Meditation Technique and Suggestion for Drug Abuse." *Mental Health Reports–5*, National Institute of Mental Health, Department of Health, Education and Welfare, December 1971.

22 BENSON, H. "Yoga for Drug Abuse." *New England Journal of Medicine*, Vol. 281, No. 20, 1969, p. 1133.

23 BENSON, H., B. P. Malveila and J. R. Graham. "Physiological Correlates of Meditation and Their Clinical Effects in Headache: An Ongoing Investigation." *Headache*, April 1973, pp. 23–24.

24 BENSON, H., and R. K. Wallace. "Decreased Blood Pressure in Hypertensive Subjects Who Practiced Meditation." Supplement 11 to *Circulation*, Vols. XLV and XLVI, October 1972. Abstracts of the 45th Scientific Sessions.

25 BENSON, H., and R. K. Wallace. "Decreased Drug Abuse with Transcendental Meditation: A Study of 1862 Subjects." *Proceedings of the International Symposium on Drug Abuse*, C. J. D. Zarafonetis (ed.), Philadelphia, Lea and Febiger, 1972, pp. 369–376. *Congressional Record*, Serial No. 92–1, Washington, D.C., U.S. Government Printing Office, 1971.

26 BERGIN, A. E. "Evaluation of Therapeutic Outcomes." *Handbook of Psychotherapy and Behavior Change*, A. E. Bergin and S. L. Garfield (eds.), Chapter VII, New York, John Wiley & Sons, 1971, pp. 217–270.

27 BLASDELL, K. "The Effect of Transcendental Meditation Upon a Complex Perceptual Motor Test." *Scientific Research on Transcendental Meditation: Collected Papers*, D. W. Orme-Johnson, L. H. Domash, and J. T. Farrow (eds.), Los Angeles, MIU Press, 1974.

28 BLOOMFIELD, H. "Assertive Training in an Out-patient Group of Chronic Schizophrenics: A Preliminary Report." *Behavior Therapy*, Vol. 4, No. 2, March 1973, pp. 277–281. Also in *Annual Review of Behavior Therapy: 1974 edition*, New York, Brunner, Mazel Publishers, 1974.

29 BLOOMFIELD, H. H., M. P. Cain, D. T. Jaffe and A. E. Rubottom. "The Psychophysiology of Transcendental Meditation." *What Is Meditation?*, J. White (ed.), New York, Doubleday, Anchor Books, 1974.

30 BOESE, E., and K. Berger. "In Search of a Fourth State of Consciousness: Psychological and Physiological Correlates of Meditation." Pennsylvania State University Medical School, 1972.

31 BOUDREAU, L. "Transcendental Meditation and Yoga as Reciprocal Inhibitors." *Journal of Behavioral Therapy and Experimental Psychiatry*, Vol. 3, 1972, pp. 97–98.

32 BOWERS, M. K. "Observations on TM." New York, New York, April 1973.

33 BRAUTIGAM, E. "The Effect of Transcendental Meditation on Drug Abusers." Research Report, City Hospital of Malmo, Sweden, December 1971.

34 BRECHER, E. M. *Licit and Illicit Drugs*. New York, Consumers Union, 1972.

35 BROSSE, T. "A Psychophysiological Study of Yoga." *Main Currents in Modern Thought*, July 1946, pp. 77–84.

36 BROWN, B. B. "Recognition of Aspects of Consciousness Through Association with EEG Alpha Activity Represented by a Light Signal." *Psychophysiology*, Vol. 6, 1970, pp. 442–452.

37 BROWN, F. M., W. S. Stewart and J. T. Blodgett. "EEG Kappa Rhythms During Transcendental Meditation and Possible Perceptual Threshold Changes Following." Presented to the Kentucky Academy of Sciences, Richmond, Kentucky, November 13, 1971, revised January 1972.

38 BROWN, N. O. *Life Against Death*. Middletown, Conn., Wesleyan University Press, 1959.

39 CALDER, N. *The Mind of Man*. New York, The Viking Press, 1970

40 CAMPBELL, A. *Seven States of Consciousness*. London, Victor Gollancz Ltd., 1973.

41 CAMPBELL, A. (ed). "Towards Pinning Down Meditation." *Hospital Times*, London, May 1, 1970.

42 CAMPBELL, A. "Who Are We?" *Creative Intelligence*, No. 2, Regeneration Movement Publications, London, 1972, pp. 39–47.

43 CARRINGTON, P., and H. S. Ephron. "Meditation as an Adjunct to Psychotherapy." *The World Biennial of Psychotherapy and Psychiatry*, Sancti and G. Chrzanowski (eds.), New York, John Wiley & Sons (in press 1974).

44 CARTER, H., and P. C. Glick. *Marriage and Divorce: A Social and Economic Study*. Cambridge, Mass., Harvard University Press, 1970.

45 CATTELL, R. B., and J. H. Scheier. *The Meaning and Measurement of Neuroticism and Anxiety*. New York, Ronald Press, 1961.

46 CAYEDO, A. *India of Yogis*. Delhi, National Publishing House, 1966.

47 COLLIER, R. W. "The Effect of Transcendental Meditation upon University Academic Attainment," *Proceedings of the Pacific Northwest Conference on Foreign Languages*, Seattle, Washington (in press 1974).

48 COREY, P. W. "Airway Conductance and Oxygen Consumption in Human Subjects via a Wakeful Hypometabolic Technique." National Jewish Hospital and Research Hospital, Denver, Colorado, April 1973.

49 COX, S. B. "Transcendental Meditation and the Criminal Justice System." *Kentucky Law Journal*, Vol. 60, No. 2, 1972.

50 CRISSWELL, D. "Feedback and States of Consciousness: Meditation." *Proceedings of Biofeedback Research Society*, Panel 5, 1969.

51 CUNNINGHAM, M., and W. KOCH. "Transcendental Meditation, A Pilot Project at the Federal Correctional Institution at Lompoc, California." *Scientific Research on Transcendental Meditation: Collected Papers*, D. W. Orme-Johnson, L. H. Domash and J. T. Farrow (eds.), Los Angeles, MIU Press, 1974.

52 DANIELOU, A. "The Influence of Sound on Consciousness." *L'Age Nouveau*, November 1968.

53 DATEY, K., S. Deshmukh, C. Dalvi and S. Vinekar. "Shavasan: A Yogic Exercise in the Management of Hypertension." *Angiology*, Vol. 20, 1969, pp. 325–333.

54 DEIKMAN, A. J. "De-automization and the Mystical Experience." *Altered States of Consciousness*, Charles T. Tart (ed.), New York, John Wiley & Sons, Inc., 1969, pp. 23–44.

55 DEIKMAN, A. J. "Experimental Meditation." *Altered States of Consciousness*, Charles T. Tart (ed.), New York, John Wiley & Sons, Inc., 1969, pp. 199–218.

56 DEIKMAN, A. J. "Implications of Experimentally Induced Contemplative Meditation." *Journal of Nervous and Mental Disease*, Vol. 142, 1966, pp. 101–116.

57 DEMENT, W. C. "Effects of Dream Deprivation." *Science*, Vol. 131, 1960, pp. 1705–1707.
58 DEMENT, W. C. "Eye Movements During Sleep." *The Oculomotor System*, M. Bender (ed.), New York, Harper and Row, Publishers, 1964, pp. 316–366.
59 DEROPP, R. S. *The Master Game.* New York, Dell Publishing Co., Inc., 1968.
60 DOMASH, L. "Physics and the Study of Consciousness: Does Transcendental Meditation Induce a Macroscopic Quantum State in the Nervous System?" Dept. of Physics, Maharishi International University, Santa Barbara, California, 1974.
61 DOUCETTE, L. C. "Anxiety and Transcendental Meditation as an Anxiety Reducing Agent." McMaster University, Hamilton, Canada, January 1972.
62 DOVE, W. F. "A Study of Individuality in the Nutritive Instincts." *American Naturalist*, Vol. 69, 1935, pp. 469–544.
63 DRISCOLL, F. G. "TM as a Secondary School Subject." *Phi Delta Kappan*, Vol. LIV, No. 4, December 1972, pp. 236–237.
64 ELLUL, J. *The Technological Society.* New York, Alfred A. Knopf, 1964.
65 ERIKSON, E. H. *Childhood and Society.* New York, W. W. Norton, 1963.
66 ERIKSON, E. H. *Identity, Youth and Crisis.* New York, W. W. Norton, 1968.
67 EYSENCK, H. J. *The Effects of Psychotherapy.* New York, International Science Press, 1966.
68 FARROW, J. T. "Enhancement of Psychophysiological Adaptability Through the Science of Creative Intelligence." Dept. of Neurobiology, Maharishi International University, Santa Barbara, California, 1974.
69 FARWELL, L. "Effect of Transcendental Meditation on Level of Anxiety." Dept. of Psychology and Social Relations, Harvard University, Cambridge, May 1973.
70 FEHR, T., U. Nerstheimer and S. Torber. "Study of 49 Practitioners of Transcendental Meditation with the Freiburger Personality Inventory." *Scientific Research on Transcendental Meditation: Collected Papers*, D. W. Orme-Johnson, L. H. Domash and J. T. Farrow (eds.), Los Angeles, MIU Press, 1974.
71 FERGUSON, P. D., and J. Gowan. "The Influence of Transcendental Meditation on Anxiety, Depression, Aggression, Neuroticism and Self-Actualization." *Journal of Humanistic Psychology* (in press 1974).
72 FINDLAY, J. "The Logic of Mysticism." *Ascent to the Absolute*, London, George Allen & Unwin Ltd., 1970.

73 FISCHER, R. "A Cartography of the Ecstatic and Meditative States." *Science*, Vol. 174, No. 4012, November 26, 1971, pp. 897–904.

74 FLISHER, M. "Science and Objectivity." *Creative Intelligence*, No. 1, Spiritual Regeneration Movement Publications, London, 1970, pp. 29–35.

75 FOREM, J. *Transcendental Meditation, Maharishi Mahesh Yogi and the Science of Creative Intelligence.* New York, E. P. Dutton & Company, Inc., 1973.

76 FORT, J. *Alcohol: Our Greatest Drug Problem.* New York, McGraw-Hill Book Company, 1973.

77 FREEMON, F. R. *Sleep Research: A Critical Review.* Springfield, Illinois, Charles C. Thomas Publishers, 1972.

78 FREUD, S. *An Outline of Psychoanalysis*, trans. by J. Strachey. New York, W. W. Norton, 1969.

79 FREUD, S. "Analysis Terminable and Interminable" (1937). *The Standard Edition of the Complete Psychological Works of Sigmund Freud*, trans. by J. Strachey. London, Hogarth Press, 1953–1966.

80 FREUD, S. *Beyond the Pleasure Principle*, trans. by J. Strachey. New York, Bantam Books, 1967.

81 FREUD, S. *Civilization and Its Discontents*, trans. by J. Strachey. New York, W. W. Norton, 1962.

82 FREUD, S. *New Introductory Lectures on Psychoanalysis*, trans. by J. Strachey. New York, W. W. Norton, 1965.

83 FREUD, S. *The Interpretation of Dreams*, trans. by J. Strachey. New York, Basic Books, 1959.

84 FREW, D. R. "Transcendental Meditation and Productivity." *Academy of Management Journal* (in press 1974).

85 FRIEDMAN, M. *The Pathogenesis of Coronary Artery Disease.* New York, McGraw-Hill Book Company, 1969.

86 FRIEDMAN, M., and R. H. Rosenman. *Type A Behavior and Your Heart.* New York, Knopf, 1974.

87 FROMM, E. *Zen Buddhism and Psychoanalysis.* New York, Harper and Row, Publishers, 1970.

88 FULLER, R. B. *Education Automation.* New York, Doubleday, 1971.

89 FULLER, R. B. *No More Secondhand God.* Carbondale, Illinois, Southern Illinois University Press, 1963.

90 FULLER, R. B. *Operating Manual for Spaceship Earth.* New York, Simon & Schuster, 1970.

91 FULLER, R. B. Transcript of Fuller-Maharishi Press Conference, Science of Creative Intelligence Symposium. University of Massachusetts, Amherst, July 22, 1971. (Available thru SIMS.)

92 FULLER, R. B. *Utopia or Oblivion: The Prospects for Humanity.* New York, Bantam Books, Inc., 1969.

93 GABOR, D. *The Mature Society*. London, Secker and Warburg, 1972.
94 GATTOZZI, A. A., and G. G. Luce. "Physiological Effects of a Meditation Technique and a Suggestion for Curbing Drug Abuse." National Institute of Mental Health, Department of Health, Education and Welfare publication No. HMS 72–9042, December 1971, pp. 379–388.
95 GAZZANIGA, M. S. "The Split Brain in Man." *Scientific American*, Vol. 22, 1967, pp. 24–29.
96 GELLHORN, E., and W. F. Kiely. "Mystical States of Consciousness: Neurophysiological and Clinical Aspects." *Journal of Nervous and Mental Disease*, Vol. 154, No. 6, 1972, pp. 399–405.
97 GELLHORN, E., and W. F. Kiely. "Autonomic Nervous System in Psychiatric Disorder." *Biological Psychiatry*, Joseph Mendels (ed.), New York, John Wiley & Sons, 1973. Chapter 11, pp. 235–263.
98 GHISELIN, B. *The Creative Process*. New York, New American Library Inc., 1952.
99 GLUECK, B. C. "Current Research on Transcendental Meditation." Rensselaer Polytechnic Institute Symposium on "The Science of Creative Intelligence and Management Science." Troy, New York, March 13, 1973.
100 GLUECK, B. C. "A Psychodynamic and Neurophysiologic Assessment of Transcendental Meditation." Presented at the International Symposium on the Science of Creative Intelligence, Fiuggi Fonte, Italy, April 12, 1972.
101 GLUECK, B. C. "Research Review Committee Memorandum." Institute of Living, Hartford, Connecticut, January 5, 1972.
102 GLUECK, B. C. Quoted in "Doing Something About Stress." W. McQuade, *Fortune*, May 1973, pp. 250–261.
103 GLUECK, B. C., and C. S. Stroebel. "The Use of Transcendental Meditation in a Psychiatric Hospital," presented at the 127th Annual Meeting of the American Psychiatric Association, Detroit, Michigan, May 1974.
104 GOLDSTEIN, K. *The Organism*. New York, American Book Company, 1939.
105 GOLEMAN, D. "The Buddha on Meditation and States of Consciousness, Part II: A Typology of Meditation Techniques." *Journal of Transpersonal Psychology*, Vol. 4, No. 2, November 2, 1972.
106 GOLEMAN, D. "Meditation as Meta-Therapy: Hypotheses Toward a Proposed Fifth State of Consciousness." *Journal of Transpersonal Psychology*, Vol. 3, No. 1, 1971, pp. 1–25.
107 GOODALL, K. "Meditation as a Drug-Trip Detour." *Psychology Today*, March 1972, p. 5.
108 GRACE, W. J., and D. T. Graham. "Relationship of Specific Attitudes

and Emotions to Certain Bodily Diseases." *Psychosomatic Medicine*, Vol. 14, 1952, pp. 253–261.

109 GRAHAM, J. "Auditory Discrimination in Meditators." *Scientific Research on Transcendental Meditation: Collected Papers*, D. W. Orme-Johnson, L. H. Domash and J. T. Farrow (eds.), Los Angeles, MIU Press, 1974.

110 GRAHAM, R., M. Peterman and R. Scarff. "Insights into the Richmond Community." British Columbia, Canada, Summer 1971.

111 GREEN, E., A. Green and E. D. Walters. "Voluntary Control of Internal States: Psychological and Physiological." *Journal of Transpersonal Psychology*, Vol. 2, No. 1, 1970, pp. 1–26.

112 GRIFFITH, F. "A Review of the Physiological and Psychological Literature on Meditation." Dept. of Psychology, Yale University, May, 1972.

113 HANKEY, A. "Symmetry and Particle Physics." *Creative Intelligence*, London, Spiritual Regeneration Movement Publications (in press 1974).

114 HARMAN, W. "The New Copernican Revolution." *Stanford Today*, Winter 1969, pp. 1–10.

115 HARTMANN, E. *The Biology of Dreaming.* Springfield, Illinois, Charles C. Thomas Publishers, 1967.

116 HASKELL, E. F. "Assembly of the Sciences into a Single Discipline." *The Science Teacher*, December 1970.

117 HEATH, D. "Affective Education." *School Review*, May 1972.

117a HEATON, O. P., and D. W. Orme-Johnson. "Influence of Transcendental Meditation on Grade Point Average: Initial Findings." *Scientific Research on Transcendental Meditation: Collected Papers*, D. W. Orme-Johnson, L. H. Domash, and J. T. Farrow (eds.), Los Angeles, MIU Press, 1974.

118 HEBB, D. O. *A Textbook of Psychology.* 3rd. ed., Philadelphia, Saunders, 1972.

119 HERZBERG, F. *Work and the Nature of Man.* New York, New American Library, 1973.

120 HJELLE, L. A. "Transcendental Meditation and Psychological Health." Dept. of Psychology, State University College, Brockport, New York, 1972.

121 HOLT, J. C. *How Children Fail.* New York, Pitman, 1964.

122 HOPE, A. (text), with L. Nilsson (photographs), and F. Armitage (drawings). "The Brain." *Life* magazine. Part I, October 1, 1971, pp. 42–59; Part II, October 22, 1971, pp. 42–64; Part III, November 12, 1971, pp. 55–76.

123 HUCKABEE, W. E. "Relationships of Pyruvate and Lactate During Anaerobic Metabolism." *Journal of Clinical Investigation*, Vol. 37, 1958, pp. 244–254.

124 HUME, R. (trans. from Sanskrit). *Thirteen Principal Upanishads.* Rev. 2nd ed., reproduction of 1931 ed., London, Oxford University Press, 1971.

125 HUXLEY, A. *The Doors of Perception.* New York, Harper and Row, Publishers, 1954.

126 HUXLEY, A. *The Perennial Philosophy.* New York, Harper and Row, Publishers, 1970.

127 ILLINOIS HOUSE OF REPRESENTATIVES. "Resolution Supporting Transcendental Meditation and Maharishi's World Plan." Resolution No. 677, offered by Mr. Murphy, May 24, 1972.

128 JACOBSEN, E. *Anxiety and Tension Control.* Philadelphia and New York, J. B. Lippincott Company, 1964.

129 JACOBSEN, E. *You Must Relax.* New York, McGraw-Hill Book Company, 1957.

130 JAMES, W. *The Principles of Psychology.* New York, Dover Publications, Inc., 1950.

131 JAMES, W. *The Varieties of Religious Experience.* London, Longmans, Green and Company, 1929.

132 JAMES, W. *William James in Psychical Research.* G. Murphy and R. V. Ballou (eds.), New York, The Viking Press, 1963.

133 JASPERS, K. *The Idea of the University.* Boston, Beacon Press, 1959.

134 JONES, M., and V. Mellersh. "Comparison of Exercise Response in Anxiety States and Normal Controls." *Psychosomatic Medicine,* Vol. 8, 1946, pp. 180–187.

135 JUNG, C. G. *Aion: Researches into the Phenomenology of the Self,* trans. by R. C. F. Hull. Vol. 9, collected works, Bollingen XX, Princeton, New Jersey, Princeton University Press, 1959.

136 JUNG, C. G. *Analytical Psychology: Its Theory and Practice.* New York, Vintage Books, 1970.

137 JUNG, C. G. *The Structure and Dynamics of the Psyche,* trans. by R. C. F. Hull. Vol. 8, collected works, Bollingen XX, Princeton, New Jersey, Princeton University Press, 1959.

138 JUNG, C. G. *Two Essays in Analytical Psychology,* trans. by R. C. F. Hull. Vol. 7, collected works, Bollingen XX, Princeton, New Jersey, Princeton University Press, 1959.

139 KAMBE, T., and K. Sato. "Medical and Psychological Studies on Zen; Electroencephalogram and Electromyogram During Zen Practice." *Proceedings of the 26th Convention of JPA,* No. 289, 1962.

140 KAMIYA, J. "Operant Control of the EEG Alpha Rhythm and Some of Its Reported Effects on Consciousness." *Altered States of Consciousness,* C. T. Tart (ed.), New York, John Wiley & Sons, Inc., 1969, pp. 507–517.

141 KANELLAKOS, D. P. "Transcendental Meditation." *The Highest State of Consciousness*, J. White (ed.), New York, Doubleday, 1972.

142 KANELLAKOS, D. P. "Voluntary Improvement of Individual Performance, the Psychobiology of Consciousness: A Literature Survey." Final Report, IR&D Project Number 933531–01–AFB, Stanford Research Institute, Menlo Park, California, February 1972.

143 KANELLAKOS, D. P., and W. Bellin. "The Practice of Transcendental Meditation as a Means to the Fulfillment of the Ideals of Humanistic and Transpersonal Psychology." Presented to American Psychological Association, 1972.

144 KANELLAKOS, D. P., and P. Ferguson. "The Psychobiology of Transcendental Meditation (an annotated bibliography)." Maharishi International University, Los Angeles, California, Spring 1973.

145 KANELLAKOS, D. P., and J. S. Lukas. *The Psychobiology of Transcendental Meditation: Literature Survey*. W. A. Benjamin Co., Reading, Pennsylvania, 1974.

146 KASAMATSU, A., and T. Hirai. "An Electroencephalographic Study of the Zen Meditation (Zazen)." *Altered States of Consciousness*, C. T. Tart (ed.), New York, John Wiley & Sons, Inc., 1969, pp. 489–501.

147 KASAMATSU, A., and T. Hirai. "Science of Zazen." *Psychologia*, Vol. 6, 1963, pp. 86–91.

148 KATKIN, E. S. "The Relationship Between Manifest Anxiety and Two Indices of Autonomic Response to Stress." *Journal of Personality and Social Psychology*, Vol. 2, 1965, pp. 324–333.

149 KATKIN, E. S. "The Relationship Between a Measure of Transitory Anxiety and Spontaneous Autonomic Activity." *Journal of Abnormal Psychology*, Vol. 71, 1966, pp. 142–146.

150 KATKIN, E. S., and R. J. McCubbin. "Habituation of the Orienting Response as a Function of Individual Differences in Anxiety and Autonomic Lability." *Journal of Abnormal Psychology*, Vol. 74, 1969, pp. 54–60.

151 KATZ, V. "Some Basic Insights of the Present Revival." *Creative Intelligence*, No. 1, Spiritual Regeneration Movement Publications, London, 1970, pp. 9–17.

152 KETY, S. S. "A Biologist Examines the Mind and Behavior." *Science*, Vol. 132, No. 3443, December 23, 1960, pp. 1861–1870.

153 KLEITMAN, N. *Sleep and Wakefulness*. Revised and enlarged ed., Chicago, University of Chicago Press, 1963.

154 KLUMOUS, I. M. "Changes of Marginal Gingivitis in Meditators and Controls During an Interval of 25 Days." College of Health, Physical Education, and Recreation, Pennsylvania State University, 1973.

155 KNIFFKI, D. K. *"Transzendentale Meditation—TM a.u. eine nechte-chemische Methode gegen Drogenmissbrauch."* Niedersachsisches *Anzteblatt*, No. 24, 44 Jahrgang, Hanover, Germany, December 22, 1971, pp. 805–809.

156 KOESTLER, A. *The Ghost in the Machine*. New York, Macmillan, 1967.

157 KOESTLER, A. *The Invisible Writing*. New York, Macmillan, 1954.

158 KOESTLER, A. *The Roots of Coincidence*. London, Hutchinson, 1972.

159 KORY, R. "Toward a Theory of Consciousness: a Return to the *Veda* by Way of Psychoanalysis." Dept. of Philosophy, Yale University, July 10, 1972.

160 KRIPPNER, S., and D. Rubin (eds.). *Galaxies of Light*. New York, Doubleday, 1973.

161 KRIPPNER, S. "The Plateau Experience: A. A. Maslow and Others." *Journal of Transpersonal Psychology*, No. II, 1972.

162 KRIS, E. *Psychoanalytic Explorations in Art*. New York, Schocken Books, 1964.

163 LAING, R. D. *The Politics of Experience*. New York, Ballantine Books, 1967.

164 LAZARUS, A. A. *Behavior Therapy and Beyond*. New York, McGraw-Hill Book Company, 1971.

165 LAZARUS, A. A. "Multimodal Behavior Therapy: Treating the 'BASIC ID.'" *Journal of Nervous and Mental Disease*, Vol. 156, No. 6, 1973, pp. 404–411.

166 LAZARUS, A. A. "Notes on Behavior Therapy; The Problem of Relapse and Some Tentative Solutions." *Psychotherapy: Theory, Research and Practice*, Vol. 8, 1971, pp. 192–194.

167 LEDAIN, G., *et al.* "Treatment," in a Report of the Commission of Inquiry into the Non-Medical Use of Drugs, Information Canada, Ottawa, 1972.

168 LEONARD, G. *Education and Ecstasy*. New York, Delacorte Press, 1968.

169 LEONARD, G. *The Transformation*. New York, Delacorte Press, 1973.

170 LESH, T. V. "Zen Meditation and the Development of Empathy in Counselors." *Journal of Humanistic Psychology*, Vol. 10, No. 1, 1970, pp. 39–83.

171 LEVI, L. (ed.). *Emotional Stress*. New York, American Elsevier Publishing Company, Inc., 1961.

172 LEVI, L. (ed.). *Stress: Sources, Management, and Prevention*. New York, Liveright Publishing Corp., 1967.

173 LEVINE, P. "Transcendental Meditation and the Science of Creative Intelligence." *Phi Delta Kappan*, Vol. LIV, No. 4, December 1972.

174 LEVITT, E. E. "Psychotherapy with Children: A Further Evaluation." *Behaviour, Research and Therapy*, Vol. 1, 1963, pp. 45–51.

175 LORENZ, K. *On Aggression,* trans. by M. K. Wilson. New York, Harcourt, Brace and World, 1966.

176 LOWEN, A. *The Language of the Body.* New York, Macmillan, 1971.

177 LOWEN, A. *Physical Dynamics of Character Structure.* New York, Grune & Stratton, 1958.

178 LUCE, G. G. *Current Research on Sleep and Dreams.* Department of Health, Education and Welfare, Public Health Service Publication No. 1389, United States Government Printing Office, Washington, D.C., 1965.

179 LUCE, G., and E. Peper. "Mind over Body, Mind over Mind." *The York Times Magazine,* September 12, 1971.

180 LUCE, G. G., and J. Segal. *Sleep,* New York, Lancer Books, Inc., 1967.

181 MacINTOSH, G. R. "Transcendental Meditation and Selected Life Attitudes." University of Calgary, Canada, 1972.

181a *Maharishi International University Catalogue, 1974/75,* MIU Press, Germany, 1974.

182 MAHARISHI Mahesh Yogi. *Love and God.* Spiritual Regeneration Movement Publications, Oslo, 1965.

183 MAHARISHI Mahesh Yogi. "A Message." *Creative Intelligence,* No. 1, Spiritual Regeneration Movement Publications, London, 1970, pp. 2–5.

184 MAHARISHI Mahesh Yogi. *On the Bhagavad-Gita: A New Translation and Commentary, Chapters 1–6.* Baltimore, Maryland, Penguin Books, Inc., 1969.

185 MAHARISHI Mahesh Yogi. *The Science of Being and the Art of Living.* Spiritual Regeneration Movement Publications, Stuttgart, Germany, 1966.

186 MAHARISHI Mahesh Yogi. Video-taped course on *The Science of Creative Intelligence.* Tapes available through International Film and Tape Library (IFTL), Academy for SCI, Livingston, New York.

187 MAHARISHI Mahesh Yogi. Video-taped residence course lecture series 1970–1973. Tapes available through IFTL.

188 MAHARISHI Mahesh Yogi. International Symposium on the Science of Creative Intelligence, Maharishi International University, Los Angeles, California, 1972.

189 MAHL, G. F. "Physiological Changes during Chronic Fear." *Annals of New York Academy of Science,* Vol. 56, 1952, pp. 240–252.

190 MARZETTA, B. R., H. Benson and R. K. Wallace. "Combating Drug Dependency in Young People: A New Approach." *Medical Counterpoint,* September 1972, pp. 13, 32–36.

191 MASLOW, A. H. *The Further Reaches of Human Nature.* New York, The Viking Press, 1971.

192 MASLOW, A. H. "New Introduction: Religious Values in Peak Experiences." *Journal of Transpersonal Psychology*, No. II, 1970.

193 MASLOW, A. H. *Religions, Values, and Peak Experiences*. New York, The Viking Press, 1970.

194 MASLOW, A. H. "A Theory of Meta-motivation: The Biological Rooting of Value-Life." *Readings in Humanistic Psychology*, A. J. Sutich and M. A. Villch (eds.), New York, Free Press, 1969.

195 MASLOW, A. H. "Theory Z." *Journal of Transpersonal Psychology*. Fall 1969, pp. 31–47.

196 MASLOW, A. H. *Toward a Psychology of Being*. New York, D. Van Nostrand Co., 1968.

197 MAULSBY, R. "An Illustration of Emotionally Evoked Theta Rhythm in Infancy: Hedonic Hypersynchrony." *Electroencephalography and Clinical Neurophysiology*, Vol. 31, 1971, pp. 157–165.

198 McQUADE, W. "Doing Something About Stress." *Fortune*, May 1973, pp. 250–261.

199 McQUADE, W. "What Stress Can Do to You." *Fortune*, January 1972, pp. 102–107.

200 MEAD, M. *And Keep Your Powder Dry*. New York, William Morrow and Co., 1971.

201 MIGDAL, S. "The Holistic Ideal of Education and Its Realization by Maharashi International University." Dept. of Literature, Maharishi International University, Santa Barbara, California, 1974.

202 MILLER, N. E. "Learning Visceral and Glandular Responses." *Science*, Vol. 163, January 31, 1969, pp. 434–445.

203 MISKIMAN, D. E. "The Effect of Transcendental Meditation on Compensatory Paradoxical Sleep." Dept. of Psychology, Trent University, Ontario, Canada, August, 1973.

203a MISKIMAN, D. E. "The Treatment of Insomnia by Transcendental Meditation." *Scientific Research on Transcendental Meditation: Collected Papers*, D. W. Orme-Johnson, L. H. Domash and J. T. Farrow (eds.), Los Angeles, MIU Press, 1974.

204 MORUZZI, G., and H. W. Magoun. "Brain Stem Reticular Formation and Activation of the EEG." *Electroencephalography and Clinical Neurophysiology*, Vol. 1, 1949, pp. 455–473.

205 NARANJO, C., and R. E. Ornstein. *On the Psychology of Meditation*. New York, The Viking Press, 1971.

206 NIDICH, S., W. Seeman and T. Dreskin. "Influence of Transcendental Meditation: A Replication." *Journal of Counseling Psychology* (in press 1974).

207 NIDICH, S., W. Seeman and M. Seibert. "Influence of Transcendental Meditation on State Anxiety." *Journal of Consulting and Clinical Psychology* (in press 1974).

208 NORMAN, D. A. (ed.). *Memory and Attention.* New York, John Wiley & Sons, Inc., 1969.

209 OATES, J. C. "New Heaven and Earth." *Saturday Review,* September 4, 1972, pp. 51–54.

210 OLDS, J. "Self-Stimulation of the Brain." *Science,* Vol. 127, 1958, pp. 315–324.

211 OLDS, J., and P. Milner. "Positive Reinforcement Produced by Electrical Stimulation of the Septal Area and Other Regions of the Rat Brain." *Journal of Comparative Physiology and Psychology,* Vol. 47, 1954, pp. 419–427.

212 OLDS, J., and M. E. Olds. "The Mechanisms of Voluntary Behavior." *The Role of Pleasure in Behavior,* R. G. Heath (ed.), New York, Harper and Row, Publishers, 1964, pp. 23–54.

213 ORME-JOHNSON, D. W. "Autonomic Stability and Transcendental Meditation." *Proceedings of the First International Symposium on the Science of Creative Intelligence.* Humboldt State College, Arcata, California, August 1971.

214 ORME-JOHNSON, D. W. "Autonomic Stability and Transcendental Meditation." *Psychosomatic Medicine,* Vol. 35, No. 4, July-August 1973, pp. 341–349.

215 ORME-JOHNSON, D. W., and D. P. Heaton. "Influence of Transcendental Meditation on Grade Point Average: Initial Findings." *Scientific Research on Transcendental Meditation: Collected Papers,* D. W. Orme-Johnson, L. H. Domash, and J. T. Farrow (eds.), Los Angeles, MIU Press, 1974.

216 ORME-JOHNSON, D. W. "Transcendental Meditation Is the Solution to the Drug Abuse Problem." Dept. of Psychology, Maharishi International University, 1973.

217 ORME-JOHNSON, D. W. Transcendental Meditation For Drug Abuse Counselors," *Scientific Research on Transcendental Meditation: Collected Papers,* D. W. Orme-Johnson, L. H. Domash and J. T. Farrow (eds.), Los Angeles, MIU Press, 1974.

218 ORME-JOHNSON, D. W., D. McFadden and F. Giordan. "Meditation as Psychotherapy." Maharishi International University, Santa Barbara, California, 1973.

219 ORME-JOHNSON, D. W., J. Kiehlbauch, R. Moore and J. Bristol. "Personality and Autonomic Changes in Meditating Prisoners." La Tuna Federal Penitentiary, Texas, August, 1972.

220 ORNSTEIN, R. E. *The Psychology of Consciousness.* San Francisco, W. H. Freeman and Company, 1972.

221 ORTEGA y GASSET, J. *Mission of the University.* trans. by H. L. Nostrand. New York, W. W. Norton Company, 1966.

222 OTIS, L. S. "If Well-Integrated but Anxious, Try TM." *Psychology Today,* Vol. 7, No. 11, April 1974, pp. 45–46.

223 PELLETIER, K. R. "Altered Attention Deployment in Meditators." Psychology Clinic, University of California, Berkeley, 1972.

224 PENFIELD, W. *The Excitable Cortex in Conscious Man.* Springfield, Illinois, Charles C. Thomas, 1958.

225 PENFIELD, W., and T. Rasmussen. *The Cerebral Cortex of Man: A Clinical Study of Localization of Function.* New York, Macmillan, 1950.

226 PERLS, F. S. *Gestalt Therapy Verbatim.* LaFayette, California, Real People Press, 1969.

227 PERLS, F. S., R. F. Hefferline and P. Goodman. *Gestalt Therapy.* New York, Delta Publishing Company, 1951.

228 PITTS, F. N., Jr. "The Biochemistry of Anxiety." *Scientific American,* Vol. 220, February, 1969, pp. 69–75.

229 PROSSER, R. "Transcendental Meditation and Physical Reality." *Creative Intelligence,* No. 1, Spiritual Regeneration Movement Publications, London, 1970.

230 REICH, C. *The Greening of America.* New York, Random House, 1970.

231 REICH, W. *Character Analysis.* London, Vision Press, 1948.

232 REICHART, H. *"Plethsmographische untersuchungen bei konsentrations und meditations ubugen artliche forsche."* *Artliche Forsch.,* Vol. 21, 1967, pp. 61–65.

233 RIESMAN, D. *The Lonely Crowd.* Yale University Press, New Haven, Conn., 1950.

234 RITTERSTAEDT, H. P. "A New Effect in Infrared Radiation of the Human Skin Through TM." Düsseldorf, Germany, 1966.

235 RITTERSTAEDT, H. P., and H. Schenkluhn. "Measuring Changes of the Skin Temperature During the Practice of Transcendental Meditation." Max Planck Institute, Düsseldorf, Germany, 1966.

236 ROGERS, C. *On Becoming a Person.* Boston, Houghton Mifflin Co., 1961.

237 ROSENMAN, R. H. "Emotional Factors in Coronary Heart Disease." *Postgraduate Medicine,* Vol. 42, September 1967, pp. 165–171.

238 ROSZAK, T. *The Making of a Counterculture.* New York, Doubleday, 1969.

239 ROUTT, T. "Transcendental Meditation and Relaxed States: A Pilot Study Comparing Physiological Parameters." Huxley College of Environmental Studies, Western Washington State University, Bellingham, September, 1973.

240 ROUTTENBERG, A. "The Two-Arousal Hypothesis: Reticular Formation and the Limbic System." *Psychology Review,* Vol. 75, 1968, pp. 51–80.

241 RUBOTTOM, A. E. "Transcendental Meditation." *Yale Alumni Magazine,* February 1972.

242 RUBOTTOM, A. E. "Transcendental Meditation and Its Potential Uses for Schools." *Social Education,* December 1972.

243 SCHACHTER, S., and B. Latane. "Crime, Cognition, and the Autonomic Nervous System." *Nebraska Symposium on Motivation,* D. Levine (ed.), Lincoln, Nebraska, University of Nebraska Press, 1964.

244 SCHACHTER, S., and J. E. Singer. "Cognitive, Social and Physiological Determinants of Emotional States." *Psychology Review,* Vol. 69, 1962, pp. 378–399.

245 SCHRÖDINGER, E. *Mind and Matter.* London, Cambridge University Press, 1969.

246 SCHULTZ, T. "What Science Is Discovering About the Potential Benefits of Meditation." *Today's Health,* April 1972.

247 SEABOND, G. T. "Uneasy World Gains Power Over Destiny." *The New York Times,* January 6, 1969.

248 SEEMAN, W., S. Nidich and T. Banta. "The Influence of Transcendental Meditation on a Measure of Self-Actualization." *Journal of Counseling Psychology,* Vol. 19, No. 3, 1972, pp. 184–187.

249 SELYE, H. *The Stress of Life.* New York, McGraw-Hill Book Company, 1956.

250 SERINO, G. S. *Your Ulcer: Prevention, Control, Cure.* Philadelphia and New York, J. B. Lippincott Company, 1966.

251 SHAFII, M. "Adaptive and Therapeutic Aspects of Meditation." *International Journal of Psychoanalytic Psychotherapy,* Vol. II, No. 3, 1973, pp. 364–382.

251a SHAFII, M. "Silence in the Service of the Ego: Psychoanalytic Study of Meditation." *International Journal of Psychoanalysis,* Vol. 54, 1973, pp. 431–443.

252 SHAFII, M. "Smoking Following Meditation." Dept. of Psychiatry, University of Michigan Medical Center, Ann Arbor, Michigan, 1973.

253 SHAFII, M., R. Lavely and R. Jaffe. "Meditation and Marijuana." *American Journal of Psychiatry,* Vol. 131, No. 1, 1974, pp. 60–63.

254 SHAPIRO, D., B. Tursky, E. Gershon, and M. Stern. "Effects of Feedback and Reinforcement on the Control of Human Systolic Blood Pressure." *Science,* Vol. 163, February 7, 1969, p. 588.

255 SHAW, R., and D. Kolb. "One Point Reaction Time Involving Meditators and Non-Meditators." *Scientific Research on Transcendental Meditation: Collected Papers,* D. W. Orme-Johnson, L. H. Domash and J. T. Farrow (eds.), Los Angeles, MIU Press, 1974.

256 SHEAR, J. "Parallels Between the Philosophy of Plato and the Science of Creative Intelligence of Maharishi Mahesh Yogi." Dept. of

Philosophy, Maharishi International University, Santa Barbara, California, 1974.

257 SHEAR, J. "The Conscious Source of Thought." *Creative Intelligence*, No. 1, Spiritual Regeneration Movement Publications, London, 1970, pp. 45–54.

258 SHELLY, M. W. (summarized by G. Landrith). "A Theory of Happiness as It Relates to Transcendental Meditation." Dept. of Psychology, University of Kansas, Lawrence, Kansas, 1972.

259 SHELLY, M. W. *Sources of Satisfaction*. Lawrence, Kansas, University of Kansas Press, 1973.

260 SHELLY, M. W. *The Counter-Evolution*. Lawrence, Kansas, University of Kansas Press, 1973.

261 SHERRINGTON, C. S. *Man on His Nature*. London, Cambridge University Press, 1951.

262 SIMEONS, A. T. W. *Man's Presumptuous Brain*. New York, E. P. Dutton & Co., 1960.

263 SPERLING, G. "Three Models for Short-Term Memory." *Memory and Attention*, Donald A. Norman (ed.). New York, John Wiley & Sons, Inc., 1969.

264 SPERRY, R. W. "The Great Cerebral Commisure." *Scientific American*, Vol. 117, 1964, pp. 42–52.

265 STACE, W. *Teachings of the Mystics*. New York, New American Library, 1960.

266 STERNBACK, R. A. *Principles of Psychophysiology*. New York and London, Academic Press, 1966, pp. 27–41.

267 STROEBEL, C. F. "Psychophysiological Comparison of Alpha Biofeedback and Transcendental Meditation in Normal Subjects and Psychiatric Patients." Presented at American Psychiatric Association symposium on "The Psychobiology of Meditation," May 1973.

268 STROEBEL, C. F., and B. C. Glueck. "Biofeedback Treatment in Medicine and Psychiatry: An Ultimate Placebo?" *Seminars in Psychiatry*, Vol. 5, No. 4, November 1973, pp. 379–392.

269 SUGI, Y., and K. Akutsu. "On the Respiration and Respiratory Change in Zen Practice." *Japanese Journal of Physiology*, Vol. 26, 1964, pp. 72–73.

270 SUZUKI, T. "Electroencephalographic Study During Zen Practice." *Proceedings of the 15th Convention of JPA*, 1963, p. 346.

271 SYKES, D. E. "Transcendental Meditation as Applied to Criminal Justice Reform, Drug Rehabilitation and Society in General." *University of Maryland Law Forum*, Vol. 3, No. 2, Winter 1973, pp. 37–53.

272 SZENT-GYORGI, A. Address Before the Conference on Interdisciplinary Science Education, Washington, D. C., January 23, 1969.

273 TART, C. T. (ed.). *Altered States of Consciousness.* New York, John Wiley & Sons, Inc., 1969.

274 TART, C. T. "A Psychologist's Experience with Transcendental Meditation." *Journal of Transpersonal Psychology,* Vol. 3, No. 2, 1971, pp. 135–140.

275 TART, C. T. "States of Consciousness and State-Specific Sciences." *Science,* Vol. 176, June 16, 1972, pp. 1203–1210.

276 THOMPSON, W. I. *At the Edge of History.* New York, Harper & Row, Publishers, 1971.

277 *Time.* "The Rediscovery of Human Nature." April 2, 1972, pp. 79–87.

278 TIMMONS, B., and J. Kamiya. "The Psychology and Physiology of Meditation and Related Phenomena: A Bibliography." *Journal of Transpersonal Psychology,* Vol. 2, No. 1, 1970, pp. 41–51.

279 TJOA, S. H. "Some Evidence that the Practice of Transcendental Meditation Increases Intelligence as Measured by a Psychological Test." *Scientific Research on Transcendental Meditation: Collected Papers,* D. W. Orme-Johnson, L. H. Domash, and J. T. Farrow (eds.), Los Angeles, MIU Press, 1974.

280 TOFFLER, A. *Future Shock.* New York, Random House, 1970.

281 TRUCH, S. "Transcendental Meditation: A Boon for Teachers." *Alberta Teachers' Association Magazine,* Canada, May–June 1972.

282 VAN DER BERG, W. P., and B. Mulden. "Psychological Research on the Effects of Transcendental Meditation on a Number of Personality Variables Using the N.P.I." *Scientific Research on Transcendental Meditation: Collected Papers,* D. W. Orme-Johnson, L. H. Domash, and J. T. Farrow (eds.), Los Angeles, MIU Press, 1974.

283 VANSELOW, K. "Meditative Exercises to Eliminate the Effects of Stress." *Hippokrates,* Verlag Stuttgart, 39 Jahrgang Heft, 13, 1972, Seite 462–465.

284 VARGIU, J. G. "A Model of Creative Behavior." *Fields within Fields within Fields,* Vol. 5, No. 1, New York, The World Institute Council, 1972.

285 WADDINGTON, C. H. *The Nature of Life.* London, George Allen & Unwin Ltd., 1961.

286 WALLACE, R. K., "Physiological Effects of 'Transcendental Meditation." *Science,* Vol. 167, March 27, 1970, pp. 1751–1754.

287 WALLACE, R. K. *The Physiological Effects of Transcendental Meditation.* Ph.D. Thesis, Dept. of Physiology, University of California, Los Angeles, 1970.

288 WALLACE, R. K., and H. Benson. "Physiological Effects of a Medi-

tation Technique and a Suggestion for Curbing Drug Abuse." Mental Health Program Reports, Thorndike Memorial Laboratory, Harvard University School of Medicine, December 5, 1971.

289 WALLACE, R. K., and H. Benson. "The Physiology of Meditation." *Scientific American,* Vol. 226, No. 2, February 1972, pp. 84–90.

290 WALLACE, R. K., H. Benson and A. F. Wilson. "A Wakeful Hypometabolic Physiologic State." *American Journal of Physiology,* Vol. 221, No. 3, September 1971, pp. 795–799.

291 WALLACE, R. K., H. Benson, A. Wilson and M. Garrett. "Decreased Blood Lactate During Transcendental Meditation." *Proceedings of the Federation of American Society for Experimental Biology,* Vol. 30, No. 2, March–April 1971, p. 376.

292 WALRATH, L. C. "Psychophysiological Studies of Transcendental Meditation." Dept. of Psychology, Eastern Washington State College, 1973.

293 WATTS, A. *Psychotherapy East and West.* New York, Ballantine Books, 1961.

294 WEIL, A. *The Natural Mind.* Boston, Houghton Mifflin Company, 1972.

295 WENGER, M. A., and B. K. Bagchi. "Studies of Autonomic Functions in a Practitioner of Yoga in India." *Behavioral Science,* Vol. 6, 1961, pp. 312–323.

296 WENGER, M. A., B. K. Bagchi and B. K. Anand. "Experiments in India on 'Voluntary' Control of the Heart and Pulse." *Circulation,* Vol. 24, 1961, pp. 131–132.

297 WENGER, M. A., T. L. Clemens and T. D. Cullens. "Autonomic Functions in Patients with Gastrointestinal and Dermatological Disorders." *Psychosomatic Medicine,* Vol. 24, 1962, pp. 267–273.

298 WERTHEIMER, M. *Productive Thinking.* New York, Harper & Row, Publishers, 1959.

298a WESTCOTT, M. "Hemispheric Symmetry of the EEG during Transcendental Meditation," *Scientific Research on Transcendental Meditation: Collected Papers,* Vol. 1, D. W. Orme-Johnson, L. H. Domash, and J. T. Farrow (eds.), Los Angeles, MIU Press, 1974.

299 WHEELER, J. A. "The Princeton Galaxy." *Intellectual Digest,* June 1973.

300 WHYTE, L. L. *The Next Development in Man.* London, The Cresset Press, 1944.

301 WILHELMJ, M. S., and H. H. McCarthy. *Dietary and Neural Factors in Hypertension.* Springfield, Illinois, Charles C. Thomas Publishers, 1963.

302 WILSON, A. F., and R. Honsberger. "The Effects of Transcendental Meditation Upon Bronchial Asthma." *Clinical Research,* Volume 2, No. 2, 1973.

303 WINQUIST, W. T. "The Effect of the Regular Practice of Transcendental Meditation on Students Involved in the Regular Use of Hallucinogenic and 'Hard' Drugs." Dept. of Sociology, University of California at Los Angeles, 1969.

304 WITKIN, H. A., R. Dyk, J. F. Faterson, Dr. Goodenaugh and S. A. Karp, *Psychological Differentiation.* New York, John'Wiley & Sons, 1962.

305 WITKIN, H. A., and P. K. Oltman. "Cognitive Style." *Inter. Journal of Neurology,* Vol. 6, 1967, pp. 119–137.

306 WOLF, S., and H. G. Wolff. *Human Gastric Function.* London, Oxford University Press, 1943.

307 WOLFF, H. G. *Stress and Disease.* 2nd ed., Springfield, Illinois, Charles C. Thomas Publishers, 1968.

308 WOLPE, J., and A. A. Lazarus. *Behavior Therapy Techniques.* New York, Pergamon Press, 1966.

309 WOOLRIDGE, D. E. *The Machinery of the Brain.* New York, McGraw-Hill Book Company, 1966.

INDEX